THE LIONS' ROAR

by

CRAIG McGILL

LIPSTICK PUBLISHING

The Lions' Roar

First Edition published 2006 by:
Lipstick Publishing
West Knockenbaird Croft
Insch, Aberdeenshire.
Scotland. UK. AB52 6TN
Tel: UK: 01464 821954
Fax: UK: 01464 821954
Web: www.lipstickpublishing.com
E-Mail: admin@lipstickpublishing.com

A record for this book is available from the British Library

ISBN 1-904762-15-8

Contents

The Author

Craig McGill is the author of three books – Football Inc: How Soccer Fans are losing the Game, Do No Harm: Munchausen Syndrome by proxy and Human Traffic: Sex, slaves and immigration.

He has been a sports reporter for The Lanarkshire People newspapers and acerbic sports column in The Scottish Daily Mirror. These have all helped him to be crowned Allmediascotland.com's Media Personality of the year 2004.

He also covered the 2000 World Cup for TIME Magazine and website.

His work has also appeared in many newspapers and magazines across the globe with projects for 2006 including the first biography of Scottish writer and chaos magician Grant Morrison, a book on the Irish Loyalist hit list 'Know the Provo' and further fiction work.

He can be reached through cmcgill@gmail.com and one day promises to get content up on www.craigmcgill.com

Further praise for Craig McGill:
Football Inc:
"A cry for the soul of the game." Michael Grant, Sunday Herald
"There is a need for a book like this." The Independent
"McGill is football's John Pilger." Amazon.co.uk

Do No Harm:
"This has to be the least biased book I have ever read covering this topic. The author portrays MSBP in a very thought provoking manner. He leaves the media hysteria behind and searches for the truth in these cases where the truth is hard to find." Amazon.co.uk

Human Traffic:
"McGill has firmly grasped the nettle and revealed an international underworld that few of us could even imagine existed." Amazon.co.uk

Acknowledgements

Writing a book is really like playing in a football team with a great striker – one person gets most of the glory while there are a lot of people behind him doing all the work.

First off, obvious thanks to everyone at Livingston – fans, players and others for their help, time and patience in helping me put together this book. Similar thanks go to everyone else mentioned in the book, who may no longer be part of the club, but were still of help. And thanks to everyone at Lipstick for their incredible patience.

Many people were also reluctant to help with the book, feeling that a tabloid journalist could only be out to do a hatchet job on the club. Hopefully now they will see that is not the case and would be willing to be more forthcoming for future print runs of the book.

Remembering the game is a pleasure, but it's the people behind the game that truly shows what makes each club unique.

Off the pitch metaphorically, thanks must also go to a number of people including Rob Bruce of Tennents' Lager, Shaun Milne and Mike Graham at *The Mirror* newspaper, Alan Hodge at Archant Newspapers Glasgow, Alan Muir at *The Sun*, Iain Ferguson and many, many other.

Also, many thanks to sporting colleagues for helping fill in the blanks at times and as such – as well as a portion of this book's profits going to the club and Livingston for Life – my own proceeds from the first print run of this book will be going to journalistic charities.

A number of newspapers, websites, radio stations and TV shows also helped in part so thanks to *The Scottish Daily Mirror, The Scottish Sun, The Daily Record, Sunday Mail, News of the World, Mail on Sunday, Daily Mail, Daily Express, Fourfourtwo, The Herald, The Scotsman, The Evening Times. The Evening News, The Press and Journal, the official Livi website, Liviforlife, the ultralivis, Radio Clyde, Radio Forth, FiveLive, BBC Scotland –* sport, news and website *and The Sunday Post.*

And as always, thanks to my close friends and family for their support when I was nothing more than a bad-tempered git as deadlines were approaching. I won't forget your help and greatly appreciated that you knew when to just leave me alone to get on with the work. Similarly, everyone who got in the road when deadlines loomed, I'll remember that too.

Craig McGill

INTRODUCTION

"Livingston? Why would you want to write a book about them? Even more so, why would anyone want to read about them?" This was the common reaction when it was announced this book was going to be written.

While some people might think that it's an understandable sentiment, I don't think so. Livingston embodies everything that makes football a great game. This is a small team that didn't exist just over a decade ago but since then, have been third in The Scottish Premier League beating teams who have won European cups, taken points off the Old Firm, and earned a place in the UEFA Cup.

People might shrug their shoulders and say "So? They didn't win the cup," but that is to miss the point. As any real football fan knows, the beautiful game is a game for romantics. It's where dreams come true. Where Partick Thistle beat Celtic in cup finals, where Qatar beat France in the World Cup. Most football fans suffer week in and week out as their teams get beat, but still they go to the games. Why? In the hope that this is the week it all changes; this is the week the team wins and they go on to better things.

In that sense, Livingston are the football equivalent of Rocky, or any other sporting film, where the underdog comes up and that is what makes their story so fantastic – they have lived the dream, though at times it has been a nightmare, losing promotion on the last day of the season just a few years ago.

And for other detractors to say, "They'll go nowhere from here. Hibs were third once and they were fighting for their lives the next year," is to miss the point even more spectacularly. This is a club that rose from nowhere to the top in just six years. Some clubs haven't managed third place in sixty-six years.

What makes it even better though is the fact that we constantly hear about how only the big clubs can win now. If you're not Real Madrid, Celtic, Arsenal or one of the other big clubs then you don't stand a chance as you don't have the money or the legions of fans who will buy anything associated with the club. Livingston – and to an extent Chievo in the Italian Serie A – have shown that's not the case. The little club can still come up and compete.

Of course, while the Italians were praised, the Scots, being a tad more reticent about this sort of thing, said Livi were going up only to come back down.

As Jim Leishman himself pointed out: "We were constantly being written off as relegation material – Chievo were the same but they have also proved their doubters wrong."

Yes, the churlish may point out that the club has had a little help in the form of the likes of John McGuiness, the Scottish lottery winner who put in a cash injection of £1 million, but let's be fair about this. In this day and age, in a football premier league, that's not a lot of money. Yes, it will have helped, but as Motherwell FC showed at the end of 2001/2002 season, having someone inject a lot of money into a club is no guarantee of success. John Boyle put £11 million into Motherwell before selling up, so McGuinness's million is put into perspective. Money alone does not make a footballing success, so if nothing else we can state with conviction that Livingston are a wonderful example and incentive to so-called lesser clubs all over Europe and a reminder that clever transfer and tactical policy when combined with shrewd coaching can reap benefits.

But it hasn't been plain sailing, especially after the pinnacle of reaching third in the league. The club went into administration – but again survived, confounding the many nay-sayers who were convinced the club was doomed. The club has also struggled in the SPL – but crucially it has stayed in the SPL, something most teams who come up through the leagues struggle to do.

Livingston – just like the town – have shown that they are survivors. It hasn't always been beautiful, but it's certainly been interesting, and here, looking back at the hundreds of games played, you get a sense of that surviving spirit at the club.

So let people slag off the club – half the time they're just jealous. Livingston have demonstrated what can happen in football if a few people dare to dream. And it's that dream which makes us all football fans in the first place.

CHAPTER
1

THE GAME

"Jim! Jim, we're in Europe!"

"I know, but that's no excuse for breaking mah specs."

Indeed, the fourth goal for Livingston had seen a problem posed for Jim McIntyre. John, who sat beside him, had punched up in the air as Jim had gone forward. The clenched fist just missed his nose but did catch the bridge of his glasses, the force breaking them in half.

"Sorry mate. But we're in Europe! I'll buy you a new set in France or wherever we end up!"

It was a day full of expectations and anticipation. It had been a long hard season for the small club called Livingston. At the start of the season most of the experts had written off their chances, saying that they would be lucky if they managed to stay up.

Yes Jim Leishman and David Hay were talented managers, but they were coming up with a small team. Perhaps they would come up, go back down, and then come back up to struggle along in the bottom half of the SPL. That was the general consensus.

And it was wrong.

The die-hards knew that if they could win this game against Dunfermline, it would mean they were the first side to win the First Division championship and then secure a UEFA Cup place the following season.

On that day, Livingston finally – or so they thought – put paid to all their critics by coming from nowhere to qualify for a place in Europe in their first season.

And in doing so, they gave a wheelchair-bound girl enough ability to take the first steps of her life.

The weather didn't inspire most of the fans, some of whom were annoyed at Sky Television having moved the time slot from a Saturday to a Sunday so that the game could be televised. It was overcast and gloomy. The superstitious would have stayed at home in bed.

To make matters even worse, from before the kick-off, it was fairly obvious that the game wasn't going to be a sell-out, despite the cheap tickets on offer. Fears were rising that this was going to be a bad day for the club and the closest the players or fans would get to Europe would be on a summer holiday and not part of any footballing tournament. But just over 9,000 fans ended up coming.

The team took to the pitch in a 4-3-3 formation with the fans easily able to see the players who had brought them so far this season: Broto, Brinquin, Andrews, Rubio, Santini, Makel, Quino, Lovell, Xausa, Wilson and Fernandez.

The game started off at a frantic pace and a scare for Livi when the Fifers' Stevie Crawford had a great chance at goal. Fortunately he headed wide, but it gave the visitors encouragement to take the game to the euro-chasers.

But as Dunfermline tried to break down Livi, Lovell controlled the midfield, prompting action from his strikers with long passes that made sure Dunfermline didn't have the whole game to themselves.

At this point, Broto was the hardest-working player on the park, constantly dealing with trouble in or near the goalmouth.

While Broto was busy, it was the goalkeeper at the other end who provided the first controversial moment of the game. Marco Ruitenbeek picked up the ball when he shouldn't have and even though it was well spotted, referee Mike McCurry took ages to react before finally blowing for a free-kick.

However that came to nothing – though Fernandez's free-kick was powerful – as Ruitenbeek got to it, determined to make up for his stupid mistake in causing the free-kick in the first place.

Quino then had a chance at the far post but it shot straight into the arms of Ruitenbeek.

But then an opener came in the 28th minute in the shape of Lovell, after Barry Wilson sent in a corner from the left of the post and Lovell got up to it and nutted it into the net.

And while this fired the crowd up, it seemed to have the opposite effect on the home players while Dunfermline charged forward time after time with only Broto managing to keep the score at 1-0 for the Lions.

And while his defence didn't seem much help to him, one thing that was useful was the shocking finishing by Dunfermline, who were squandering chances left, right and centre.

Jason Dair powered a close-range drive past the despairing hands of Broto after the home defence had failed to deal with a Sean Kilgannon attempt at levelling the scoreline.

Kilgannon then ran on to a short ball from Stevie Crawford, to unleash a shot that forced a fine diving one-handed save from Broto before Lee Makel cleared the loose ball.

Broto also proved he was the day's saviour when he brilliantly beat out a Scott Thomson header and then had to rely on Phillipe Brinquin to make a goal-line clearance from a mistimed header from Marvin Andrews.

As half-time approached, it was looking as if the home team could hang on, but in the 41st minute, all the plans were changed and again, Kilgannon – who had been causing problems throughout the whole game – sent a long cross to the far post where Barry Nicholson headed the ball back across the face of the goalmouth, where a lurking Jason Dair thumped it into the net, to make it 1-1, which the scoreline stayed at going into half-time.

As the second-half kicked off, Dunfermline still looked like the more inspired team, pushing forward, but to the detriment of their defence.

Barry Wilson exploited this to try and restore the home lead. His first chance came in the 48th minute when Fernandez took the ball from Crawford to set up Wilson inside the area, but the attempt came to nothing as it shot into the side netting. Two minutes later, Fernandez again slid the ball through to Wilson, who from a similar position, fired his shot across the face of the goal.

Minutes later, Dunfermline broke free and Crawford fired in a great cross from the right with only Broto to beat. It was one of those goals that looked harder to miss than score, but Nish managed it, putting the ball past the far post instead of tapping it into the empty net.

Ten minutes later, as the game reached the hour-long mark, Barry Wilson took a corner that he hit low for Davide Xausa to slot home and make it 2-1 for Livi, who were now facing a ten man team after Dunfermline's latest signing Karnebeek limped off.

In the 73rd minute Broto – yet again! – was the man of the moment, with a fantastic save of a Barry Nicholson shot.

Realising the threat Dunfermline still posed, Livi started to up the gears to show why they were the team challenging for Europe and they started to show it quickly.

The score became 3-1 after Xausa fired in his second goal – an 18-yard belter – after a set-up from Fernandez in the 75th minute.

That was Xausa's last contribution to the game as he was replaced by Bingham in the 78th minute.

And while that had the fans starting to chant about going to Europe, the club's elevation to the European elite was confirmed in the 83rd minute with some dramatic work by Fernandez and Quino.

Fernandez had beaten three defenders to force a save from Ruitenbeek, who could only clear it as far as Quino, who got the ball in the air and volleyed it in from inside the penalty box, to make it 4-1.

For Leishman the fourth goal was when he let himself believe that he had helped guide a club into Europe for the first time in his career.

"It wasn't until Quino's goal went in that we could relax because we knew Dunfermline wouldn't score three. So that was when it all began to sink in," he said.

Fernandez then came off for the last five minutes for an eager Caputo.

And in the dying seconds an incredible chip by Lee Makel wowed the crowd, but it came off the Dunfermline crossbar instead of making it five.

As the whistle blew, people were in shock – they had done it! There had been jokes at the start of the season about getting to Europe, but here they were, going to Europe!

The following week would see them confirm third place – behind the Scottish giants of Celtic and Rangers – who had been hinting about leaving the SPL. If they had already gone, Livingston would have won the SPL in their first season there!

Of course, for one player it wasn't a surprise. In fact as the whistle blew super-keeper Broto made a point of going over to pass a message on to Chairman Dominic Keane.

Broto had expected Europe so much so that the previous year when he had been negotiating his contract, he had told Chairman Dominic Keane, "This is fine, but there is no mention of a bonus for getting into Europe."

Keane had thought Javier was half-kidding because neither he – or Leishman or Hay – had thought that Livingston would be in a European position.

"Frankly, I thought he was daft," he said. "At the time we were in a good position in the First Division but we still had a lot of work to do to get promoted. Europe was never a part of even the most optimistic projections we indulged in."

But here was big Javier on the day running over to the director's box, lifting off his top to show a t-shirt which read 'Dominic,

Mission Accomplished." Keane could afford to laugh, even though he knew that in football the mission is never accomplished and it's never full-time when you're trying to keep a club afloat. As he would sadly learn one day.

Broto never did get his bonus for the European placing, though the players were rewarded with a handsome bonus for ending up in third place in the league, which they achieved the week after getting the Euro spot.

For Leishman, it was a dream day. "This beats everything in a long career for me," he said.

"Everyone has played a part and there have been a few tears. We'll savour the moment and then move on. We can't stop with this success. Winning championships is great, but all my success previously had come in the lower leagues with both Livingston and Dunfermline."

Of course, Jim being Jim, he wouldn't take all the praise.

"I have to say that Davie Hay is a genius. He is the most knowledgeable football man that I have ever worked with. He deserves a major share of the credit of what has been achieved by this club in the last couple of years. The rest of the staff have also been magnificent – it's been a real team effort.

"I really am delighted and I'm so proud of all the players as well. They had put themselves in a position where they could qualify and they went out there and did it.

"They had taken some stick for their performances but they worked hard and went out and made sure they achieved that European place.

"We will enjoy this but, come Monday morning, we will be planning for the future. That is the way it is at Livingston. It is what Dominic Keane and his directors' demand . . . and they are right."

And Keane was already making plans for the next season.

He said, "We are working particularly hard on our income away from the football side and, at the moment, more than 50 per cent of our income is generated from non-football activity.

"We have a thriving business with conferences, weddings, funerals and other functions that will continue to drip income whatever the state of the game's finances.

"Our wages here are realistic but the bonus payments are very generous and that's the way we have to keep it. Everything has to be performance-related. We have to remember that our customers

5

come from normal working life and they cannot relate to players who are earning £20,000 or £30,000 a week.

"We will not be sucked into paying money we can't afford and placing in jeopardy the good work that has already been done.

"Everyone who works for this club will get a good Living, doing a job that they enjoy, but the overall well being of the club remains paramount.

"We've achieved so much in a relatively short time span and this next experience is a little added bonus that none of us had bargained for."

"It's going to be really exciting. It may be that the whole thing has come too early for us, but the players have earned this chance and we must make the most of it.

"People said at the start of the season that we'd go straight back down again, but we forced them to change their tune.

"Of course, there is lots of work to be done and we have not had a lot of money to spend on players. But the infrastructure here, and all the facilities we have been developing the nightclub, office block and hotel - these are all geared towards helping the club on the pitch."

"Right from day one we tried to invest in the things that matter and hopefully, in 10, 30 or 40 years, there will still be full-time football – and Livingston FC - in Livingston."

"Leishman also revealed his emotional side, to show why people deserved to celebrate on days like those when Livi won the UEFA space, and in doing so, also showed why people call him 'Gentleman Jim.' These days have to be relished, for it is so hard," he said. "Good people like Sandy Clark, Billy Davies and Eric Black have all lost their jobs during the season."

And one other man who was ecstatic at the result was Honorary Vice-President John Bain.

John was the longest link with the club, having looked after it throughout two previous incarnations. He was manager of the Ferranti Thistle in 1952 which became Meadowbank Thistle, which then became Livingston.

His history with the club dated 50 years and the Dunfermline game was one of his proudest, and it brought back an incredible amount of memories for the 79-year-old.

He said, "I can remember on our first pitch at Crew Toll, the Ferranti players were lucky to get their expenses paid. I didn't get a penny - I was a paid employee of Ferranti. The players would get their bus or train fares for training. It maybe amounted to enough to buy themselves a pie and a pint after the sessions."

And it was a family effort in the Bain household.

"My wife Catherine was also 100 per cent behind the club. She washed the strips and even came down and made tea at half-time and things like that."

"Never in my wildest dreams did I think we would ever be looking at Europe."

But despite all the jubilation, there was one celebration stronger than the rest.

Diehard Livi fan Mandy Stalker had been watching the exciting game, as enraptured as everyone else. The fourteen year old – well known at Livingston for her cookery column in the fanzine – had been on the edge of her chair throughout the 90 minutes causing her mum, Beryl, worry as she feared her daughter might fall and hurt herself.

This was because Mandy was born three months prematurely and was given only six weeks to live by doctors. She suffered from necrotising fascitis and suffered a brain haemorrhage which impaired her ability to control her limbs.

Throughout her life, she had endured more than 30 operations so that she could live a normal, healthy life, but one thing it seemed she would never be able to do was walk, as expert after expert had said it would never be possible.

As the last goal went in, Mandy felt she could get up, though her mum panicked. Beryl remembers: "I nearly had a heart attack when Mandy got up. I grabbed her, thinking she might hurt herself."

The club lottery man spotted that Mandy had been getting up and came over, asked her if she thought she could get across the wall and she said she would give it a try.

And she did, eventually walking out to near the half-way line and meeting some of the players including her favourite, David 'Bingo' Bingham.

And while that was a delight for her, mum Beryl was in tears at hearing her daughter say something she thought she'd never hear. "Mum, I did it. I can walk."

For Mandy, taking those steps topped a great day for her.

She told the *Scottish Sun* newspaper who exclusively revealed the tale: "I wanted to get out of the wheelchair and run on to the pitch. I was so excited. I'd do anything for the club. I love football and Livi are the best."

"Walking after the win was the greatest moment of my life. I got off my seat and felt good as the shot went in and I managed to walk from the dug-out. At that moment, I knew that I could do it - and I did."

And Jim Leishman, who has always been level-headed enough to know that there's more to life than football while still knowing the effect it can have on fans pulled out a surprise for the young girl, saying the club would mark her achievement by inviting her to travel with the players to their first away match in the UEFA Cup.

As he said, "She is a remarkable girl. She's our top fan and we're hers. Everyone knows what she has been through and she's an inspiration."

And Brave Mandy's efforts sum up what seems to be the attitude for the club and its supporters: "I don't think anything's impossible."

And no matter what followed – for there were some dark days for the Lothian club – no one could take away from the fact that they had brought joy to that young girl – and thousands of others throughout the region, including Jim McIntyre, who never did get a pair of glasses from his old friend.

CHAPTER
2

HISTORY

But where did this little club that roared come from? The people of Livingston didn't just wake up one morning and there was a team sitting, waiting to be supported. No, Livingston did not come out of a vacuum, from nowhere, to run up to the heights of the Scottish Premier League. But the tale of their formation shows how the persistence of just a few men over a few years can change the landscape of Scottish football.

To say the club started in the mid-1990s would be accurate in a sense when talking about Livingston FC but the club has roots a little further back – still shorter than most football clubs – though the pedant could argue that the club actually started in 1943 with the formation of a works football team.

Ferranti was one of the giants of the wartime industries, with its technologies being used in many fields.

As many works did then – and continue to do to this day – a football team was set up by the men of the firm.

One of the men instrumental in the setting up of that team was John Blacklaw. The former RAF wing commander was a consultant to Ferranti when he persuaded them to sponsor the team and help it on its way.

Another person who came in at the beginning was a worker called John Bain, who had no idea of the lifetime association he was setting himself up for.

As he recalled: "When I joined in 1952 I was happy to play for fun. My real work was with Ferranti and the football was just a release."

It may just have been fun, but the team did well enough that they decided to join the local and regional league of the East of Scotland League in 1953 and it continued to do moderately well, winning cups and being fairly well supported. It was never going to win the European Cup, but it did OK.

The future for the club looked uncertain – cynics of today would say that some things never change. But in 1969 Edinburgh's then council revealed plans for building a college at the site where

Ferranti played their games. To make up for it, the council offered another ground not far away but it would take some cash to get it working.

One way of saving money was by getting wives to wash strips, which is where the Bain household came in.

John said: "It was all done for the love of the game. Not a penny came my way. My bosses at the work prohibited me from taking any wages and I was not allowed to even claim travelling expenses. It actually cost me money to be involved, but there was never any question that I would turn my back on the team."

Ferranti coughed up some of the money for the improvements, including much-needed changing facilities.

Another thing the club gained was company, as the Hibs Reserves moved in 1971. While some people complained about this, it was actually a very important event – and a positive one as it helped Ferranti achieve a much-attempted entry to the Scottish Football Association, better known as the SFA, the ruling body of the game in Scotland. However joining the SFA did not mean that the team were able to join the league and that took a little more than help from Hibs, which had been the case in getting into the SFA.

Two things helped Ferranti more than anything. The first was Third Lanark going out of business in 1967 and subsequent plans for league reorganisation to make up the shortfall.

The second was a concerted press campaign by some Scottish newspapers, especially the much-loved Edinburgh newspapers: *The Edinburgh Evening News* and *Scotsman*.

One of the factors that the papers were quick to play up was that Ferranti were centrally based and able to get to most of the other grounds, unlike some of the other clubs that were jostling for the vacant spot, especially the Highland-based clubs.

And for the so-far-unpaid John Bain, this meant more work

"When the chance came to join the league we jumped at it. I got serious. I spent months scouting for votes from the big clubs. I went around them all and tried to play my PR bit, telling them we'd be good for the league. The likes of Inverness and Elgin City were battling against us and they put us down because we were just a works team."

"But something we said must have struck a chord because Hibs, Hearts and Tom Devlin at Celtic backed us up and we were admitted."

Of course, the only way for the matter to be sorted was through an AGM and at that meeting there were seven clubs to choose from: Elgin City; Ferranti Thistle; Forres Mechanics; Gateshead United; Hawick Royal Albert; Inverness Thistle and Ross County.

This was knocked down to two clubs – Ferranti and Inverness – who both pulled in 13 votes each, with all the others polling much less. The second round of voting went in favour of the capital team, beating Inverness 21 votes to 16. Historians of the club could claim that this was the beginning of the rivalry between the two – a rivalry that would continue into the 21st century!

But the victory did not come without problems – specifically the club's name – that was seen as an endorsement of the company and almost a type of sponsorship, given that the company had been putting some support and funds into the club. This was a problem because no type of sponsorship was allowed in those days, so the most obvious way round all of this was for the club to change its name, but to what?

At the time John Bain was quite vocal in the problems as he told the *Evening News*.

He shrugged off talk of the club name changing to Edinburgh Ferranti FC or Edinburgh City FC and he even pointed out that "the SFA accepted us as Ferranti Thistle when we qualified for the last two Scottish Cups. If they can do it why can't the Scottish League follow suit?"

But it was for nothing and the club were told that if they wanted to play in the top Scottish leagues then the name would have to change.

The *Evening News* got back in the act and called for a new name for the club. It also revealed that the club would be playing at the then-quality ground of Meadowbank Stadium, which was looked after by the council.

A number of wild suggestions were made, including reversing the Ferranti in Ferranti Thistle, but the eventual name chosen was that of Meadowbank Thistle, with John Bain being the first boss of the newly named team.

And he had some good shoulders to lean on for support if he needed it – including a future European Cup winner.

"I got a lot of support from guys like Alex Ferguson at that time," said Bain.

"He was at East Stirling and I'd phone him for advice on tactics and stuff. Alex Smith, then at Stirling Albion, was the same."

"There was a camaraderie between football people that pulled us all through the troubles."

Bain had one year in charge at senior level before joining the board on Ferranti's instructions. John Blacklaw was the club's first chairman.

Former Hibs's player Willie McFarlane took over the running of the club in 1978, bringing in with him Terry Christie, who found out the hard way what it was like to co-run a club.

In fact things were so bad, he resigned after one year, promising only to return on the basis that things would change.

"They were still an East of Scotland amateur team at heart and didn't have a clue what they were doing in senior football," he recalled years later.

"One of the biggest struggles I had with the board was to ban our supporters travelling on the first team bus to away games. We used to pick up our supporters and they'd sit on the bus with the players, then we'd collect them again afterwards and take them home.

"It was also impossible trying to persuade even non-league players to join us. In my early days at Meadowbank we couldn't sign juniors because all the East Coast lads felt Bonnyrigg Rose and Linlithgow Rose were bigger clubs and paid better wages."

Of course things looked to pick up when the team signed a Scottish internationalist for a goalie.

The only problem being was that he played volleyball.

Christie remembers: "Willie McFarlane reasoned that because Connie Johnston was a big lad, had played in goal for Spartans and played volleyball, he must be useful with his hands."

Christie became the club's fourth boss in 1980 and he found that as well as manager he was often the groundskeeper because the financially-strapped council had got rid of the ground's full-time groundskeeper.

His first task on a match day was replacing divots caused by javelin throwers and shot-putters who had gouged holes in the playing surface, as the stadium tried to cater to more than just footballers.

Christie said, "One cup tie I turned up, having to replace huge patches of turf. Meanwhile a massive shot-putter was waiting to finish his training session."

"Eventually he lost the plot and confronted me and angry words were exchanged. He became so heated it became clear to me the incident was going to come to blows."

"I got my retaliation in first and did a runner. It was lucky for me the guy was a shot-putter rather than a sprinter because he was too big to catch me!"

Another problem was the lack of decent football facilities, with proper changing room not being built until the mid-1980s, though Christie felt that this sometimes helped the team, as no-one wanted to be at Meadowbank and play.

Another problem was that the council – as the owners of the land – very often threw games into chaos, something Bain will never forget.

"At Ferranti we could just play football on the public parks, but at Meadowbank we had to go by council rules. That meant if they wanted a function on under the main stand they could put it on at a minute's notice and scupper our football."

"Sometimes I'd get a call a week before a game saying 'You can't play next weekend because we're having a cat show.'"

"Dog shows, flower shows, you name it. There were all sorts of reasons for games being cancelled and it was really starting to upset the Scottish League."

Despite all of this, the club still had its moments. In 1983 they were promoted to the First Division and in 1987, history could have turned one way and changed the way everything would happen in terms of forming Livingston, after Meadowbank were second in the First Division.

Some years this could have been enough to get up – or at least force a playoff – but this was not one of those years.

In 1988 John Bain retired from working and was presented with a TV set as a present. On it was an inscription: "This present will enable you to sit back in comfort to watch your team play in the Premier League."

But the Premier League looked a long way away then. It seemed as if things were just going to go on with the club achieving some small successes for the very small but faithful number of fans, but it would never be third in the top Scottish league, or travel to Europe.

But in 1991, one man had a different idea. And that man was Bill Hunter, a businessman who owned shops, pubs, a plant hire firm and other interests. And over time he sold these off to look after the club, but at that point he was only the Secretary of Meadowbank Thistle.

Bill knew that the club couldn't go on as it had been for the previous decade. He knew there had to be complete change in the club.

His plans included leaving Meadowbank Stadium because games were being put off because the council had other events it wanted to hold.

According to Bill: "What happened was, I was invited to join the board of directors after having been going about the club since 1978. That's 13 years I was going about the club. I was a supporter, but in those days, because of the profile of the club, it was like drawing teeth trying to get a sponsor and the most that Meadowbank had ever had was about £1,000 a season for a bit of sponsorship."

"I spoke to the directors and said, "Look, we've really got to try and do something with this club or they're never ever going to go anywhere, and they'll just go defunct eventually."

One of the things that Hunter considered was moving the club. He knew the club had to leave Edinburgh central. Hibs and Hearts were both struggling so his smaller club had no chance of bringing people in. Never mind the heyday of 4,000 - sometimes they were lucky to have 40 fans.

But by September 1993 things were moving on, including Terry Christie who had resigned in 1992 when he was voted off the Meadowbank board of directors.

Hunter had considered East Kilbride and Glenrothes as new venues for the club. Twice attempts were made - but soon aborted - to relocate to Musselburgh before Livingston was suggested.

Talks were at an advanced stage with the East Lothian Council and there was a plan to move Meadowbank to Musselburgh, before Livingston came on the scene. However, although East Lothian was willing it didn't really have the financial power to see the move through.

According to Hunter: "I also had option on 22 acres of land with a firm of house builders. They were going to sell me it for agricultural price. If I had got the planning permission down in East Lothian it was breaking the green belt, so they were going to have hundreds of acres of land into the green belt. That got knocked on the head because the police said it would be a traffic hazard going onto the new bypass."

"But the club had to move to a new area, where I hoped the locals would come out and support their local team instead of going to Edinburgh or further to support a team."

"I foresaw the potential for increased crowds, and subsequently more revenue, from a whole new fan base."

"I also predicted and hoped that the club, if armed with a 10,000-seat, criteria-meeting ground, would play in the Premier League within seven years."

But once Hunter had the club he could decide its fate, though a sporting Conservative would prove to be a catalyst as well.

Livingston Development Corporation's Brian Meek suggested that instead of looking to the east of the city, why did he not look west, specifically to the new town of Livingston.

According to Hunter, that had been considered before and knocked back – but that was in the Seventies.

Hunter remembers: "They were a new town and the West Lothian Development Corporation was winding down and had money to spend. They saw the opportunity to leave Livingston the legacy of a football stadium as too good an opportunity to miss and there is no doubt it has brought the town a sense of identity."

"Meek overcame my mild concerns by promising the bulk of the stake money for a new £5.1million stadium. Meek's corporation was being formally disbanded, but had significant funds remaining."

However, from there Bill went from being secretary to the top man at the club as he bought the majority of the club's shares after converting it into a limited company.

"I decided to try and take control of the club after the chairman asked me to look into options for saving the club, including making it a limited company. I got permission from the club's founder members – not as easy as it sounds because they were all over the world - and I underwrote the shares."

"The founder members were given the first option of buying the shares. That left 62 per cent of the shares and I bought them. With that out of the road, I started opening talks with anyone that I thought could save the club."

But fans launched a shock takeover bid for the club at this point, as some knew of Hunter's plans for the club.

David Baxter, a founder member of the Thistle Action Group as well as an ex-editor of the club programme and editor of an excellent fanzine called The Thistle, said, "This bid is funded by people who do not wish to see the club die. The supporters are virtually 100% behind us."

"We don't like the way it's being handled and are concerned about the lack of communication from the club. We don't feel they've been level with us."

And to be fair, the protesters had at least one valid point: "The reason that fans from other clubs have supported us is that this will be the first franchise in Scottish football - Clyde did not have to change their name when they moved to Cumbernauld so why should we?"

And a petition was signed by over 4,200 people to politicians to express their concern at the move. If only these people had been going to the games every week, some pointed out, then it might never have been in financial dire straights.

But Hunter pressed on.

Hunter called Meek up and set up meetings with the LDC. Within one week of gaining control of the club, a tentative deal had been set up for the club to move to Livingston.

Of course, it wasn't easy. Yet again, the club name was the problem. 'Meadowbank' would obviously have to go – the problem was 'Thistle'. The word had links back to the Ferranti days and some of the older people were reluctant to see it go and felt that getting rid of it was a betrayal.

The abuse Hunter took was animalistic and undeserved. Family members were spat at, death threats were made, his car was scratched and some people chanted, "If you've shagged Bill Hunter's daughter clap your hands."

Hunter ended up banning daughter Cathy from games to protect her. At the time he said, "I can take all they throw at me. But enough is enough when they chant obscenities at my 15year-old daughter."

But the reasons for the name change were quite simple, including the fact that the LDC would not put up cash otherwise. This was money earmarked for Livingston as Hunter recalls.

He said, "The name 'West Lothian' was never mentioned. Being Livingston Development Corporation, and they were putting the money up, they wanted 'Livingston'. If I had wanted to make it 'West Lothian,' they wouldn't have gone along with it."

While the problems with the name were a disgraceful end to that chapter of the club's small but dignified history, it only strengthened Hunter's resolve ("At every game I got abuse, but

I've no regrets. Nobody can take it away from me, that it was my vision.") And the name 'Livingston FC' was settled on, pending approval from Scottish football bosses, which was granted in April 1994 with the name to take effect from the start of the 1995-96 season.

Of course, now that off the pitch was settled, Hunter had to look to on the pitch and what was going to happen there. Specifically, who was going to manage the club?

Hunter's choice was made for him one Monday night in March 1995 at a sporting event in West Lothian.

Jim Leishman was there with Davie Cooper – who would die just days later – and George McNeill, who was the chairman for the night.

What settled it for Hunter was when McNeill said that Jim should be the next manager of Meadowbank.

According to Hunter: "The response Jim got that night persuaded me. People were chanting for him to be made manager. I wanted a man the community could identify with."

"There is a charisma about Jim and it was vital we appointed a man who would work well within the community."

Leishman was well-known and loved in Scottish football.

After a double leg-break ended his playing career at the age of 25, Leishman became the youngest Premier League manager when he once guided Dunfermline back into the top flight a few weeks after turning 33.

It was while at Dunfermline that he first attracted media attention for the power of his oratory – something which would come back to haunt him over the years as puns grew about his poems.

But while some people thought he was being wacky, Leishman had a reason for the way he acted.

"When I arrived at Dunfermline in 1983 the club was fourth bottom of the second division. Yet in the Sixties they'd been cup semi-finalists. Consequently, we'd rate about one paragraph in the national papers - if we were lucky. When I started the Shakespeare and Churchill thing we started getting a quarter of a page, then half a page, then a full page. It brought us the publicity we needed at the time to give the players a bit of confidence in themselves and pride in what had been a great club."

After being sacked from Dunfermline he had spells with Inverness Thistle and Montrose before ending up with Fife junior outfit Rosyth Recreation for 18 months before Hunter approached him and it was good timing, as Leisman told reporters.

He said, "For the past six months I have been itching to return to senior football, and getting in at the start of something like moving to a new town is tremendous."

"There are similarities here to Dunfermline, with a community that needs to be galvanised behind their team."

"My immediate job is to try to keep us in the Second Division, but long-term I have to attract people to watch Livingston FC next season. We will have a smashing new stadium and I want to fill it."

And in a mantra that would become very familiar over the years, he said, "There are thousands of Rangers, Celtic, Hearts and Hibs fans living in Livingston who don't get to games. I want them to adopt us."

Leishman's first signing was Cowdenbeath midfielder Willie Callaghan for £15,000, showing the club was serious about the future.

Work started in December 1994 and it was hoped that the stadium would be ready in time for the new season, but it wasn't, though there was still a lot to look forward to – a new team in a new town.

Who knew where it would end? Or how well the team would do?

CHAPTER
3

AND SO IT BEGAN

And so it began on August 5 1995 with the first Livingston game – the first round of the league cup against Montrose, and things started promisingly with a 2-0 win for the newcomers.

It was a memorable game – and not just for the fans. For Stewart Williamson, it gave him an insight into why people were so ready to give everything for Jim Leishman.

"Jim gave us his Braveheart speech, which had nothing at all to do with football, but it was all about passion and having the will to win," he recalled.

"He went on about how we could be fighting in Bosnia or down a pit and that we had our fitness and health and we should enjoy having them.

"As the season went on, I learned that he had all sorts of speeches before games that make you go out on a different plane, totally psyched up for it.

"After the game he cracked a great line as well - that we'd won every game in the club's history and how many teams could say that. That sort of line was Jim all over. He knew how to make you feel as if you'd accomplished something special."

Leishman's ten-minute speech was dramatic and passionate not just for the players, but also for himself because it was his first time at Montrose since resigning as manager three years earlier.

And in true soap opera fashion, his rival in the home dugout was a man that Jim had got rid of at one point - Andy Doran.

Montrose had some excellent build-up play but Livi were the hungrier of the two teams

And the closest they came in the opening half-hour was a McDonald header that bounced off the back of Livi goalkeeper Horace Stoute.

The first-ever Livingston goal came from former St Johnstone player Jason Young in the 22nd minute, who ran all over the pitch constantly, tiring out players but never himself, summing up this new fresh air that had been breathed into Scottish football.

In the second half, the home team nearly forced the equaliser from a well-directed Mailer header, but Williamson headed it off the line and Livi broke off on the attack. Young passed the ball to Grant McMartin, grabbing the second in the 61st minute to set up a second round game against St Johnstone.

Afterwards a member of the crowd turned round and shouted, "Hey, Leishman, that's the first victory you've ever had at Links Park!" and according to those who were there, the manager just couldn't resist bursting into a grin at the comment.

And to show that everyone was in the party mood with the result, on the way back to Meadowbank Stadium to drop the players off, Bill Hunter rewarded the players by stopping the coach for a quick celebratory drink.

The first league game was against a team that over the years would prove themselves to be the club's biggest thorn – Inverness Caledonian Thistle, but between them they also provide some of the most entertaining matches Scottish football has seen.

And while the first manager Livingston had faced up to and had been an old Leishman associate, it was nearly the case that Livingston were facing against Big Jim this day as he revealed at the time: "If it hadn't been for the travelling I could have ended up in charge at Caley."

And he added prophetically: "They will be one of our main challengers."

Anyway, Livingston – and their small travelling support - left the Highlands a happy team that day, having won by three goals.

Then it was time to play with the big boys on August 19, for a game against St Johnstone took place at McDiarmid Park.

Both teams were hungry for it but Livingston took the edge when Grant McMartin's shot bounced out of a crowded goalmouth for Lee Bailey to be able to whack it in the 8th minute.

But St Johnstone kept battling away and were rewarded with an equaliser when George O'Boyle made it one-one after a set-piece cross by Twaddle.

Despite some fierce battling and exciting play – more so by St Johnstone as the game went on – it ended up a draw, not just after full-time but also after extra time, taking the newcomers to their first dramatic penalty shootout.

Four Livingston players managed to hit the net, including Mark Duthie, who turned 23 on the day. He later quipped that his scoring

– and Stoute saving two of the St Johnstone penalty shots – were two of the best birthday presents he could get.

For the newspapers, this was great stuff. Big Jim Leishman's return to football had already pulled off a giant killing act and while it was great news, the big issue facing the club at that point was the fact that their next game – against Morton – was meant to be a home game, but the new Almondvale Stadium was still incomplete, and would stay that way until November.

This meant the club had to return to the charmless environment of their old ground at Meadowbank for a game against Morton, which they won 1-0. For fans who had dreamed of the glory days to come, going back there was a brutal reminder of the past and very few turned up for the old games, despite the club's winning streak.

It might be that the stadium actually helped the club, though as Morton boss Allan McGraw confessed: "Playing there is like playing in a ghost town."

That winning streak continued with a 3-1 massacre of Arbroath and fans were looking forward to the game against Partick Thistle.

By now people were starting to take things seriously, given the results that had gone their way to that point. And while Jim couldn't shake off the newspaper jibes about his poems from days gone by, he was concentrating on making the club a force to be reasoned with on and off the park.

"There is no secret to our success. It's down to hard work, pure and simple," he said as he carried out a bunch of press interviews to convince people about Livingston. At one point he quipped: "I'm like a missionary trying to convert people to our cause - like Dr Livingston you could say."

And while he was banning any talk of promotion so early on in the season, he was taking a slightly long term view himself, professing: "We have the population and multi-national firms based in the town to build the foundations to take us into the Premier League."

But the SPL was a long distance away that night as the club tasted their first defeat against Partick Thistle on August 30 with a game which ended 2-1, and while the Thistle fans may have been gloating at the time, over the years it would be Livingston who would have the last laugh, with a better stadium, support and financial situation than that of the old-style supposed romantic team of Scottish football.

September 1995 started well for the club with a crowd of 409 watching a 2-1 win against East Stirlingshire in the league where Dwyer nabbed a goal in the 29th minute for East Stirlingshire while Young nabbed two goals for the Lions' in the 47th and 74th minutes to get the points.

Then there was a two-nil win against St Mirren in the Challenge Cup. Two-nil ended up being the best way to sum up September as Livi went on to win games against Alloa – with Williamson and Smart getting the goals in the 22nd and 49th minutes in front of a muted crowd of 349 - and Queen's Park by that score line too, but something went slightly wrong in the next game on September 23 as Albion Rovers managed to grab a goal, but Livingston still won by scoring two.

Off the pitch there was also some cause for celebration as Jim was named Bell's Third Division Manager of the Month, where he revealed that he was as amazed as anyone to be getting the award.

He said, "A year ago I thought it was adios for me and football, but it's great to be recognised like this. This one's for Livingston, the fans and the players who have been magnificent, but it's important we keep up the good work."

One thing Jim did let slip was that he was getting sick of his detractors though.

"I know some people still think I'm a joke character - but I've always said that I'd invite any of them round to my house and show them my medals; then we'll see if they're still laughing.

"After all, how many other managers can say they have been at the top of every division? I won the second and first with Dunfermline, I'm top of the third with Livingston and I was on top of the Premier with Dunfermline for three days."

The end of September saw a battling – but tired looking – Livingston lose against Stirling Albion, but the club picked themselves up for the next game, against Cowdenbeath, banging out a plucky 1-0 win.

October however started with a run of draws. The first of these was a 1-1 result with Ross County on October 7. Milne scored a penalty in the opening minutes while Young grabbed an equaliser in the dying seconds to make sure of a share of the points.

This wasn't as bad a result as many people made out as Leishman had warned that Ross County would be fighting for promotion. However the result left Livi six points clear at the top.

That was followed up one week later with a 0-0 against Brechin City at Meadowbank with 272 people making the effort to come out.

The club recovered some form – and more importantly three points – at the next game, a one-nil win against Queen's Park with Young grabbing the goal in the 7th minute in front of 590 people.

Arbroath ended the month for Livi on a dismal note though, beating them 1-0 but the club were still seven points ahead at the top of the league - and with the season starting to go on, the memories of the giant killings at the start seemed to be dismissed by some as flukes rather than genuine football achievements, proving that even when you are ahead, there is always someone glad to see you fail.

November saw Alloa roll over and be beaten 2-0 with Duthie grabbing two goals in the space of six minutes.

The next time the Lions' made the news was not mid-month with the eventual opening of the ground, as most thought it would be, but when Celtic chief Fergus McCann slagged off the club.

McCann described Leish's lads as "Livingston Thistle" on a Scot FM radio programme about the state of Scottish football.

And as part of his argument for restructuring the game he claimed some clubs should be killed off.

McCann said, "How many people want to watch the likes of Livingston Thistle anyway?"

It didn't take Big Jim long to fire out a reply. "He should get his facts right. Doesn't he realise we're moving into our new stadium next week? We expect between 2000 and 3000 fans for our first game against East Stirling on Saturday."

"We are backed by world-known organisations Mitsubishi and Russell Athletic and we're providing senior football for a catchment area of 160,000 people."

"And by the way, we are Livingston FC - not Livingston Thistle."

And then, finally, it was the big day. November 11, 1995. The day the Lions' were complete by being able to move into Almondvale Stadium.

Billy Connolly has often joked that the Queen thinks the world smells of paint because wherever she goes, that is the smell that greets her. If that's the case then Livi fans were certainly treated like royalty because the smell of fresh paint was everywhere.

Management and the board had originally said that if they got more than 1000 people then they would be happy campers. They ended up with more than 4000.

For Bill Hunter, it was vindication. He had shown that with some vision and ambition, it was possible to take a dying club and then remake them successfully. The best comparison was the American Football style of taking a club to somewhere they can have proper facilities and decent support.

For Jim Leishman, it was a day to find a goalkeeper, as Stout was injured, and Steve Ellison wasn't playing. Rab Douglas – later to play with Celtic and Dundee – ended up between the sticks.

The Almond View summed up the day perfectly. "The first game in the new stadium attracted a capacity crowd which led to an electrifying atmosphere. The game kicked-off late to allow the large crowd into the ground on a very wet day.

"The game started with a crescendo of noise and the players looking a little nervous. After a great run by McMartin early on that nearly produced a goal the visitors started to show. They had two excellent chances to open the scoring of which the second was brilliantly saved by Douglas. After the first ten minutes the game settled into a pattern with both sides creating openings but not threatening the goal-keepers much.

"By the half-hour the expectation of a goal had dimmed and the bigger cheers were reserved for the ball being kicked out of the ground. Both McMartin and Duthie looked dangerous on the wings with Bailey doing well in the centre.

"The second-half saw Livingston looking more composed, and in the 50th minute McMartin created havoc in the opposition penalty area with the ball being scrambled away for a corner. Then the moment everyone had been waiting for; Bailey got the ball out on the right, moved forward, looked up and played an intelligent ball to the feet of Young who made no mistake and hit the back of the net."

"Livingston then took control with both Sorbie & Bailey nearly increasing the lead. Then in the 69th minute the roof fell-in with East Stirlingshire equalising."

"The ball came over from the right and McLean was left unmarked at the back-post giving Douglas no chance to save his bullet-header. Livingston went in search of a winner - with McLeod hitting the post offering the best of the chances."

24

After a draw in the opening game, the pressure was on for a home win the following week. Unfortunately the complete opposite happened with Cowdenbeath being party poopers and scoring a goal to take all the points.

Then the team went and played away and on the journey must have found their winning streak beating Albion Rovers 2-0 with Young getting both goals – one in the 14th minute and one in the 54th minute, scoring from the penalty spot – to depress most of the 433 crowd that turned up for the late November game.

Then it was back home for a friendly against Kilmarnock, for the official game to celebrate the switching-on of the Almondvale lights.

Again, the lights helped the team find their winning way as it was a 5-2 drubbing of the full strength Premier League team.

An own goal by Neil Whitworth set the homeboys on their way and further goals came from trialist Cona Hislop, Graham Harvey, Gordon McLeod and Mark Duthie. Derek Anderson and John Henry scored for Killie.

More than 3,400 turned out for the next home game on December 2 against Ross County. Sadly, it wasn't the best of games, ending up as a nil-nil draw but form was well and truly recovered the following week for the first round of the Scottish Cup against Stranraer.

Former Airdrie and Dundee striker Graham Harvey was the inspiration for Livingston as they won the only Scottish Cup tie to survive the weather of the day.

He gave the Third Division leaders the lead after 31 minutes and was instrumental in the build-up to their second goal, scored by Duthie eight minutes later.

Second Division Stranraer, who hadn't been beaten at home this season, huffed and puffed in the second half, but when Douglas saved Duncan's penalty their chance of a comeback was lost and Harvey scored the visitors' third in the final seconds.

And who was it in the next round? Inverness Caledonian Thistle.

Before that saw a league game against Brechin, but the club were rocked hours before kick-off with rumours of cash problems at the club. Skipper Gordon McLeod fumed at the reports that claimed players were ready to strike over a cash row on bonuses and what the players would be paid if they won the league.

McLeod told reporters: "It's rubbish. We are currently involved in amicable negotiations with Chairman Bill Hunter over bonuses."

Nonetheless the carping and sniping by those out with the club took its toll and the team lost 2-0 – hardly the perfect Christmas present for the fans.

The New Year brought a new player to the club - former Dundee defender Steve Campbell from Irish side Coleraine.

Caley wanted revenge for the defeat earlier in the season and they got it thanks to one man.

Caley boss Steve Paterson had paid £15,000 for striker Brian Thomson because he was missing top scorer Iain Stewart for the clash, and he repaid him as Caley won 3-2.

Livingston never had time to dwell on the defeat though with three games needing to be played in the space of a week. First up was a three-one win Queen's Park on January 10. But after that it was three defeats as Albion Rovers beat the Lions' one-nil with 2500 watching the home team get beat as Crawford scored the only goal in the 76th minute. Then Caledonian Thistle and Brechin came to Almondvale and walked away with three points each, Caley winning two-nil and Brechin winning one-nil, leaving the club with only having won one game from their first seven games at their new home.

A win against Alloa at Almondvale on February 10 silenced some critics as did the news that Jim Leishman had signed a new three-year deal to stay at the club.

The next game was an away match against Ross County and the points were shared by the teams as it ended a two-each draw.

Then it was a game against East Stirlingshire which ended on a happier note, but not for most of the 472 crowd made up mostly of East Stirlingshire fans, as the Lions' won 3-0 despite the absence of Graham Harvey, who had a groin injury. Young grabbed two goals in the 17th and 66th minutes and Sinclair nabbed one in between during the 22nd minute.

This put the club back on top of the league through virtue of goals scored, as Brechin could only manage a 0-0 draw at home to third-placed Ross County.

By February 24, the pressure was starting to be felt, especially as that day's games saw the four top sides face each other. Livingston faced Arbroath.

Big Jim summed it up perfectly when he said, "It's exciting for the fans, but nerve-wracking for the bosses."

Livingston won 2-1, with David Alleyne shooting the winner.

A game against Cowdenbeath was equally exciting the following week when the Lions' beat them three-nil.

At the same time Jim Leishman revealed he was in talks with education chiefs with a view to running coaching sessions in local schools.

Leishman said, "The club wants to become part of the community and coaching pupils in the local schools is a step in the right direction."

The club also signed former Hearts and Falkirk midfielder George Wright until the end of the season.

And then it was Inverness Caledonian Thistle again, Living up to their reputation as being a thorn, with a stirring second-half performance to clinch a draw which kept them in touch with the leaders, who threw away a 2-0 lead.

A rather turgid first half was illuminated momentarily after 11 minutes, when Livingston's Grant McMartin crossed and Jason Young scored.

The home side, unchanged for the last three games, then staged a solid defensive performance which limited the visitors to only a couple of weak shots on target, although towards the end of the half Caley Thistle managed to build some attacking moves.

Half time broke the team's flow though and at the start of the second half Lee Bailey put Livingston 2-0 ahead with a curling right-foot shot.

Livingston twice went close at nabbing another goal, first through Bailey whose dipping shot in the 56th minute was tipped over by James Calder, the Caley goalkeeper, who then made another excellent in the 79th minute to deny Grant McMartin.

However in the 80th minute Colin Mitchell's through-ball to fellow substitute Charlie Christie resulted in Chris Sinclair putting the ball through his own net.

Just as Livingston were getting over the shock of conceding a goal, the visitors then drew level after 86 minutes, Michael Teasdale glancing in Graeme Bennett's low-driven corner.

The club picked themselves up from that for a March 9 win over Albion Rovers with a first-half goal from Alleyne securing the points in the 33rd minute.

Clever footwork from Bailey almost brought a second goal shortly before half time but his shot was too close to Moffat.

Early in the second half, Bailey was just short of connecting with a McMartin cross and Alleyne was not far away with a 20-yard shot but Albion showed more resilience when their substitutes Strain and Bell came on.

As time wore on, it became clear they would have to settle for their solitary goal but the final whistle was nevertheless greeted with a roar by the large Livingston support who welcomed it as another step towards the championship.

A match report in one of the tabloids noted that "Livingston are a First Division team masquerading in the Third Division."

A home game against Cowdenbeath was next with the East coast team winning 2-1.

March was rounded out by two league draws – a 1-1 win against Alloa Athletic and a similar result on March 30 against East Stirlingshire.

A home game against Ross County – and a 2-1 win – saw the team go 12 points clear at the top but Jim warned against early celebrations.

He said, "No way will I claim promotion if we win this one. There would still be four games to go - and 12 points to play for."

"The season doesn't end until May 4 – that's where you assess what you've done."

Stewart Williamson added: "Talk of promotion never comes into the changing room. The gaffer has it drummed into us to take one game at a time and not to look too far ahead."

An away win against Brechin was followed by an April 20 0-0 draw against Queen's Park, setting up the last home game for the end of the season.

Livingston were without Stout and David Alleyne, who was on international duty, and injured Craig Smart, but still managed to win 3-0 to clinch the championship and promotion.

And despite his talk of not mentioning the future, manager Leish let slip: "Coming to Livingston has been great for this club, even if it took us a while to get used to our new stadium."

"We've settled in now and we can't wait to get in among the Second Division clubs next season."

However the season ended on an ominous note. The club were so worried that West Lothian councillors would change their minds on a cash pledge to help build a new 1850-seat stand at Almondvale Stadium that Bill Hunter asked local MP and Livingston supporter Robin Cook to step in.

CHAPTER
4

CHANGES

There were some changes at the start of the season with Tommy Callaghan from Dunfermline joining and Steven Ellison and Stuart Wilson leaving, to go to Stenhousemuir and Queen of the South. Another thing that seemed to have changed was the club abandoning its winning ways.

The first result was a howler with the club losing 5-2 to Ayr United in the Coca Cola League Cup, but at least it wasn't a dull game, especially as the club learned that Steve Kerrigan - who scored twice for United – shouldn't have been playing. The striker should have been serving a one-match ban slapped on him before his close season switch from Stranraer.

Livingston protested that the game should be replayed but SFA chiefs threw that decision out and instead Ayr were fined £12,000, leaving Bull Hunter very unhappy.

He said, "I accept the decision - but I'm not happy. We were in a similar situation when we were fined £5000 for fielding Paul Rutherford against Stenhousemuir at a time when our attendance was only 200 a game."

"Possibly the £12,000 fine reflects that Ayr can look forward to a good financial return from their tie against Kilmarnock. That does not help us for we have missed out on the chance of extra cash."

From that it was on to a game against Inverness Caledonian Thistle in the Challenge Cup.

Everyone at the club was up for facing their old foes, but it was the second cup defeat in a week for the club, made all the worse because it was a home defeat, being beaten 2-1 in literally the dying seconds of the game.

Brian Thomson gave the visitors the lead with a 16-yard effort after 10 minutes. Livi's Mark Duthie blew a chance for the team to go ahead when he missed a penalty after 59 minutes, but they looked to have forced extra time when Jason Young scrambled in an equaliser 11 minutes later.

But Paul Cherry sent Caley Thistle through with a crashing volley – just 15 seconds from time.

Leishman told people that yes they were disappointed to be out of both cups, especially as the income would have been more than welcome, but it now left the players free to concentrate on the league and that's exactly what they appeared to do, winning six of their first eight games and drawing the other two with the first loss coming against Ayr United, who were starting to look like the jinx team for the season.

But the first of the games was against Queen of the South and one player who was looking forward to it was Stuart Wilson, who was with Queens and facing his old team mates. He told newspapers at the time that he felt Jason Young was the danger player to watch, but in the end he wasn't, and a glorious day which saw the league flag unfurled at Almondvale was made complete with a 3-1 win.

Their goals, which all came in the first half, were scored by Grant McMartin, Mark Duthie and Graham Harvey. Craig Flannigan's goal for Queen of the South in the 81st minute was too little, too late.

The next game was a 2-1 away win against Stranraer and then before the club's next game - a home leg against Hamilton Academical - the team continued their role as being part of the community by going to a civic reception and celebration designed to mark their promotion. Afterwards though, fun was swapped for physical exercise as the players got ready for the game, which had an added edge to it for the managers involved as it was the first time Jim Leishman and Ian Munro would face off since their split at Dunfermline six years ago.

To be fair Munro said, "I don't think there are any grudges between Jim and me – we've spoken often enough since then."

Both sides had doubts for their starting, but in the end the Lions' had nothing to worry about as a Graham Harvey header saw the Lions' go to the top of the Second Division with a 100% record.

September started with a game against Brechin City and beforehand Jim revealed his winning strategy for the team: "I don't worry about being in front. I simply stick to the formula that won us the Third Division title last season - worry about one game at a time."

Brechin boss John Young was also up for the game and he praised Livi's storming start. He said, "They are the team of the moment and they deserve to be. They've got off to a flier whereas we are finding our feet in this division."

"But last season we beat them once and managed two draws, so we're relishing facing them again. We're underdogs, but that was the case last term too."

And they stayed underdogs as Livingston won 2-1 win at home to maintain their 100% league record.

The next game saw Dumbarton get walloped 4-2, but the club followed that up with a draw against Stenhousemuir, though September ended on a high with three points from Berwick after the club won 2-1.

October kicked off with a draw against Clyde and an away loss to Ayr, but form seemed to come back with a 2-0 win over Stranraer and a 5-0 gubbing of Dumbarton taking the club into November.

And while things were unpredictable on the pitch, off pitch things were proceeding nicely.

Bill Hunter announced that anyone caught using harsh language would be turfed from the stadium and this helped bring in more families, impressed with the man's candour and efforts to make it a family ground and family team.

But he also revealed that he had came close to chucking it all in as at times he felt he was completely unappreciated by some.

"I thought of packing this whole thing in - particularly when we were getting abuse during games," he said.

And he also let slip that the club could have perhaps kept the old name, much to the ire of some.

"I suppose I could have dug my heels in a little more to keep the name Meadowbank, but part of the key to success here has been in calling the club Livingston."

Plans were also nearing completion for the third stand with seating for around 2000 fans and Hunter announced he was planning to give away 1000 seats to local youngsters for every home game from December to the end of the season.

He also revealed that by the end of 1996 he had put in more than £400,000 to the club, ending up with 74 percent of the shares and despite the fact that doctors told him to take it easy after heart surgery in 1994 he was putting in 70 hour weeks to make sure his dream came true.

But he also hinted that he would be prepared to step aside if the right offer came in.

Prophetically he said, "This club will go on with or without me.

31

"I've put a lot into this club, both in time and money, and if somebody with money was prepared to come in and buy me out then so be it. I would hope to be involved, but if I wasn't then I've done my bit."

The mid-November game against Berwick, which followed a no scoring draw against Brechin, saw a meeting of two old minds - Leishman versus Berwick boss Jimmy Thomson, who was caretaker manager at Dunfermline for a spell in the early 80s when he asked Jim to take over the reserve team – and within a couple of months Jim had the manager's job.

Livingston won 2-1 at Berwick thanks to two goals in the first half from Tom Callaghan. Ayr United stayed at the top of the Second Division by just one point after a 1-0 victory over Stranraer. Alain Horas, their French trialist, scored the game's only goal in the 73rd minute.

The game against Clyde gave Livingston the chance to keep the pressure on Ayr, but a howler of a match saw them lose by two goals. Miller Mathieson's first-half header gave Clyde the lead and Eddie Annand tied up the win in the last minute. To make matters worse, Grant Tierney broke two ribs and looked set to be out until the New Year and Hamilton beating Brechin meant that the Lions' slipped to third place in the league.

Midfielder Tom Callaghan was of the opinion though that the game served as a wake-up call to the team.

He said, "Maybe we were getting a bit cocky and this is just the slap in the face we needed. It has brought us all back to earth."

As always Jim Leishman put it into perspective: "There is no pressure on us, remember we've just come up from the Third Division."

The team were all fired up for the early December game against Stenhousemuir winning 2-1 at home. A lacklustre first half from Livingston allowed Stenhousemuir a half-time lead through Ian Little's 33rd-minute header, but the team pulled it together to get the three points.

Meanwhile the *Sunday Mail* newspaper exposed a hate campaign against Bill Hunter.

Scotland's top selling Sunday newspaper revealed a divinity student was involved in a hate campaign against Hunter.

Minister's son Diarmid Campbell-Jack, 21, used the internet to post allegations about Bill Hunter's personal and business life. And he used his Edinburgh University student e-mail account to keep in touch with others who share his views.

Hunter was furious. "This is damaging to the club when we are trying to raise money through commercial activities," he said.

When the *Sunday Mail* tracked down Campbell-Jack, he offered to take the webpage down and added: "I am not the only one involved and I don't necessarily agree with everything stated. If Mr Hunter is offended by anything we have said, I can only apologise."

Back on the pitch, the next game against Ayr would prove to be a vital one for all concerned. Ayr needed the points to stay at the top, while Livi needed the points to keep the pressure on the leaders.

Livi gave Grant Tierney and Graham Davidson last minute fitness tests while Ayr were without suspended pair Jock McStay and Steve Kerrigan.

And while everyone was thinking of going top, Jim Leishman said being top at Xmas wasn't what mattered, adding: "It would be good to go top but being there on May 10 is all that counts."

It was a tight game but Livi managed to win 1-0 nabbing all three points, but there was one more game before the Christmas break, against Queen of the South, that looked set to be as tough as the Ayr game.

Queens boss Rowan Alexander decided to field an experienced team including Jim Brown, Steve Leslie and David Kennedy.

The Queens boss said, "This is not a job for the young boys - we need experience for this one."

Meanwhile Livi were without Grant Tierney, Graeme Davidson, Tom Callaghan and Gordon McLeod.

Livingston took the points, winning 2-1, to go five points clear at the top but that result was not without sweat, graft and toil as Queen of the South bombarded the Livi goal in the second half.

Graham Harvey had an off day by his standards – after all, he didn't score - but he still played a massive role in the game.

Mark Duthie's cross from the right midway through the first half picked out the unguarded Grant McMartin who hit a weak shot through David Mathieson's legs and over the line.

The second goal arrived eight minutes from half-time when the unfortunate David Kennedy, who should have been policing McMartin at the first goal, played his part again when he almost put the ball past his own goalkeeper. When Mathieson saved it, referee John Rowbotham ruled that it was a back-pass. Steve Campbell rolled the ball forward for Duthie to provide the finish.

And Queen of the South gave Livi a boost when George Rowe felled Harvey and was shown the red card.

They still managed to pull a goal back, scored by Craig Flannigan, before half-time and then saw the two teams levelled to ten men when Livingston defender Stewart Williamson was sent off in 63 minutes for fouling.

Most fans treated the January 1 game against Berwick Rangers as a formality. After all, the Rangers were bottom of the league and 32 points separated the teams.

Jim Leishman warned people that it wouldn't be a foregone conclusion. He warned: "Although we are sitting at the top and Berwick are at the bottom it would be totally unprofessional to go into the game expecting to win this match easily."

"I watched Berwick against Ayr United last week and for a long period in the match it was very even.

"My players know that they can't be complacent - that would spell disaster."

They must have forgotten though because the Lions' were given a New Year slap and hangover with the end result being a draw, proving Leishman right that there are no sure things in football.

The fact that Berwick made it at all made the game even more amazing as a number of players had flu or failed to turn up because of poor weather.

Bill Hunter then had to kill some New Year happiness by warning the young fans to behave at games.

Some of the children benefiting from the free tickets being handed out were misbehaving so much during games that police pleaded with Chairman Bill Hunter to make an announcement before each game telling the kids to sit down and behave.

Hunter put the blame on who decided to use Livingston games as a nursery – a move which didn't endear him to many.

The draws continued with a nothing-each game in the Scottish Cup against Brechin.

The next league game saw the team face off old familiar Terry Christie who said he would be able to predict some of the team plan as he had signed a bundle of the players during his time at Meadowbank, like Stewart Williamson, Duthie and Thomson.

Unfortunately for Christie the team he had out wasn't as good as the team he had help sign and they were beaten 3-1. Gordon

McLeod and Graham Harvey scored for Livingston before Ian Little pulled one back, but a Steve Campbell penalty wrapped it up.

Two days later, Livi crashed out of the Scottish Cup, losing 2-1 in the replay against Brechin, but the consolation, as some fans tried to dress it up as, was that this left the club free to concentrate on the league and winning a promotion place, though according to Big Jim, no-one was discussing such things - they were just looking at it one game at a time, he said, trotting out his usual line.

But it seemed to have a demoralising effect on the team as they followed that up with a string of poor performances. That or they were still hung over from New Year.

First up was a disappointing draw against Clyde. While fans of positive thought pointed to the fact that it was the eighteenth league home game without defeat, the harsh truth was that without Rab Douglas in goal, this could have been a hammering for Livi.

But the club managed to stay top thanks to Hamilton losing and Ayr drawing with Dumbarton, meaning Livingston stayed at the top of the table.

Douglas was on form again the following week but it wasn't enough to stop a one-nil defeat at the hands of Ayr but the team came back from no points to grabbing one point the next game in a tough battle against Hamilton. One goal from Stevie Campbell and two from Mark Duthie gave the Lions' three but Hamilton countered with three goals to share the points.

A win against Dumbarton on February 8 perked the fans up a little, but it was a dramatic 90 minutes with Mark Duthie's early lead being surrendered by the end of the first half as the Sons grabbed two goals. A fired-up Livi came out in the second half though and nabbed goals from Graham Harvey and Gordon McLeod to get all three points and a timely boost.

And while fans hoped to keep the winning run going, it was not to be as they drew with Stranraer. It was a scrappy game, played in a strong wind that had little of memorable note.

February ended with a home leg against Brechin that did not leave the home fans in a happy mood, ending in a 3-2 defeat. Most fans and commentators put the defeat down to the absence of Tom Graham and for once Graham Harvey scoring was not enough to save the day.

Graham returned for the next game - against Stenhousemuir - but it wasn't enough as a lacklustre and tired Lions' folded 3-1 with the Livi goal coming from Lee Bailey.

The following week saw Ayr fire ahead at the top after a 1-0 win at Stranraer. Livingston needed a Tom Callaghan goal, just minutes from full-time, to salvage a point at lowly Berwick, and Hamilton lost 1-0 at Queen of the South, but the league was still all there to play for.

In an attempt to bolster the squad, the club tried to land veteran Hearts winger John Colquhoun but it failed as Livi couldn't meet the fee - thought to be £50,000.

Two more poor results followed - a 1-1 draw against Berwick Rangers and a defeat at the hands of Clyde.

Then, to everyone's surprise, the club announced a friendly against Akranes from Iceland, managed by former Dundee United boss Ivan Golac.

And while some questioned the wisdom of playing during the league run-up, it turned into a morale booster as the Lions' left with a 2-1 win.

Mark Duthie hit the first direct from a corner after 24 minutes and added a second with a 30-yard rocket eight minutes later.

Leishman said afterwards, "I'm pleased with the result and it was a chance to give a few of the boys a run before Sunday's game against Hamilton. That's the big one."

And it was.

Second-top Hamilton headed for West Lothian with a three-point lead over Livingston.

Accies boss Sandy Clark claimed: "There's a bit more pressure on Livingston because a victory would see us open up a six- point gap. If we lose, we'll still be ahead of them on goal difference."

"There's a lot to play for, and you can only give credit to Leish and his players. They've come up from the Third Division and made an impression on everyone."

And one Livi player certainly made an impression after the passionate and hotly contested game.

The Second Division crunch game turned on a penalty awarded to Accies after Quitongo crashed in the box following a tackle by Grant Tierney, who insisted he didn't touch the winger saying, "Quitongo conned the referee."

This sparked off a war of words with Clark replying: "If Tierney wants to look at people breaking the rules he should look at his own team for they had five players cautioned.

"Jose is not a cheat. In fact, he is the opposite for he takes sore abuse regularly and does not go down.

"He is an honest lad and he has the marks on his legs to show that. He had to stand up to some really hard tackling all through the game.

"Tierney was fortunate not to be cautioned for the penalty and he was yellow-carded later for another foul.

"The referee was Hugh Dallas who is reputed to be the best in Scotland. He has handled an Old Firm game recently and will be in charge of the Scottish Cup final. He saw it as a penalty - and it was.

"I would hope the SFA would look very carefully at these remarks and I would like Livingston to take the appropriate action against their player.

"I am sure their chairman, Bill Hunter, and their manager, Jim Leishman, must be embarrassed by them. There are too many people outside the game criticising football without people inside it joining in.

"It is very unfair to Hamilton and our players who performed so well to get such a good result.

"We played football and deserved the win. But the after-match comments certainly took away any joy we felt."

And the row wouldn't die down in the week after the game as hate mail started being sent to Sandy Clark and Quitongo.

Leishman was raging.

"The game is finished and Accies won fair and square.

"Whoever is sending the mail is crazy – it's stupid and they should stop immediately. If we find out who is responsible I'm sure the chairman would ban them from the club. It's an embarrassment to us.

"I've spoken to Sandy Clark and apologised."

Clark revealed that the mail was coming in bearing Livingston postmarks.

He said, "The letters are marked 'Clark is a liar' and 'Quitongo is a cheat.' It's very upsetting and I'm sending them to Livingston to let them see what has happened as they allowed one of their players to make these accusations."

"It will also let Mr Tierney see the kind of situation that his words have put fellow professionals in."

After that, it was a high-pressure game against Ayr, who knew that a win would put them 15 points ahead of Livi and with only five games left afterwards, would make it hard for the Lions' to catch them.

Livi won 2-1 to keep them in the running but they then threw it away with defeats against Brechin and Dumbarton. It was the Dumbarton game that cost it. Despite taking an early lead when Gordon McLeod turned in Stewart Williamson's long throw, they lost 2-1. Dumbarton's goals came from Jim Meechan and Lee Sharp late in the second half, but their spirit came from manager Ian Wallace.

The season tumbled to an end with wins against Queen of the South and Stranraer, but it was too little too late and the last game of the season against the Accies had fans wondering what could have been as the Hamilton fans celebrated going up. The only consolation was that the club had performed well over the season and with a few changes, could improve the following season and go up.

No-one though could have predicted just how many changes there would be. It would be a year where literally no one was safe at the club and everyone's job was on the line – including Bill Hunter's.

CHAPTER
5

MOST DIFFICULT SEASON

Season 1997/1998 would prove to be Livingston's most difficult, both on and off the field since the club's rebirth as the cost of challenging for honours and developing a new senior team virtually from scratch began to take their respective tolls on the club's wellbeing.

Signs of the impending turmoil were apparent from the start of the season, for those who knew where to look. Many of the squad had been released, while influential goalkeeper Robert Douglas took his first steps up the league after being signed by Dundee for £60,000 and the wide player Kevin Magee.

Despite the departures, however, many expected that this season would see them progressing to the next level in Livingston's evolution and make it into the first division. Pundits, rival managers and the home support were all tipping Livingston and newcomers to the league – and old enemies - Inverness Caledonian Thistle as the runaway favourites for the title. Ironically, the sides were scheduled to clash in Livi's first league match of the season.

One of the few to play down Livingston's chances as per usual was Jim Leishman, who admitted as the season kicked off: "Personally, I prefer to be the underdog - then you can say you've beaten the best. But this will be a tough season and division. There are some very good teams around."

After a lacklustre pre-season, which included a 4-0 Almondvale drubbing at the feet of Manchester City, things got underway in earnest when Livi and Caley clashed in the Highlands.

Livingston's domination of their opening match of the season on August 6 1997 came to little more than a point after seeing their rivals steal a share of the spoils with just seconds remaining to end the game one-all. Magee made an immediate impact in his debut for the side, providing the corner for Tom Graham's unchallenged header in the 43rd minute after a first half which had seen Livi have the upper hand throughout the game.

However, despite their dominance the Lothian men failed to capitalise, and gave the Inverness side far too much time and space to come back into the match. Eventually Ian McCaldon found himself beaten on the stroke of full time by a Brian Thompson equaliser, knocked in after a perfectly played long pass from Barry Wilson.

Leishman found himself having to put all thoughts of disappointment out of his head, however, as the club geared up for an immediate, and far more difficult, challenge. The Coca-Cola League Cup draw had thrown up the mouth-watering prospect of a tie against nearby rivals Hearts at Almondvale. The Lothian derby took on an added resonance for one new member of the Livingston coaching staff.

Craig Levein had joined the backroom team at Almondvale following his retirement from Hearts because of injury, and was now helping out with coaching the first team at the invitation of his long-time friend Jim Leishman. A hero to the legions of Jambos, and would be again when he managed the club, the former Scotland star found himself in the unenviable position of immediately having to help plan the downfall of his former side, although Leishman found himself having to deny he had recruited Levein purely to help prepare his side for the arrival of Jim Jeffries' side.

Hearts were already looking strong in the Premier Division, and Livi knew it faced a tough test if it wished to progress further in the League Cup and draw another big name, money-spinning tie, something made tougher without the commanding presence of Stewart Williamson at the heart of the Livi defence. Even forcing a replay back at Tynecastle was out of the question with the cup's single match knockout format. Sadly, it was to prove a forlorn hope.

Two virtually identical headed goals from Neil McCann assured Hearts a place in the last sixteen of the League Cup.

McCann showed the gulf in class between Premier League wingers and second division defenders when he found himself in a vast area of space to head home Steve Frail's perfectly placed cross in the 25th minute. As if still not satisfied at demonstrating to Livingston the step-up they would need to make to face sides like Hearts on a regular basis, he repeated the trick almost exactly just two minutes later.

It could have been more than two if Hearts had found themselves able to convert more shots, but poor finishing meant that Livi realised they had much to learn if they wanted to play with the big boys without getting too much of a humiliating beating.

Just days afterwards, the club found themselves winning in another cup though – the Challenge Cup. They beat Stenhousemuir on penalties after drawing 1-1 in normal play.

Out of the league cup prematurely, Livingston found themselves focusing on their second division campaign. Graham Harvey had missed his chance to play in the League Cup side after arriving late at Almondvale. He was determined not to make the same mistake again, and after being reinstated to the team by Leishman repaid his manager in the best manner possible, scoring the 80th minute winning goal against a stubborn Stranraer in the club's first home league match of the season.

Off the park the club was also looking to build for the future. Cameroon international midfielder Constantin Etot was the latest high profile transfer target for a club whose increasingly obvious ambitions were beginning to take their financial toll. Eventually Leishman found himself forced out of the transfer market for the player, ironically by his old club Dunfermline, leaving the way clear for him to focus on the next game with Stenhousemuir.

The need for transfer activity was becoming apparent. With the release and sale of players during the close season, the Livingston squad was far smaller than it had been, and already injuries were beginning to take their toll on the side. Graeme Davidson, Gordon McLeod, Ryan Heggarty and George Wright were all absent for the trip to Ochilview, and the side struggled to eke out a less than impressive draw against the basement side.

Quickly the club found itself facing another cup tie, this time in the Scottish League Challenge Cup. Despite its lesser status, many of the lower league sides took the competition very seriously. Livingston found themselves facing Brechin City - and being shown up by them.

As early as the 4th minute the Angus outfit found themselves ahead after good play by Marcus Daily who squared the ball across the face of Livingston's goal. The resultant knock back found Ralph Brand, who blasted his shot just inside the post and shock the Lothian side. A deserved rollicking from an irate Leishman on the touchline saw his side fired back into action, with Laidlaw twice coming close but seeing his shots denied by the woodwork. Craig Feroz put the Brechin into a 2-0 lead before Steve Raynes got one back for Livingston with a 30-yard shot, but it was too little too late and Livi were out of another cup at in the early stages.

Clearly something needed to be done to turn about Livingston's fortunes. Despite not losing in the league, the side was struggling to score goals or kill off opposition who should have been easily brushed aside. Having missed out on strengthening his side, Leishman had to look to within the team for the answer. He found it, and an emphatic one at that, in the form of Graham Harvey. His response to the Challenge Cup defeat was to ensure his name would go down in the history of Livingston's history. The club needed goals, and he was, it seemed, the man to get them.

Harvey ensured his name would forever appear in pub quizzes and football trivia books by becoming the first hat-trick hero for the West Lothian side. The 35-year old postman nabbed all three goals in Livingston's comprehensive defeat of Queen of the South, thoroughly justifying the tag of Harvanelli hung on him by his team mates

Harvey had much cause to celebrate. Getting towards the twilight of a solid journeyman career, it had been nearly five years since the veteran forward had bagged himself a hat-trick.

The results so far had kept the club in the top half of the league, and the outcome of the Queen of the South and results elsewhere helped propel the team towards number one slot. As Harvey would admit afterwards, "At least it gives the fans something to shout about."

Going into the match with Brechin, with vengeance for the challenge cup exit on his mind Leishman found himself without the useful services of Heggarty and Davidson, who had been joined on the casualty list by David Lane and Billy Wright.

At the away game, Graham Harvey continued his prolific Harvanelli efforts in front of the opposition goal to ensure Livingston gained their revenge.

Things looked bad for Livi when Craig Feroz rattled the post early on, but Livingston refused to go under. Twelve minutes after their scare, a neat cross from Kevin Magee found the postie, who twisted, jinked and turned past the Brechin defence before letting fly.

Just to ensure the ball found its target, young rookie Gordon Forrest added his own powerful touch to the shot. Harvey then returned the favour for Magee, setting the former Dundee winger up in the 32nd minute with a neat flick which brought Stuart Garden rushing from his goal line. Magee nipped in and, finding himself in space, laid the ball off to Jason Young who had little to do to extend their lead.

The club was beginning to hit form, something Harvey himself acknowledged after the game.

He said, "A lot of teams won't come to Brechin and manage to play as well as we did and once we get two or three players back fit then we will surprise a lot of teams."

Spectators too were pleased with the result as Livingston started to show the class many had expected from the get-go. The standard of play in the team, from front to back, was far higher than had been demonstrated in earlier matches in the season, and hopes were building once again that Livi could well be challenging. They were sitting close to the top of the league, showing signs of strength and power necessary to escape the physical demands of the second division, yet with a touch of skill that suggested the club could do well in a higher league.

Word leaked out that Livingston's aims were even loftier than just success in division two. Following the pre-season friendly against English giants, Manchester City, the Scots club had made overtures towards them about establishing a feeder network, which would give Livi the chance to loan veterans seeking first team football and the next generation of English wunderkinds.

Livingston's chairman Bill Hunter admitted he felt establishing feeder networks and collaborations between big name clubs and lower league sides was the only way of securing the future of the underdogs in the Scottish game which he was realistic to acknowledge that Livingston were.

He said, "I think it is the only way for the smaller Scottish clubs to move forward, and it could be a back-door into Europe for some of the English sides who can't get there. It would be easier being an English team in Scotland.

"Because of the strength of the Old Firm in Scotland, feeder clubs could also eventually make for a real challenge to Rangers and Celtic, which clubs cannot do at the moment. It could help make us a force in Scottish football."

Although the deal would eventually come to nothing, the combination of publicity-seeking and big name star-searching would help lay the foundations for Livingston's future success and show that the club were, if nothing else, ambitious.

At the time, however, it brought into focus the problems the lower league sides were facing. Livingston, like many clubs, were concerned about the implications of a new break-away Scottish Premier League being planned by the country's top ten league sides.

The new league was designed to maximise revenues for the Old Firm, and the other big name sides, but its structure gave much concern to the 29 clubs outside the proposal, who felt they had been blatantly and brutally ignored by the game's senior figures.

Hunter put himself at the forefront of the push to oppose the formation of the SPL and its breakaway from the Scottish League. The 11 clubs involved - the SPL members and Raith Rovers - had given notice they planned to depart the Scottish Football League structure at the end of that season, establishing their own TV deal, sponsorship deals and promotional ventures.

For Hunter, this was a worrying development, and he went on radio to denounce the plans in the strongest possible terms.

"They are giving a courtesy to us to see what the proposals are but we don't have a say in it, that's really what he is saying, and I just hope the press and media pick up on this because we know what happened to Hitler don't we?"

His words understandably attracted much criticism, with the media picking up on the Hitler comparison, but Hunter was unrepentant: "It comes down to a simple word, money. At the present time the Top Ten receive 87.5% of all revenues that come in to Scottish football and they want to remove the structure of the SFL so that they are then in control of all negotiations and in control of all monies that come in."

"The dynamic new football structure that they are going to put in place, four leagues of ten, is already existing, and I don't see how any extra money coming into the Top Ten is going to make them any more dynamic than at the moment.

"I don't have any doubt that there is a hidden agenda there and I believe that some of the smaller clubs will go to the wall sooner rather than later. At this moment the 29 other clubs are shoulder to shoulder on this and if they stick together they will not be able to break the rule that they will have to give the two years' notice."

Amid the background of the SPL dispute, Livingston found themselves travelling to Bayview for a tight match with East Fife. The heated game saw the referee producing his red card three times - twice for East Fife and once for Livingston, as defender Stewart

Williamson was dismissed. Despite the sending off, Livingston managed to take all three points, placing Livingston on top of the league for the first time that season.

But there was also some bad news. Craig Levein had, until that point, remained on the coaching staff in a voluntary capacity, taking little to no reward for his work. Even so, the club was struggling to be able to afford his presence, and the finances at Livingston were starting to look more threadbare.

Levein was having to pay for his own involvement in the club, and with no steady income following his premature retirement from playing, the costs were starting to become prohibitive. Much as he was keen to keep Levein in place, and much as the former Hearts star was showing signs of coaching prowess, Jim Leishman was forced to admit he would not be able to keep him on.

After a draw with Clydebank which showed Livi had problems finishing games off, they lost their first game of the season to Clyde. The hard-fought 1-0 victory by the home side at Broadwood, with Livi still suffering from their ongoing injury problems, was a minor blip on the club's momentum, however, as the spirit built up by Leishman and his players took the aggression of their defeat out on the next side to visit Almondvale.

Veteran striker Wayne Foster showed he had lost none of the skill and touch which had been cultivated in premier division spells with Hearts and Partick Thistle when he turned out for Livi, bagging the first of the club's four goals in just 40 seconds during the October 25 game against Forfar Athletic.

Foster, brought in by the Almondvale side as a trialist, played his way into a contract with the side by catching Forfar by surprise.

Goals were then exchanged on a seemingly tit-for-tat basis as Forfar equalised through a Ben Honeyman volley, before Gordon McLeod and Kevin Magee gave Livingston the lead.

Martin McLaughlin brought the score back to 3-2, but Lee Bailey stepped in and side footed home the fourth to restore the Lothian side's two goal cushion. That cushion would last just a few minutes, however, as Honeyman popped up to net Forfar's third.

The result would put Livi two points clear at the top of the league, but the shine was taken off that by the dire financial reality at the club.

Bill Hunter was admitting the club was financially struggling and would have to be open to offers for its best players.

"I am now at the stage that I need others to come into this club," he would admit, sewing the seeds for future investment.

"I have proved that I can take a small club and build it up into a successful business. It now needs another push."

On the pitch, the club was indeed enjoying that push. Almondvale was rapidly becoming the second division's hardest ground to play at, developing the kind of fortress reputation which many clubs envy.

On the back of the Forfar victory, Livingston then beat Stenhousemuir 2-1 with Gordon McLeod and Jason Young bagging the Lions' goals.

Then it was Stranraer and the two sides clashed at Stair Park where Keith Knox would prove to be both hero and villain for the home team, managing to find a way through a far more solid Livingston defence than earlier games had shown, before slipping up himself to allow Kevin Magee the chance to whip in a sharp cross for Gordon Forrest to head home.

The following match, however, would prove to be Livingston's undoing. Leishman's men faced a Queen of the South side which had lost the Challenge Cup final then taken a midweek battering from the ever-improving Clydebank. Leishman admitted going into the match that his table-topping side would be the ideal team for Queen of the South to defeat in a bid to regain their confidence. He wasn't proved wrong and the club had their second defeat of the season, despite having a lot of the game's play and possession.

But the loss of three points seemed only to spur Livingston on and Brechin City faced a Livi ready to take someone apart. The five goals scored by Livingston came with swagger and style, though Brechin managed to nab two.

But while the club's home form was stirring, away games were always less certain. Playing Clydebank in the last game of November Wayne Foster was needed to grab a goal three minutes from the end to earn Livingston a point in a game where they had played the far poorer football, giving the Bankies a boost in their own title aspirations.

And then Bill Hunter revealed he was off at the end of the season.

It turned out that Livingston's position was fiscally insecure despite everything with debts approaching a quarter of a million pounds.

With Hunter going, the club would need to find another backer -
and ideally one with as deep pockets as the current incumbent.
Edinburgh plumber-cum-bookmaker John Jeromson immediately
announced an interest in taking a stake in the club, while investors
from north and south of the border sized up the Almondvale outfit
for a potential takeover. On paper, the club looked a good
investment. A well developed stadium, with potential for further
growth. Substantial non-footballing derived income facilities such
as a nightclub and restaurant. A good playing and managerial
team, which sat on the top of the second division and was enjoying
substantial success. If someone was looking to get into the Scottish
soccer market, there could be few better clubs to sign up to.

However, the problems with the club were equally apparent.
Crowd figures, despite its success, could at best be described as
disappointing, even with the support of local school kids given
freebie tickets. There was a hefty debt for a second division club,
which would have to be cleared reasonably soon, with a projected
loss on the books for the current season. And with the small
attendances, and the club's relatively new existence in an area
without a natural support for the team, little in the way of on-pitch
revenue generation.

Among the ideas mooted for developing Almondvale further, and
bringing in extra cash to the club's coffers, was the installation of a
dog track - something Jeromson was keen to moot in the press.

Hunter's decision to step down had been forced on two fronts.
The stress of running the club was proving hazardous. And the
proposed breakaway of the SPL was proving a massive headache
for the lower league clubs, which had appointed Hunter to act as
their representative.

"I am totally sickened by what is going on," he confirmed at the
time. "I am putting all my shares up for sale. I am three years into
a seven-year plan here - and I believe that we are ahead of our
targets. But how can we look ahead and plan for that in the present
set-up? As far as I am concerned the Scottish League constitution
is the bible - but if that's not there these people can do what they
like."

Things became more problematic as the next couple of weeks
progressed. The atrocious weather that hit Scotland as November
gave way to December resulted in Almondvale being washed out.
At a time when the club could ill-afford to not stage matches, the
cancellation of its match against East Fife posed a real headache -

especially with the first round of Scottish Cup games coming up the following weekend. The Fifers wanted a clear week to ensure their players were fit and rested ahead of their clash with Stranraer. Livi, meanwhile, wanted the match to go ahead midweek, as per SFL rules. In the end, the dispute had to be settled by the Scottish League, which came down on the side of the Lothian club and the game was played on December 3.

As if to rub salt into the wound over their victory in having the game played, Livi took all three points from their midweek encounter with the Fifers, and gave Lee Bailey his 50th goal for the club.

Bailey, who had demanded to be placed on the transfer list following the signing of Wayne Foster, continued his current purple patch by shining in the December gloom and firing home a spectacular lob over keeper Willie McCulloch from 25-yards out after a neat pass from Mark Duthie. Duthie came close to doubling the score line minutes later, and when Livi had a clear-cut penalty chance ruled out by the referee, it served only to underline the dominance of Leishman's men in the match-up.

The result put Livi back on top of the second division, much to the delight of Jim Leishman, and continued the club's unbeaten run at Fortress Almondvale. Things were coming together again on the pitch, and as the club geared up for the run-in to the hectic Christmas and New Year period - keeping one anxious eye on the weather all the while - the attendance reflected an ever growing concern at the club.

The number of fans through the turnstiles - or "bums on seats" as Leishman would have it - had been steadily dropping despite the club's success. Audiences of less than 1000 people were now not uncommon at Almondvale, and worryingly there could regularly be found more away fans perched on the yellow and black plastic seats than home support. Crowds of around 3000 people were needed for breakeven, but more often than not half that number would be in attendance at matches. The club's relocation, rebirth and rebranding may have been a critical success and won many friends in the media, but for Joe Public, the attractions of West Lothian were not enough to keep fans in the region from travelling through to Glasgow or Edinburgh to see the bigger, more established outfits.

Of greater concern was the fact that such small crowds meant the club was losing money faster than before, at a rate which gave

48

cause for concern to both players, management and boardroom. Things weren't helped when the Inland Revenue came calling with an overdue, unpaid bill, which they sought immediate repayment of. The threat of sequestration, and possibly even going out of business, was already hanging over the newest club in Scottish football.

A new share issue was launched, making 200,000 shares at £2 a piece available to the public and to investors, in a bid to try and generate much needed cash, while emergency meetings with the Bank of Scotland - due £140,000 and growing worried over how and when it would receive that sum - and West Lothian Council were arranged.

The club's close relationship with West Lothian Council was highlighted yet further when the council agreed to send in a team of financial advisers at its own expense to spend the next month going over the books, assets and facilities, to draw up a report and prepare a rescue plan for the club. Having invested so much time, money and effort in bringing a senior football club to the new town, West Lothian Council was determined to ensure the club stayed there.

Leishman was worried, yet in one of his light-hearted comments was a rather prophetic statement: "I'm just keeping my fingers crossed - we all are - that someone will come in with the investment we need. You never know what's round the corner. Maybe I'll win the lottery jackpot and then all our problems will be over."

The off-field problems seemed to be taking their toll on the club's on-field activities, however. Over the next few games, Livingston would take just 10 points from a potential 21, losing their unbeaten home record in spectacular style. Having remained resolute so far in the season, two of their next three home games would be defeats against sides challenging for the championship. The results, coupled with the winter break, all but killed the momentum that had been building up for the Almondvale men, and would dent further their chances of taking the second division trophy home at the end of the season.

Things got off to an average start with a 2-2 draw against Forfar at Station Park on the Saturday after the emergency financial meetings. Having led the match early on, Livi found themselves 2-1 down in the second half, before Jason Young earned himself the old cliché of supersub with a header from Kevin Magee's cross.

And while the club toiled on the Angus pitch, Chairman Hunter toiled off of it.

Hunter was asked to leave the ground after responding to verbal barracking from a Forfar supporter by giving him the V sign

He admitted after the match: "Basically, this person was an idiot and I admit I gave him the V. I was fed up with his shouting and bawling. After Livingston equalised he kept on screaming abuse at me, ranting on about the financial difficulties facing our club. That sparked off a bit of a rammy and at one stage our manager Jim Leishman told the supporter to shut up."

"After that, I went into the Forfar boardroom for a cup of tea. When David McGregor came in a few words were exchanged and I was asked to leave before I had time to take my coat off."

"But as I've said, these things happen in the game. I just feel that the Forfar stewards and policemen could have done something to stop this fan hurling abuse. One thing is certain, it would never have been allowed to happen at Almondvale."

The negative publicity could not have come at a worse time for either the club or for Bill Hunter, making the headlines less than a week after the problems at Almondvale became common knowledge. In a bid to counter the falling attendances, Livingston decided to take the age-old step of slashing entrance prices for their crunch match with Clyde the following week

Then, just five days before Christmas, Livingston surrendered their lead on the second division in apathetic fashion after offering the visitors Clyde a two goal Christmas present, neatly gift wrapped in yellow and black ribbon.

The unbeaten home record Livi had been so proud of up to this point was shattered by a mix of incompetent defending and inconsistent finishing.

Livingston bounced back from the defeat in the best way possible, taking all three points at Stenhousemuir through some goalkeeping heroics by Ian McCaldon on December 27. But the damage had already been done.Fortress Almondvale, previously the impenetrable barricade upon which Livi had built their on-field success that season, had now been breached, and at the worst possible time.

The collusion of supporters' apathy, financial woes and occasional lapses on the pitch, had cost the club dearly. Now no longer top of the league, Livingston would have to go into 1998 with its once unassailable lead now overturned.

The Christmas week did bring with it one unexpected piece of cheer, however. The dining facilities at Almondvale, and the nightclub which formed a part of the complex, had done respectable business thanks to the revelries, and over the holiday fortnight pulled in around £20k in funds. The money was a massive boost for the cash-strapped board, guaranteeing the wages of the players for some time. Bill Hunter felt moved enough to express his thanks to punters, seeing it as an encouraging sign that things could yet be turned around by the people of the new town.

As the club entered the New Year, and turned its attentions towards a Scottish Cup second round tie against Borders outfit Berwick Rangers, hellish bad weather saw the possibility of the game being postponed. Again the decision was one which left the Board wringing their collective hands, and sounded a warning as the club tried to regroup its financial position. At that time, they could ill afford even one cancelled league game. To see a cup game disappear into the ether, albeit temporarily, and the prospective revenue Livingston could generate by drawing a big name in the third round go with it, was something they could ill-afford to contemplate.

In the end the match went ahead - just. Conditions were comparable to quicksand as the melting frost and continued downpours turned grass and skills into mud and chaos. The conditions contributed much to the nature of the game, which became more about physical abilities than silky skills. Eventually Livingston managed to gain the advantage, Graham Harvey once again delivering the killer blow with a shot from Magee's cross. Berwick briefly levelled through Neil Irvine, before Wayne Foster turned provider for Grant McMurray to slot home. For their efforts, the reward was a trip to lowly Albion Rovers - hardly the lucrative cash cow that Livi had prayed for.

Throughout the match Berwick's support made much of the noise, and the vast majority of that was directed at Bill Hunter and the club's perilous finances. Rumours were continuing to circulate that the Bank of Scotland was getting ready to bring the curtain down on Livingston's performances for good, and that West Lothian's dabbling with senior football would prove to be short-lived. While the chants were little more than what could be heard at any cash-strapped side up and down the country, for Livingston they were cutting closer to the bone than anyone would have liked.

The accountants had finished their report – and found that £120,000 would need to be found in savings as soon as possible if Livingston was to have any kind of long term survival. Hunter acted immediately, and sacked five of the club's peripheral staff. The bar manager, a member of the ground staff, and some of the cleaners who kept Almondvale respectable were shown the door in a cost-cutting effort. The move saved around £7500 immediately, but there were still far more problems and other solutions were sought.

Faced with entering the New Year on such a low, Hunter admitted the club's plight had worsened, and efforts were continuing to rectify it. "The rest of the money we shall try to find by increasing turnover, not by more cuts," he said. But it is not true that the bank is about to close this club. We want to find a way out of this, but I believe there are people who would love to see me fall flat on my face."

He would go on to hint cryptically in the press that Hunter and Livingston were at the centre of a witch-hunt, with lies being told about just how bad the club's plight was in order to deter any potential investors.

One story to emerge, which underlined how bad things were, was that Livingston was considering legal action against West Lothian Council over the continuing pitch problems at Almondvale. The club's close relationship with the local authority was being put under threat while the pitch continued to deteriorate in the weather. Estimates put the cost of postponed and threatened games at around £80,000 - a massive sum for a club in Livingston's condition, and the drainage problems that left the ground like a swamp were, in Hunter's eyes, the responsibility of the council which owned the stadium.

Investigations revealed the wrong type of sand had been mixed with the soil when the playing surface was initially laid two years previously, and the error was coming back to bite the club.

The impact of the pitch problems was brought home when another game was called off, this time against old rivals Inverness Caley Thistle.

Already postponed once because of the ground conditions, referee Martin Clark decided to call the rescheduled midweek match off at lunchtime because of the state of the pitch, in order to save the Caley fans a long and fruitless journey from the

Highlands. Yet it cleared up within a few hours, and by 5pm that night was playable once again, much to the chagrin of Hunter.

Worse was to come. With no games having been played at the ground in more than a week, funds were starting to run dry – something the pitch could have done with, and even the cutbacks and savings made on the advice of the accountants, had proved inadequate. If any more games were called off, the club faced the worrying prospect of not being able to pay players or staff.

The decision by match officials to postpone the top-of-the-table Clydebank game on January 17 was to be the final straw for Hunter and he put his controlling interest in the club up for a token fee.

"I'm looking for somebody to take a controlling interest and I'd sell my majority shareholding for a pound if somebody was interested," he announced. "I'd like somebody else to take this club forward. I've got angina and my doctor has told me I could have a major heart attack if I don't ease up."

The club had just managed to avert disaster, raiding the takings from the nightclub and restaurant at Almondvale in order to pay the players, but the danger was growing more present, and the stresses of trying to juggle the finances of an ambitious club still in its youth, and without the benefit of a substantial support, was finally grinding Hunter down.

On field, the problems with the pitch were also being felt. Having had no competitive league action in the best part of a month, the players were in danger of losing their sharpness, and faced a backlog of fixtures once the conditions at Almondvale had cleared up - if there was still a club to complete them by then. Meanwhile they had the difficult task of preparing for their forthcoming match with Albion Rovers, which they had to win as victory would put them into the fourth round, and closer to a big money tie with one of the Old Firm.

It didn't work out that way though with a draw being grabbed in the dying seconds – and that draw literally cost the team players as the club was forced to get rid of players due to cash problems. Mark Duthie, who had proved a vital cog in the club's midfield throughout the season and was one of the club's longest serving players, was sold to Ayr United for £35,000. It may seem a paltry sum, but it was enough to boost the club and ensure people were paid.

The move didn't suddenly mean Jim Leishman was free to start spending again in the transfer market, but it did ease some of the concerns which had been building up about even the short term future of the side.

With a replay against Albion Rovers looming, the club needed to keep its best players and ensure the cohesiveness and team spirit which had formed in the face of adversity was not prematurely eroded.

Things, as always with Livi, became complicated however.

Cliftonhill, never the most advanced of stadia, was suffering from electrical problems and would not be able to use its floodlights for the midweek replay. The Scottish Football Association ordered the match be played at 1pm instead - which brought with it its own problems. The Albion Rovers players, and staff, were part time, and the combination of injuries, suspensions and work commitments meant they would not be able to field a team for the game. With a tie against Hearts - and the potential for a Lothian derby once more - Livingston were prepared to go along with any way of getting the game replayed. Eventually a compromise was brokered. The match would take place at East Stirlingshire's Firs Park during the evening.

Before that game could go ahead, however, Livi had the small matter of a league match against East Fife - their first league game since December 27. With such a long lay-off and only a smattering of football played during that time, the concern among fans was that the team would still be missing the edge required to win the game. They were not wrong as the team went down 2-0. It was hardly the best warm-up for their vital cup tie.

The cup game was a far cry from the powerful Livi of the opening of the season, with Rovers' keeper Steve Ross thwarting the Lions' time and time again. But it wasn't a classic game by any description and the brave souls who had made the game had their fan faithfulness tested as the game went into penalties and then sudden death as the penalties ended at 4-4.

The winners of the game faced Hearts in a tie which would bring in at least £50,000, but it wasn't to be Livi who would get the cash as Rovers won, leaving the Lions' nothing but the league.

And they posted notice that they were still determined with a home win against Forfar. The four goal thrashing suggested things were back on course for Livingston, particularly as their rivals for the top spot, Clydebank, had lost 3-2 to Inverness Caledonian Thistle.

Livi were two up inside ten minutes, and had secured their 4-0 victory scant seconds into the second half. The result set up a crunch match ahead of the rescheduled midweek fixture against the Bankies at Almondvale.

And while tension was building on the field, off it the club was starting the first stages of the next regeneration.

William Haughey and Dominic Keane, former directors at Celtic who had departed the club's board under Fergus McCann, announced their interest in buying the club for £250,000. The two die-hard football fanatics had decided to get involved in the game once again and in Livingston saw the perfect model to develop their interests.

Former Meadowbank director Walter Hey was also expressing an interest, while consortiums in Denmark and London had been sniffing around the club. But it became clear very quickly that Hunter was keen for the former Celtic men to take over - and that they were keen to get involved. Haughey began to offload some of the shares he had in Celtic to ensure there would be no barrier to their efforts to gain control of the club, as league rules restricted the involvement in ownership of anyone with a substantial share presence in another league side. To this end, millionaire lottery winner - and the third member of their Hoops-supporting triumvirate - John McGuinness was recruited to the bid.

So things were starting to progress in the boardroom, but at the same time, just as one aspect of the club's future gained momentum, another seemed in danger of stalling and while it may have been nearly Valentine's Day, there was a lack of love for Livi for the league game against Clydebank on February 10 that the club really needed to win, but didn't, and let Clydebank nab three goals and go eight points ahead at the top of the league.

Although they immediately bounced back by hammering Clyde 3-0 the following weekend, the club was still suffering from inconsistent form, and failed to secure anything more than a point when they faced Inverness Caledonian Thistle the following week. Defeat at Almondvale on Feb 25 by Stranraer, who were showing their own championship challenging form and making a late bid for the top league spot, only served to show just how bad things were getting for Livi. Having gone half a season without losing at home, three of their last four matches at Almondvale had been defeats.

Another draw against Caley Thistle made it look as if the team's next game – against Clydebank – would be the final nail in the coffin for the league hopes, especially as it was the end of an era with Bill Hunter going through with his promise of selling Livingston to new owners for just £1.

The club was sold, as had been anticipated, to the trio of Haughey, Keane and McGuinness, who immediately injected £200,000 into the club to stabilise its finances and stave off any hovering creditors. Tony Kinder took over as chairman of the board.

David Hay, the former Celtic manager - who had also left the club amid much acrimony and dispute - was brought on board as a consultant, effectively reprising his chief scout role of recent Parkhead times and it was hoped he would do as well for Livi as he had for his old club, where he had brought in many excellent signings.

The new-found stability gave Leishman the freedom to begin strengthening his squad, and showed the ambition the new owners had for their purchase. The veteran former Hearts and Airdrie winger Allan Moore was signed, while bids for Rangers midfielder Ian Durrant and Hearts striker John Robertson were launched. Although both would be rebuffed, it underlined the commitment Haughey, Keane and McGuinness had invested in the club.

"Bill Hunter has been a great visionary for Livingston but he lacked the necessary resources to take the club further," Keane said on taking control of the club. "Nobody should doubt our ambitions for Livingston. There will be no quick fix. We cannot make all the changes on day one or right or all wrongs in five the minutes. We do not want to be judged on what happens in the next two or three weeks but would prefer to be assessed over a period of three to five years."

The new management gave the club a confidence that comes from stability and knowing that you will get paid at the end of the month, and against the Bankies Livi took the lead in under ten minutes. By half-time it was 2-0, was how it stayed, and this sparked a mini-resurgence in the Livingston team, as they went unbeaten for the next four games. Following up their victory against the Bankies with an efficient 2-0 victory over Brechin City, then two draws against potential bogey teams East Fife and Queen of the South.

As Livingston went into their final run of fixtures, the title race was a three-horse contest. Clydebank still sat at the top of the league, but Stranraer's recent good form was putting them into a position to challenge Livingston's second place. In the world of footballing clichés, every game was a proverbial six-pointer.

But while the other sides were picking up their points elsewhere, Livingston's inconsistency was coming back to haunt them at a time when they needed to be firing on all thrusters. An unlikely defeat at Forfar was a crushing blow for the promotion challenge. With just six games remaining, Livingston looked to have a comfortable run-in, although their last two matches would see them travel to Stranraer, then host the side which had proved the source of so much heartache (and headaches) during Livi's short life, Inverness Caledonian Thistle.

As transfer deadline day closed in, Leishman set about strengthening the squad still further. Given the green light to bring in new players by Keane, Jim snapped up yet another striker in order to ensure the club's stop-start approach to scoring goals garnered the necessary consistency. Greg Miller was signed on a free transfer from Hibernian. The son of the former Hibs boss Alex Miller, Livi took over the last few weeks of his contract, with the lure of a longer term contract for next season should he prove himself worthy. An attempt to sign Hibs's out-of-favour goalkeeper Chris Reid - who had been training with Livi for the last few weeks - was rebuffed. But in targeting premier division talent, Leishman was setting out his stall. He wanted to guarantee promotion in the most emphatic terms possible. Lower league mainstay Sandy Robertson was also recruited to bolster the squad.

The new-look team beat Clyde 4-0 and that put Livi within touching distance of first place. With results landing favourably for them elsewhere, Livingston had moved from eight points behind the leaders to just one point away from them.

Next up would be Queen of the South. Matches between the two had been tight all season, and much was riding on Livingston's performance at Palmerston. A one-nil win, thanks to a Conway goal, was enough to secure all three points, and after Clydebank threw away their game Livingston were top of the league.

A 1-0 against Brechin saw Livi win three games on the trot, but then the consistency problem reared its head once again, going into the finishing straight of the league competition. Against Stenhousemuir the club was able only to get a draw and although the result was enough to keep Livingston on top of the second division, it underlined the problem once more that Livingston had in finishing off their opposition.

Including the part time players at Almondvale, there were eight or nine strikers available, including the club's departing veteran Graham Harvey. Harvey, who had expected, through age and part-time status, to not figure in much of the team's action, had become one of its most important players and its top scorer.

Stranraer blew the title race wide open with a comprehensive 2-0 victory which completed their almost Lazarus like resurrection from second bottom to title contenders in just three months.

Livingston's failure to find the killer touch once again allowed Duncan George to put the Stair Park side ahead in the 56th minute, striking home a rising shot from the edge of the box. Veteran forward Issac English sealed all three points for the home team in the 73rd minute when his point blank shot struck off the bar and into the net.

Despite pushing forward, Livi failed to find the net again and left an exasperated Jim Leishman fuming on the touchline.

Leishman's reaction to the game was as prophetic as it was dangerous. Irony had already taken great delight in toying with Livingston's fortunes throughout the season, so his proclamation: "I cannot wait until next week...We'll still be top of the league," should perhaps have been a warning not to take anything for granted.

The final match would be at Almondvale. A carnival atmosphere was in place for that final Saturday of the season, with the players, manager and new owners all expecting success and promotion by 4.45pm. A pleasant, mild day with one of the biggest crowds in the grounds history - some 3500 fans - seemed to indicate that everything would favour the men in yellow and black.

If ending up third in the league had been the aim, then the team achieved it that day. A combination of Caley winning 2-1 and results elsewhere saw Clydebank second and Stranraer were now celebrating as outright victors of the division.

Leishman was understandably gutted by the outcome, not just of the game but also of the season. Having seen his players come close to glory so often, and having had to overcome seemingly insurmountable odds, his players were left to reflect on what might have been, and what would have to be next season.

"I could say hundreds of things about the way we feel but the fact is that we got ourselves into a good position and just couldn't clear the final hurdle," he lamented after the match. "We got up the ladder but just couldn't get over the top. But all the machinery is in place to take the club to the next stage - watch this space."

Leishman was spot-on in his prediction. Under the direction of Keane, Haughey and McGuinness, and with the involvement of David Hay, the club was all set to progress not just to the next level, but to heights previously unimaginable for those who had supported Meadowbank Thistle all those years ago. But for now, it was back to the drawing board, and the challenge of rebuilding the team and the squad for next season. However many were just glad that the club had the chance to see another season.

CHAPTER
6

NEW FACES

And the squad and club were certainly rebuilt. In the team there were a number of new faces, including Hearts legend John Robertson who snubbed signing offers from Motherwell and Hibs to join Livingston.

He was offered better terms than Premier Division 'Well or former city rivals Hibs, again showing Livi's ambition and determination to be the best.

But there was an even bigger surprise off the park as the club moved Jim Leishman upstairs and brought in Ray Stewart as first team coach.

Leishman found the idea of moving hard at first and considered leaving the club. "I was just going to jack it in, but Dominic said, 'look Jim', he sat me down, had a chat with me which I appreciated, and told me he wanted me to look after things off the field. I thought at worst I'd learn a lot businesswise and took that opportunity."

And the pressure was certainly put on the new gaffer, who had spells in management at Stirling Albion and St Johnstone as well as being a hero at West Ham, with Dominic Keane declaring: "Livi will become the Celtic and Rangers of the Second Division."

"We have the money and the facilities to be like the Old Firm in relative terms, so everyone will be out to take our scalp."

"In fact, I can see a lot of teams raising their game when they come to play us. They'll approach it like a cup tie so the new coach must be made aware of this."

Amongst the players brought in by the new boss was Stenhousemuir striker Ian Little, Dunfermline's David Bingham, Hamilton's Jim Sherry from Hamilton.

The season began well enough with a 2-0 win over Cowdenbeath in the first round of the league cup and the first Livi goal - John Millar's strike in the 17th minute – was the first goal of the season, while the second, a David Bingham effort in the 58th minute, tied up the game for the Lions'.

The league got off to a slightly less inspiring start as the team drew 1-1 with Stirling Albion, the team Ray Stewart had just left to join Livi.

The game wasn't long in coming alive with Mark McCormick making a hell of a debut appearance with a goal in just under one minute.

Albion grabbed the equaliser within minutes though and despite efforts at both ends, there were no more goals.

Form was recovered for the next cup game though, with Dunfermline being beaten 1-0. The next round was as far as they would get though as Kilmarnock put them out on August 18, completing a few days of misery for the club as three days earlier Inverness Caledonian Thistle had beat the Lions' 2-1.

But August 18 would mark the last defeat of the club that year as they stormed to the top of the league winning all but two of their 18 league games and drawing the other two.

Queen of the South, East Fife, Arbroath, Alloa, Partick and Caley Thistles, Dumbarton and others all fell before a Lions' team determined not to lose out on promotion again. All the worries of the previous season had been put behind them and the club racked up the points.

The Dumbarton result in the Scottish Cup in December though took 180 minutes as the teams drew 1-1 in the first leg. In the second leg, the Lions' romped 3-0 to victory.

However the road to victory was not without casualties.

Ryan Haggerty had to announce his retirement from the game, just months after signing a new contract with the club. The 22 year old had to chuck it in because of a stress fracture of the spine.

The New Year brought some welcome cheer to the club though as Livi tore through Caley Thistle in the Scottish Cup, beating them 2-1 and setting up a potentially lucrative game against Aberdeen.

However the passion that people felt for Livi was clearly on show as John Robertson had a spat with Ray Stewart.

Stewart dropped Robbo for the Caley Thistle game, leaving him on the bench and accusing him of slacking.

That sparked a furious blast back at the boss from the Hearts legend, which forced Jim Leishman to step in to cool the row.

The rest of January saw the club continue its winning run but no one outside of Almondvale expected Aberdeen to have any problems against the plucky upstarts.

Oh how wrong were they.

It was a memorable game for Dominic Keane – not only because he spent a fortune in flights getting back from America in time for the game – but because of the result: Aberdeen 1, Livingston 0.

The shock goal was scored by Robbo in the 61st minute after just one pass as substitute Ian Little sent Robbo scampering clear as the Dons tried to play offside trips. Robertson drew keeper Derek Stillie and beat him with ease

Central defenders Gregg Watson and Alan McManus - rejected by Aberdeen and Hearts - inspired their team mates with ice-cool composure.

They didn't have a failure - from goalkeeper Neil Alexander, who produced one miracle 84th minute save from a Mike Newell header, to David Bingham, who ended up having to be stretchered off in 53 minutes after a shocking tackle by David Rowson.

Livingston's second goal chance arrived in the dying seconds when the impressive Charlie King broke up the park and squared across the box for Brian McPhee.

Substitute McPhee stooped for a point-blank header which Stillie parried before fellow sub Gordon Forrest blasted.

Robbie Winters fluffed a great chance when he darted into the box to meet an Ilian Kiriakov corner but headed straight at Alexander.

It was to be a nightmare afternoon for Winters. He had put an even easier opportunity wide in the 27th minute, shot straight at Alexander in the 35th minute and headed over from 10 yards in the 73rd minute.

Not that any Livi fans were concerned for him though.

Peter Thompson remembers: "We couldn't believe it as you sometimes hope for that sort of result, but in your heart of hearts you don't expect it.

"To be fair, Livi showed the same form they had throughout the start of the season, but most of the papers seem to concentrate on how duff Aberdeen were instead of praising us for giving them a walloping."

In true Livi style though, the club drew the following week, sharing a point and a goal each with Partick Thistle, but to be fair, Livi hadn't really got into the game when the Jags scored – in just 7.5 seconds.

Robert Dunn's lightning strike was the result of a mix-up between Alexander and former Jag Gregg Watson.

Livi then fired up an attack to try and take their unbeaten run to 25 games and they finally equalised through sub Brian McPhee in 78 minutes.

Fan David O'Connor remembered the game – mostly for the Jags' negative tactics: "It was a hard game as Thistle just sat in after their goal and had nine or 10 at the back."

"We had the ball a lot, but those sort of defensive tactics just kill a game. Fortunately by the time we got to the SPL we had that problem licked as we just piled right into teams that wanted to do that."

The winning streak rolled on with a 3-0 beating of Clyde but the result flattered the West Lothian squad as they were pinned back a lot and it was a goal by John Robertson on the stroke of half-time that turned the match.

Combined with the ordering off of Darren Murray, the Clyde full-back, early in the second period, it gave Livingston the belief they could win, and late goals from Charlie King and Brian McPhee made sure of it.

Then the winning streak came to an end, but not in the league, but at the hands of St Johnstone in the Scottish Cup.

The game showed one thing more starkly than anything else. If Livi wanted to compete in the Premier with the big boys, it had a little bit of growing up to do because St Johnstone took them to pieces. The Aberdeen game seemed so far behind, but the reports at the time that that result had been due to a poor Dons' team as much as anything looked quite accurate based on this performance.

Nathan Lowndes's opener had no power behind it, but Alexander took his eye off the ball and spilled it to a free running Roddy Grant, who tapped it home.

Saints poured forward at every opportunity and scored again before the interval when Philip Scott fired in the rebound after a Grant header had come back off the crossbar.

Alexander was at fault again for the third. Under pressure from Grant, he failed to collect a Scott cross cleanly and, in an attempt to prevent the ball from crossing the line, he slapped it straight to the burly striker, who had no trouble in finding the net from two yards.

The extent of their control was summed up by the fact that almost the only thing Alan Main had to do in the second half was pick the ball out of his net.

Livingston's counter came, as it had so many times in the season, through John Robertson, who expertly headed home after Gregg Watson had nodded on a Charlie King corner.

The next game, a home leg against Arbroath, saw the happy results return, but it wasn't an easy game.

The visitors nearly took the lead after 10 minutes when Kevin Tindal crashed a superb 20-yarder off a post with keeper Neil Alexander well beaten.

Charlie King then rushed into the heart of the Arbroath box but Craig Hinchcliffe beat away his fierce shot on the run.

Livi scored a minute before the break. McCormick laid the ball on for Derek Fleming who wriggled past three defenders and slotted it home.

Arbroath were cursing their luck on 72 minutes. McGlashan raced on to David Arbuckle's head flick and rammed home a low shot - but ref George Clyde ruled out his effort after spotting a linesman's flag when it looked as though Livi defender Gordon Watson had played the Arbroath striker onside.

Disgusted Arbroath manager Dave Baikie said afterwards, "Some of the Livi players even came up to me and said it was onside."

But even one disallowed goal would not have been enough to save Forfar the following week as Livi hammered them 5-0 - John Robertson and Charlie King both grabbed doubles - taking the club nearer promotion. As always though, Jim Leishman wasn't letting anyone talk about it and Ray Stewart was adopting the same tactic.

But the buzz from the game did not last long as old rivals Inverness Caley Thistle popped up at the end of February to keep pressure on Livi at the top of the table.

Livi took the lead in nine minutes when Mark McCormick curled a drive around Fridge into the net.

But Inverness hit back through Scott McLean then Bobby Wilson added a fluke second when the ball hit him and rebounded into the net. Shearer bagged the third 20 minutes from time.

Afterwards Ray Stewart, mindful of how last season had gone, said, "It's going to be a tough last quarter to the programme."

Form was improved the following week with a draw against East Fife, but the main talking point of the game was not the goals but Jim Sherry's injury.

As usual, he was diving in for tackles, but in the 22nd minute, he dived in and didn't get up as his patella bone came away from the knee cap by four or five inches in one of the most sickening injuries in recent years in Scottish football.

Jim's injury seemed to take the fight out of Livi somewhat and East Fife took the lead through a Lee Dair's goal in the 34th minute.

But former Dunfermline star Derek Fleming levelled in 54 minutes thanks to a superbly struck free-kick.

But the gap at the top of Division Two was five points in Livi's favour despite the draw as Inverness Caley's were beaten by Arbroath.

The poor run continued against Queen of the South and fans were beginning to worry that this season could be a repeat of the last – promised so much but delivered so little as players got tired near the end of the season.

Queens went ahead in the 29th minute through Derek Townsley and Charlie Adams extended their lead with a 40th minute header but Livi sub John Robertson grabbed a late consolation.

The home side's cause was not helped by the dismissal of John Millar and Queens' David Lilley was also sent off.

After the game Ray Stewart said he still believed in the team and added nerves might be playing a part.

He said, "I sometimes wonder if they are getting nervous because they are getting near the line. They might be feeling it a little. Sometimes it is easier to be chasing the title rather than be ahead but if you want the big time, then you have to cope with that."

The next game saw the Lions' play a fired-up Partick Thistle. Club icon John Lambie was still settling into his new stint as boss and the two teams had to battle for the points and at the end of the day a sharing of them was deemed a fair result by most neutrals

Livi took a 10th -minute lead when Ian Little headed in a pinpoint cross from Bingo Bingham.

But the Jags equalised just before half- time through Robert Dunn.

Paul McDonald's shot was brilliantly blocked by Livi keeper Ian McCaldon but Dunn followed up to volley in the rebound.

Promotion – and party time – was clinched the following week with a small, but significant, win against Alloa.

Brian McPhee was the 65th minute goal hero. He went on for John Robertson and almost immediately rammed home a Bingham pass.

Ray Stewart was delighted and offered the win up for the fans. "I'm happy for the fans because they've stuck by us through thick and thin and they've got behind us. It's all about the fans.

"I think the crowd showed the pressure at times and they were sometimes a wee bit anxious. At the end of the day they've got a right to be like that because they have had two years just missing out."

The winning run continued with a 2-0 win against Clyde.

Livi grabbed the opener seconds after the interval when Brian McPhee deflected luckless Clyde's Bryan Smith's pass back over stranded keeper Dave Wylie.

Charlie King clinched the points when he volleyed home Neil Bennett's cross 20 minutes from time and the club were able to go top as Caley Thistle slipped up, drawing against Stirling Albion.

John Robertson was delighted – especially as it looked as if he was about to get his first championship medal.

He said, "We know if we win our last four games we are champions. We've got the experience to see it out, but we have to show we want it."

"Our main aim was promotion this year and we've achieved that, but we don't want to finish second."

Robertson may not have scored in that game, but his goal in the next one was vital.

His 16th goal of the season – a bounce off his knee - came during a 1-1 draw with Arbroath to keep Livi two points at the top.

But he went from hero to villain in just a matter of days when he scuffed a 35th minute penalty against the legs of Stirling Albion keeper Garry Gow, and the subsequent 0-0 draw meant Livi surrendered top spot to Inverness Caley on goal difference.

With Stirling fighting relegation the game never lacked bite and the home side deserved their point despite Livi having the best chances.

Gow denied both Mark McCormick and David Bingham with wonderful stops while Albion sub Chris Wood fired a great half-volley just over the bar and hit man Alex Bone came close at the other end.

Livi midfielder Billy McDonald sent-off after a skirmish with substitute Chris Jackson in 73 minutes.

Robbo was inconsolable afterwards.

He said, "Personally, I feel I have let the boys down and I have to hold my hands up and take 99 per cent of the blame. I thought I hit the penalty well enough and you have to give credit to the keeper, but all teams live or die by their strikers' goals. I apologised to all the lads after the game."

Ray Stewart was more philosophical and refused to put blame anywhere saying, "I always knew it would go down to the last game of the season. I have asked my players if they want to be winners and it's up to them."

Fortunately Livingston still had the chance to grab the top spot back as the next game was a home leg against Caley Thistle.

Both teams were already guaranteed promotion, but you wouldn't have thought so from the battle that took place on the pitch. And without being biased, Livingston hammered their rivals at the start, getting four goals in the first 20 minutes. Even Caley boss Steve Paterson had to admit: "In the first 20 minutes I thought we were going to lose six or seven. It was the worst start I've had in 10 years of management."

And it wouldn't be his last beating at the hands of Livi as he would go on to gaffer Aberdeen later on, but that was many years in the future on that May day.

The demolition began when Charlie King took a pass from Jimmy Boyle and released a low drive which Les Fridge, the Inverness keeper, could only touch on its way to the net.

Two minutes later, King tucked inside, carried the ball skilfully round two defenders and drove it low into the far corner. After 17 minutes, John Millar created the third goal, locating Paul Deas in clear space to shoot high into the net. Then, as a shaken Inverness side failed to regroup, Brian McPhee broke through a stuttering central defence for a fiercely struck fourth.

Showing why they were top scorers in the division, Inverness managed to pull a goal back when Ian McCaldon a hash of a clearance after 37 minutes and Mark McCulloch returned the ball crisply into the net.

Inverness were spurred on to a comeback and Charlie Christie drove a low diagonal ball into the far corner after 61 minutes and Iain Stewart, who had just come on in place of Duncan Shearer, slipped in a third goal six minutes.

Suddenly, Livingston's four-goal margin had all but evaporated and a match that had throbbed from the start somehow reached new heights of intensity. After yet another error by McCaldon, only a timely block by Gregg Watson prevented McLean from giving Thistle an equality that for so long had verged on the impossible.

At the end, the reflection had to be that it had indeed been a game of two halves and that both had been wonderfully entertaining.

Fan David Black remembers it: "Probably thee best game most Livi fans have ever been to. Livi took a four goal lead 24 minutes into the game in a game which pretty much decided who would win the second division.

"A Charlie King double and a goal from Brian McPhee and Paul Deas put us in the driving seats but Caley plugged away and brought it back to 4-3 which, expectantly, resulted in a nail biting finish with Livi being the conquerers."

Nerves were high for the last game as it was still possible for either team to clinch it, but in the end it was the Lions' who roared loudest and were crowned champions, after they managed a 2-1 away win at Forfar while Inverness Caley Thistle could only draw 1-1 with Alloa.

Brian McPhee settled any nerves for Livingston with a third-minute goal. Charlie King drove home a second in the 64th minute, which was the signal for the celebrations to start in earnest. Not even an 83rd minute penalty by Martin McLauchlan, the Forfar striker, could induce the smallest of concerns amongst the visiting players.

The end of season stats looked impressive – Livi lost only three League games, earning 77 points, and scored 66 goals as well as grabbing a few senior league scalps.

And an exhausted Ray Stewart was glad to see the end of the season for his nerves if nothing else.

He said, "It has been a hard, hard season for me and I'm delighted for everyone. We've finally crossed the finishing line. We knew Caley could have overtaken us if they had won and we had lost, but we had only victory in mind for this game, which sums up our approach all season. I hope we can now go on to bigger things, but we'll have a holiday in the meantime."

One thing that he hoped would be settled before the holiday though was contract talk – specifically his own as he only had a one-year contract.

And he had plans: "I hope this is a start and that we can build from here for the future of the club," he said as he was covered in champagne.

"We have a great group of players and I believe if we can bring in a few more to strengthen the squad we can do well in the first division."

CHAPTER
7

HIGH EXPECTATIONS

Given how well the last season had gone, fans had high expectations for season 1999-2000, and as always with the Lions', it was a season of many things but dull was not one of them.

And there were some new faces as always, including Falkirk's Marino Keith, who came to Livi as he felt that they had a great chance of getting to the SPL at the end of the season.

It started off with a boost for the Livi faithful. The first game of that season was a league cup match against Cowdenbeath. Seeing them off with a competent – and attractive footballing performance – thanks to two goals from Gerry Britton meant the Lions' were up against the team they vanquished the previous season, Aberdeen. It might not have been good news for the Dons, but at Livi some took it as a sign that this was going to be a good year – especially as three clubs had the chance to be promoted to the promised land of the SPL. If nothing else, at least there would be more cash from playing a premiership team that there was in the likes of playing third division Cowdenbeath.

Paul Heron was one of the 600 or so people who made the effort to come out for the game and he remembers: "The team stopped trying in the second half. You got the impression that they felt they had done enough."

Sadly, the club's division one opener didn't have the same happy ending as the cup game with Marino Keith's goal for the club being cancelled out by a Paul Tosh equalizer in the second half for Raith. Gerry Britton also scored, but he was ruled offside.

It was a cruel start to the season, especially as the lads had been fired up for three points from the start and played the far better football.

And even though he was a new signing, Marino seemed to be full of the belief that permeated the club, telling reporters after the game that he was convinced The Lions' would be in the SPL sooner rather than later.

But Ray Stewart was thinking more of the current league, criticizing his players for using long balls and hoofing it up the park.

He said, "We allowed Raith to dominate us in that time and the second half passed us by. At this level it is all about taking your opportunities when they come along and we did not create enough or take our chances, but it is not the worst start that we could have had."

At least it was a better crowd that the Cowdenbeath game with more than 4000 people turning out for the unfurling of the league champions flag.

But whatever the club did in training during the week paid off as their first division one three points were pulled in from a game against Ayr United the following week.

Gerry Britton and David Bingham scored the goals which gave the visitors a 2-1 victory, at either end of Danny Lennon's ambitious 35-yard equaliser.

Ayr helped Livi out though as they were reduced to 10 men just after the half hour mark after Glynn Hurst was sent off for striking out at Alan McManus.

This set the team up nicely for the game against Aberdeen, but a touch of hubris on Livi's side and a hunger for revenge from the oil rig city team saw The Lions' lose 1-0. To be fair though, Livi did still give the Dons a fair fright at times.

The Dons played a very defensive game, often having eight outfield players in the box any time the Lions' pushed forward. And one of the best chances of the first half fell to Graham Coughlan who soared above Russell Anderson to meet a Charlie King corner but he couldn't get it right on target.

The visitors threatened again three minutes later when, from an Ian McCaldon clearance, Gerry Britton head flicked on and with Preece hesitant, Marino Keith stole in at an angle to fire a shot to Whyte, who just got to block for a corner.

Half time saw the Dons recover, having been the poorer side of the first half, and they came out blazing after the break and they nabbed the only goal of the game just before the hour mark, putting the Lions' out of the cup and giving the Dons their first win of the season.

Livi fans weren't left too down though as the club had shown – again – that it was able to provide entertaining football against the giants of the Scottish game and it bode well for when – few thought it was an "if" any more – the team reached the SPL.

A chance to atone for that defeat came just a few short days later when Airdrie came to Almondvale and while Livi were on form in the second half, Airdrie helped them out considerably by playing one of the worst performances the first division ever saw. And that's not bias speaking, Airdrie boss Gary Mackay thought they were awful.

To make matters worse, it was ex-Airdrie players Brian McPhee and Sean Sweeney who were on the score sheet, Brian grabbing two goals to put Livi at the top of the league.

After that the Challenge Cup was up with Livi facing off against Berwick. On paper, a first division team playing a third division team should be a no-brainer in terms of result. Someone forgot to tell the teams that.

Berwick stunned the home fans by going ahead in 37 minutes after goalie Ian McCaldon came for a corner but didn't gather it and the ball fell to Paul Paterson who put in from just 12 yards out.

A few attempts at an equalizer were squandered and in the second half, John Robertson and Charlie King came on for John Miller and Derek Fleming to try and turn things around. Just as well they came on because Robbo was instrumental in setting up Livi's 68th minute leveller, putting a corner onto Sean Sweeney, who passed on to Bingham to slot away.

Chances were created at either end but Berwick held out to force extra time.

But Bingham buried their challenge 15 minutes into overtime with a 22-yard free-kick into the top corner

The next game gave Livi a chance to go clear at the top of the league and the Lions' only had themselves to blame for it after they were two-up in just under half an hour thanks to a peach of a 25 yard goal from Marino Keith and a cute shot from John Millar. For Keith, especially that was a welcome goal – and far better than his last appearance at Cappielow where he ended up being stretchered off after a bad clash with Derek Collins.

After that though, Morton came back into it with a low shot by David Murie giving the home fans hope just before half time.

Livi were still a goal up as the second half started but squandered a number of easy chances – or thought the point of the game was to hit the posts and crossbar instead of the net - and they paid the price for it in the 71st minute when Morton equalized, thanks to loan striker Paddy Connolly.

Coach Ray Stewart lambasted Livi for throwing away the points, and said, "It shows you the standards we expect that the players are disappointed to go home with a point."

The club was still soaring high on belief in their capabilities and that was reflected in them telling Hearts midfielder Stefano Salvatori to forget any ideas he had about joining the club.

Most teams would be delighted to bring in a former AC Milan player but the fact that after the club sounded him out about the idea he said he needed a few days to think about, made them pass on him, leading to the club to look at Hearts midfielder Lee Makel instead.

Dominic Keane said, "We wanted a quick answer from Stefano today. He said he needed a couple of days to think about it, but that was not good enough for Livingston."

At the same time, other clubs were taking in interest in some of the Livi squad, specifically keeper Ian McCaldon. But Keane told him he was going nowhere.

Perhaps it was that talk that unsettled the keeper, because the next game saw all the points leaving with visiting team Dunfermline.

The first half was fantastic for Livi with a lot of good, confident attacking football, giving the, 000 or so fans something entertaining to watch in the midfield. Sadly there was a lack of direct goalmouth drama in the first 20 or so minutes with a dig by Charlie King which was blocked by Pars keeper Ian Westwater and a couple of free-kicks for Dunfermline being the only mouth-watering action.

Gerry Britton nearly gave the home fans something to cheer about at half time but his shot went wide, but as half time was blown, the Livi fans were justified in thinking that a goal was only a matter of time.

The second half was a far different affair than expected. Dunfermline started upping the pressure with wave upon wave of attacks and shots nearly going in. Disturbed at this – and as both sides pushed for a goal – tempers started to fray and there were a couple of bookings and red cards. Coughland and Petrie both going off for bad tempered moments.

The Fife team managed to keep their focus more than Livi though and they kept piling on the footballing pressure and despite

Livi throwing on three subs in the last 20 minutes – McPhee for Britton, McCann for Bingham and Keith for Feroz – as well as some great saves from McCaldon, Dunfermline nabbed a goal and the three points with just seven minutes to go.

Any thoughts that the heads were down from the result were quickly case aside though as Livi thumped Falkirk 2-0. And if Marino Keith was nervous about facing his old team he never showed it with a good chance early on that went wide.

Sadly that was to be his main contribution to the game as with just 10 minutes on the clock he was left on the ground in agony with ligament damage after a collision with defender David Sinclair.

Just as half-time dawned, Falkirk's Andy Lawrie helped change the scoreline with a weak backpass, Robertson beat Hogarth to the ball, rounded the keeper, and slotted it home.

The goal gave the Lions' a boost which they carried into the second half with them – though Falkirk didn't lie down at any point, though it must have been tempting after Bingham's goal just before the 70th minute, letting the away team go home with the three points. It also let them slot into second place in the league.

Next up was the Challenge Cup and a home leg against Raith Rovers who were swept aside in a convincing 3-1 win with the goals from Brian McPhee – who scored in the first minute, Gerry Britton and Marc Millar putting the team through to the last four.

Then it was time to face some familiar foes for the first time in the first division.

But for Caley the start of the season hadn't been as good as it had been for their central belt compatriots, languishing in the bottom two of the league, while The Lions' soared in the top two.

Just like the games of previous years, it was a thrilling encounter, and one that entertained both sets of fans, coming in at a 2-2 draw.

Brian McPhee was set to be the hero of the day, putting Livi ahead, but after that Caley seemed to take control of the game with Martin Bavidge nabbing Caley's equaliser and Paul Sheerin then firing them in front with a 38th-minute penalty.

McPhee managed to grab another one though – but blew a chance to put the Lions' ahead in the last five minutes of the game when Les Fridge superbly saved a close effort. For once it was a game where everyone agreed a draw was a fair result – though Livi did get the better of the play it has to be said.

But the club stayed confident for the clash against Clydebank a week later and any hopes the Bankies had of three points were quickly dashed after David Bingham put the Lions' two ahead nine minutes into the game, but for the second week in a row, hopes of hat tricks were thrown out the window. This one was a tad unusual though as Bingham had to come off because he was walloped by his own keeper. Ian McCaldon landed on top of him during a goalmouth struggle, leaving him bruised around the ribs.

Bingham coming off seemed to give Clydebank a little boost and they were able to attack more – mainly because they didn't have to defend so much because Bingham was off – and for the second time in the season, a handball lead to a penalty. This time, John Miller was the guilty party, in the 68th minute, and Lee Gardner had no hesitation in slotting the ball away.

Afterwards Ray Stewart said he was concerned about the fact that the team seemed to get complacent from scoring two goals so early on in the game; but there would be no complacency in the next game, a Challenge Cup tie against Caley Thistle.

A small crowd of 1025 saw an energetic first half and Livi tried to kill the game off quickly with Craig Feroz having a good chance minutes after kick off.

The pressure was kept up, but eventually the home team found their way with Dennis Wyness missing an easy shot from six yards out mid-way through the first half.

Both teams kept at it though with McPhee, Sheerin, Byers and Fleming all having the chance to take their teams one-up, but half-time saw the game as a no-scoring draw.

As the game went on, it became a more scrappy affair with fewer shots at the goals, and with both teams tiring it looked as if the game would be going to extra time at least until Caley found a burst of energy with Stuart Golabek having a run and a dig, which came to nothing, but Paul Sheerin managed to get to the rebound and put it away to get Caley the cash riches that would come from another round in the cup.

The heads stayed down for the following league game against St Mirren, which ended in a 1-1 draw. However a touch of luck ensured that they still managed to get a point instead of none.

If the team had nabbed three points from this game then they would have put the Buddies off the top of the league and taken that spot for themselves. At first all seemed to be going well with Livi taking the lead after 18 minutes thanks to a poor clearance by Scott

Walker. Charlie King got the ball, had a shot, it was blocked by Ludovic Roy, but he was unable to hold it and the rebound fell to Brian McPhee, but that came off the bar. Fortunately Gerry Britton was there to make sure it went in finally.

Livi could have made it two after McPhee had a great chance, only to put it wide.

The second half saw Livi adopt a more defensive formation and St Mirren showed they weren't going to be knocked off the top without a fight and they managed to grab an equalizer when Barry Lavety slid onto the ball to get it between the posts.

The game got a bit bad-tempered just after an hour had passed when Allan McManus was sent off, reducing Livi to ten men, for a crazy tackle on Junior Mendes.

The bad-tempers continued and a penalty was blown for against the Lions' in the 86th minute after Coughlan fouled Tom Brown. Fortunately for Livi, he took it poorly and Ian McCaldon had no problems stopping it.

While afterwards, Ray Stewart was upset at not winning the match, the club were in a good position. As the first quarter of the season ended, they were in second place and in a way, being out, the cup was a blessing, as it allowed them to concentrate on the league.

The second quarter kicked off with Livi facing a tired-looking Ayr, who had played Celtic just days earlier.

Gerry Britton nabbed the Lions' first goal after just 10 minutes, taking a cross from Andy McLaren to do so.

Nigel Jemson seemed the freshest Ayr player on the park having a number of goes at goal which came to nothing but an equaliser did silence the home support in the 33rd minute when defender David Craig took a chance with a 25-yard dig.

The second half though was one-way traffic with Mark McCormick nabbing two in under 15 minutes. The first came at the tail end of a cross by Paul in 55 minutes, while the second was a rebound from a failed first shot in the 68th minute.

The final goal – putting the game well and truly beyond Ayr who looked as they would have thrown in the towel early if it was allowed – came for Ray McKinnon after Brian McPhee crossed the ball to him.

The final game of October and all of November saw the Lions' hit a mini-slump. First up was a game against Raith Rovers that could certainly be called 'entertaining' or 'dramatic' as it had six bookings, one red card, two penalties, a player hospitalised and a debatable third goal. All that was missing was a streaker.

Both sides seemed up for a good game from kick off but Raith took the lead just after 21 minutes when Paul Browne leapt high to head one in.

Just five minutes later, Livi equalized thanks to Marc Miller slotting one away from the penalty spot caused by a soft foul on Gerry Britton.

Again, it only took another five minutes for something else to happen – another penalty as it would turn out. This time it was for Raith after Craig Dargo went one-on-one with Ian McCaldon. The ball got past the tall keeper, but Cargo certainly didn't, coming down hard after the McCaldon whacked into his shin.

Being the last man he had to go off and Brian McPhee was forced to come on as substitute keeper. Brian's many talents didn't extend to saving penalties that day and Kenny Black fired it in to make the score 2-1.

Livi didn't lie down but with their star keeper off and being down to ten men, the advantage was always going to be in Raith's favour. The killer blow came in the 75th minute when Paul Shields scored – and the goal stood despite ref George Clyde being pressured by some to concede that the goal was offside.

An incensed Ray Stewart had words with Clyde after the game and Clyde seems to have given as good as he got, telling Stewart to watch the game on telly to see how he reached the decision that the goal was legit.

After his little chat, the Livi boss fumed. "I went to see the ref after the game about their third goal and he told me I'd just have to watch it on TV. If that is what our game is coming to then things are in a bad way."

After that, the Lions' went into November trying to raise their spirits by getting three points against Falkirk. But the battling spirit of the Lions' seemed to go missing as the team took to the pitch, possibly blown away by the terrible gale-strength winds that were blowing around the new town. Livi attacked but the away team were able to soak up everything thrown at them and the opening goal didn't come until the 68th minute. Most fans at the game agreed it was worth waiting for though as Marc Millar took a free-kick of Brazillian sublime proportions in response to Andrew Lawrie fouling an outfield-again Brian McPhee, curling the ball past keeper Myles Hogarth.

If Livi thought that was all they had to do to nab three points then they were cruelly mistaken as Falkirk levelled the game just 60 seconds later as Iain Morris got to the end of a cross to ensure that both sides ended the day with a point apiece.

The Lions' had some chances to try and get the three points – notably McPhee who missed an ace chance by shooting wide after having been sent clear, and Millar having another fancy shot in the 78th minute, but this time his shot kissed the crossbar instead of going in under it.

Another game against Caley Thistle was next up, but it wasn't pretty for anyone who didn't come from Inverness as they took all three points away from this one.

It was a spirited first-half performance by Livi, but nerves seemed to take hold in the second-half and by trying too hard and pushing more players up front in search of a goal, they left themselves exposed at back and Caley were only too happy to exploit that.

A long ball from Ross Tokely from the right wing got to Stuart Golabek's feet and he whacked one in from 20 yards out, beating Ian McCaldon. The heads went down after that and Scott McLean made the misery complete just before ref George Simpson called full time.

The misery was compounded in the next game as Dunfermline took three goals and three points off the Lions' in an away game that no-one with the West Lothian club would care to remember as Dunfermline closed their gap on the top of the league to eight points.

Not for the first time in the season, Livi's game faltered after a foul lead to a penalty and a sending off.

Sean Sweeney elbowed Owen Coyle off the ball just after the half-hour mark and as Sweeney walked off, Stevie Crawford slotted the penalty to take the lead.

Ten man Livi looked as if they were holding on until half-time when just as the clock hit 45 minutes David Moss nabbed number two with a header.

The second half saw Livi fired up for the game and though they tried to pull something back, it just wasn't happening and a miserable day was made complete when Crawford nabbed a personal second with a strike just five minutes from time.

A blip in the poor run happened on November 20 as the Lions' managed to beat Morton 2-1, but it wasn't a good advert for football with a very dull first half.

The second half was a bit more sparky as Gerry Britton headed in a Derek Fleming free-kick in the 49th minute and David Bingham made it two just nine minutes later with some smooth football with Gerry Britton.

Bingo passed the ball to Britton, who back-heeled it back to Bingham, who then obliged by slotting the ball past Ally Maxwell.

Morton – a bit late – were fired up by this and started throwing more and more into the game. A panicked Livi just tried to soak up as much of the attack as they could, but in the 76th minute David Murie whacked one in.

The pressure was then on for an equalizer and in the 85th minute it looked as the 'ton would get their chance when John Millar appeared to punch the ball away from Warren Hawke inside the Livi area.

This time, luck was with the Lions' as the ref Dougie McDonald believed that the ball striking Millar had been accidental, though it was clearly a penalty under the rules of the game.

Hawke was furious: "The referee told me the ball had struck the Livingston player's hand but he felt it was accidental. I don't understand how any official can see a player reaching round an opponent to punch the ball away as being accidental."

But the luck didn't stay long as Livi found themselves on the end of another beating just seven days later. This time it was St Mirren grabbing the points to go 16 points clear at the top of the league, more or less guaranteeing promotion in practice, the theory would have to wait a few months.

The game went against Livi more or less from the start with Steven McGarry smacking in a spectacularly powerful – and wind-backed shot to take an early lead in the 12th minute.

Livi attacked, but one problem was that Bingo Bingham appeared to be neutered by Sergei Baltacha marking him out of the game, giving him little more than space to breathe for the 90 minutes.

Livi tried but the first half was not kind to them. And while Graham Coughlan made sure the Lions' didn't give in, they went two down after Barry McLaughlin headered in a corner from Gary Bowman.

Livi stayed in the game though, thanks to an own goal by Tommy Turner. That was the last that Ludovic Roy let past him though and the Lions' were denied a deserved share of the points.

Some people were starting to wonder if Livi were entering a dark period, but Dominic Keane was still convinced anything was possible, telling reporters that there was still 60 points up for grabs before the end of the season, reminding people that in the previous year the club were 13 points clear in the second division at one point but finished second.

Keane's words paid off because the club then ended the year in not only a winning fashion, but a high-scoring fashion, pulling in 11 goals in three games.

The first of these was a fantastic game against Clydebank.

It ended up 5-1 for the visiting team, but Livi could have easily scored double that with David Bingham grabbing a double in the 12th and 90th minutes while Mark McCormick scored in the 41st, Charlie King scored in the 50th and Derek Fleming grabbed the fourth in 74 minutes to inflict a heavy bruising on Ian McCall's team. Lee Gradner pulled one back from a penalty with four minutes to full-time but it far too little far too late. It was a shame that only 364 people managed to see the game, but by this point Livi were getting used to not always having big crowds see them play their best.

Next up was a horrendous game against Airdrie and questions should have been asked of referee Tom Brown allowing this game to go ahead when temperatures were hitting zero and the pitch was like concrete.

Airdrie took first blood in the game. Actually, that isn't true, the pitch claimed first blood when the home side's Gareth Evans had to come off after just five minutes injured. This allowed Davie McGuire to come on and he opened up the scoring in the 15th minute after a pass from Steve McCormick.

Livi's Derek Fleming was then the next casualty of the pitch, coming off just after the half hour had passed as his ankle buckled on the solid ground, eventually needing crutches, and McPhee came on for him. Livi kept pushing for an equalizer and got it while McPhee was still getting used to the pitch with Charlie King chipping in the ball to Mark McCormick who managed to hold off Gerry Farrell to fire in their first goal of the game.

The second half saw Livi continue to push for the points and Bingo Bingham nabbed his first of the day exactly on the hour after a Kiss cross. Airdrie pulled one back in the 84th minute, but Livi never gave up and Bingham was able to get on the end of another King cross two minutes from the end to give the visiting Lions' a well-deserved victory and three points.

As most people got ready for Xmas, Dominic Keane revealed parts of his latest plan for the club, including a £10million national youth academy. There was also mention of the £100,000 grant from SportScotland to help them build a fourth stand at Almondvale, taking their capacity to over 10,000 and allowing them into the SPL, which had become a stickler about stadium sizes, which was ridiculous as it forced many teams to work on their grounds instead of beefing up their teams.

Fleming was still crocked for the next goal thriller against Falkirk. Falkirk grabbed the game by the horns. Scoring first – and against the run of play as Livi had been the dominant team – in the 34th minute when David Nicholl scored through a mass of bodies in the box.

The next piece of drama came just before half-time as Falkirk's David Sinclair was sent off for an off-the-ball swipe at Mark McCormick.

Livingston took advantage of being a man up to attack heavily at the start of the second half and the pressure they put Falkirk under paid off when Scott McKenzie gifted them an own goal after a Charlie King shot came off him and went in the net.

Falkirk didn't take this though. They kept attacking at the other end, David Nicholls in particular having a number of chances.

And while Ray Stewart was never a fan of players losing discipline, he must be glad that McLaren was lippy to the Falkirk dug-out which lead to him being booked. Steward decided to bring him off and put on Brian McPhee.

Talk about a decision that changes a game. McPhee's first dealings in the game was to score after John Henry messed up, taking the team to 2-1 in the 65th minute.

Falkirk still weren't lying down though with Nicholls heading in a McQuilken free-kick in the 73rd minute.

Any hopes the Falkirk faithful had of a sharing of the points for some festive cheer were dashed in the 86th minute when McPhee scored his second of the day.

Fan Ann Marie McGloughlin remembers that: "Airdrie were the better team. They did a lot more attacking than us, but we just kept plodding away, waiting for a break and scoring when we could."

The New Year of 2000 would bring a lot of changes to the club, but it was a case of familiarity breeding contempt at the start of it as Livi faced off – again – against Caley Thistle. At least fans with a hangover from the New Year festivities didn't have to travel too far as it was a home game, kicking off at 1pm as well because the floodlights were out due to stadium work, but the 1-1 result might have sent them home looking for more booze.

To be fair, the game wasn't as dull as the weather with Livi having a right go against their old foes and they nearly took the lead after 14 minutes when Charlie King's corner was met by a forceful header from Graham Coughlin.

Bingo Bingham hit a half-volley, but goalie Jim Calder pulled off a fine save – and it wouldn't be his last throughout the day. King and Marc Millar continued to pile on the pressure, taking the game constantly to the visitors who found themselves only able to attack on the break.

And when they did they were dangerous with a shot from an on-form Barry Wilson, who would later play for the Lions', forcing Livi keeper Neil Alexander to parry it away. Fortunately for him there were no other Caley players nearby to get the ball and sneak it in while he was down.

Jim Calder was the hero of the second half, pulling off save after save, frustrating the home team – especially Bingham, King and Millar who he kept thwarting - and fans. Against the run of play, Caley then found themselves with a scoring opportunity and they seized it for all it was worth with Ross Tokely supplying a cross for Barry Wilson that he headed past Alexander.

But Livi didn't give in and 10 minutes later as the clock reached 82 minutes gone on the game when a three-player combo saw a sharing of the points as Charlie King ran down the left, crossed the ball over to Keith, who headed it over and down for Brian McPhee to put away.

That was it for scoring, but the game wasn't finished yet as Xausa was booked a second time – for a challenge on McManus – in the 87th minute, leaving Caley to finish the game with just 10 men.

That would be the last draw for the team in January, as they would go on for another top goal scoring run. It started on a low-key note with a win against Dunfermline which pulled the Lions' to within 11 points of St Mirren.

Marino Keith made his first start after a lengthy injury lay-off and had two early attempts which came close to being the opening goal. At the other end, Stevie Crawford had a shot saved by Livi keeper Neil Alexander before Ian Westwater saved a Brian McPhee strike at the other end in what was turning out to be a thrilling battle.

Livi took the lead in 61 minutes after Ian Westwater blundered a cross with Bingo Bingham opening the scoring account.

Paddy Kelly's delivery found its way to Bingham six yards out with Westwater flapping, and the former Pars striker easily headed his 10th of the season.

The Fifers threw everyone up to put pressure on the Livi rearguard, but they managed their first clean sheet since September.

A three goal win against Clydebank on January 22 put the club to within two points of second place, but the three points felt like a long time coming.

Thirty minutes had passed before a shot was directed on target, right-back Paddy Kelly's cross was carried goal wards by the wind, but Colin Stewart managed to get the ball. As half-time neared though, the action heated up with Charlie King setting up Marino Keith but Stewart managed to spread himself well to push the low strike to safety. A minute later, the young goalkeeper comfortably gathered David Bingham's curling free-kick from 25 yards.

But the half-time pep talk, as fan John Martin said, "Put a rocket up their arses," as Bingham tried time and time again to open the score sheet, easily beating the Bankies defence, only being constantly thwarted by Stewart. When he wasn't trying to score himself, he was setting them up sweetly for Charlie King.

But neither of these fine players opened up the goal tab. That honour belonged to Marino Keith, who got things going in the 65th minute. Eight minutes later he did it again, heading in a Millar cross.

A cross played a part in the next big part of the game, but it was Bingham being cross rather than anything else. He was taken off and replaced by McKinnon in the 82nd minute, but as he came off the pitch he spat out his gum shield, threw it away and said some harsh words to the management.

It was no long-running spat though with the player and manager clearing the air quickly.

As Ray Stewart put it: "Of course he was frustrated and I wouldn't want anyone to be pleased about being substituted. But it's my job to make decisions and players have got to like it or lump it. At the end of the day we're all working for the same cause."

Bingo added: "It just didn't happen for me and I was very annoyed. However, the management were right to take me off as nobody has a divine right to stay on the park. No player is bigger than the club."

Meanwhile on the pitch, Brian McPhee nabbed the club's third goal of the day with six minutes left on the clock, leaving the club feeling good about the possibility of playing in the SPL the following year.

Next up saw Livingston rip up their pitch at Almondvale to try and fix problematic parts of it – notably the quagmire that had once claimed to be a centre circle.

The ripping continued on the pitch as Livi tore apart Queen of the South in the Scottish Cup.

The West Lothian outfit had their task made so much easier by the 23rd minute dismissal of Steven Leslie. Marino Keith went on to score a second-half hat-trick in the space of 12 minutes.

The seven goal massacre started in the 14th minute when Ray McKinnon shot low past John Hillcoat from the edge of the box.

The Lions' were then boosted by Queens Captain Steven Leslie being sent off for a reckless challenge on Marino Keith in the 23rd minute.

That was it for first-half drama, but the second half was full of glee for Livi fans. Keith nabbed his hat-trick, scoring in the 51st, 58th and 68th minutes. Bingo Bingham followed up Keith's second goal a minute after, though some thought it was an own goal by Alan Kerr.

Brian McPhee added his name to the score sheet in 69 minutes when he scored from close up and McKinnon nabbed the seventh one minute from time.

The game was slightly marred afterwards due to claims by the 12-minute hat-trick scorer Marino Keith who claimed Queens officials tried to stop him taking the ball home. He told reporters: "I asked the referee, Hugh Dallas, if I could take it and he said it wouldn't be a problem, but Queen of the South weren't going to give it to me and said something like Livingston could afford their own balls."

"It was my first hat-trick of my career and I wasn't leaving the ground without it."

The story had a happy ending though as he got the ball and the draw for the cup saw the Lions' placed away to Partick Thistle, a team that shouldn't have been a problem for the West Lothian boys.

But before that, it was back to the league and another three points from a 2-0 victory against St Mirren

New signing Lee Richardson made his debut here and had a hard game, being jostled constantly – especially at the hands and legs of Tom Brown.

The game wasn't a classic by any description, but it was entertaining enough – if not a game for the purists – and Livi took the lead just before the half-hour when Bingham headed in a Ray McKinnon free-kick.

Livi kept pushing the pressure and it was nearly two goals in two minutes as Marino Keith found himself with a chance after a poor header pass-back by Tommy Turner. Ludovic Roy was on form though, bravely throwing himself at the feet of Keith to stop him getting to goal.

It wasn't one-way traffic though as St Mirren nearly brought themselves back into the game just ten minutes later. Mark Yardley did well to get his head onto a cross from Junior Mendes, but it was just wide.

Livi were given a boost two minutes before half time as Tom Brown found himself red carded and while there wasn't much time to capitalize on it then, the Lions' went for it in the second half.

Steve McGarry was denied a goal as Deas cleared from the goal-line in the first minute after the restart and it was all but over just before the hour. McKinnon's fantastic pass was dummied to McPhee's path by Bingham and he thumped it low into the net.

Then it was the cup game against Partick Thistle and it's fair enough to say that most fans didn't expect them to be a bother, especially after Bingo Bingham nabbed the opening goal in just nine minutes. The team looked confident from that, only to be thwarted time and time again by keeper Kevin Budinauckas. This gave the jags a boost in the arm and, growing in confidence as half-time approached, they pulled themselves onto the score sheet five minutes from the break with Albert Craig putting one by McCaldon.

This fired them up for a second half which saw the two teams battle it out. Sadly for the Lions', it was the home team that seemed to get all the breaks and after Marc Millar was sent off in the 74th minute, it looked as if the day which started so well was going to end badly.

Scott McLean nabbing Thistle's second in the 79th minute confirmed that and Livi were tumbled out the cup 11 minutes later.

Fan John Buchanan remembers it – though not fondly. "This was a game we were convinced we would canter and after Bingo put us one up in eight minutes we thought we were laughing all the way.

"The thing is Thistle thought the same as well, because after we went one up, they were scrambling around just trying to prevent us getting two or more. But the fact that their keeper kept pulling off saves, started to give them a boost – and us a knock – and we paid the price for that. If we had managed to get a second quick enough, the game would have been killed off. It was the failure to get a second that did us the damage."

"At least being out the cup allowed us to then concentrate on the league."

And while a look at the result of their next game – a February 29 game against Ayr – which was 1-0, looks as if the Lions' bounced back from their defeat, it was a tad more farcical than that.

The first half was a spirited affair with the yellow card coming out of ref Eric Martindale's pocket after just seven minutes after Mark McNally sent Derek Fleming flying to the ground.

From the free-kick, Fleming had a shot that went just wide. As well as firing up Livi, it also inspired Ayr to move up a gear and their shots were better and more on target than Livi's were.

The next yellow card belonged to Livi as Bingham was pulled up for a sore-looking challenge on Marvyn Wilson.

Ayr had a chance to take the lead at the half hour with Neil Tarrant having a great chance after a Roddy Grant pass, but he sent it just wide.

The second half kicked off with Ayr looking the better of the two teams with attempts by Grant and Hansen unlucky not to go in.

If nothing else the game was heading to be an entertaining no-score draw until the 64th minute when Ayr keeper - and Faroes internationalist Jens Knudsen lost control of a Paul Deas cross and the ball spun off David Craig and into his own net to give the Lions' one up. The score remained the same to full time and put the club in fifth spot. And while reaching the top spot was starting to look unlikely, there was still 12 games to go, so anything was possible.

The team seemed to forget that piece of self-belief though as a game against Falkirk kicked off March and was also the beginning of a slump at the club that would have massive repercussions for the team.

The game itself was a slightly dull affair – the sole goal coming in 43 minutes after the normally reliable Ian McCaldon dropped the ball from a cross by Jamie McQuilken next to Davie Nicholls and he had no hesitation in slotting the shot away. Livi had a couple of chances, including Brian McPhee being straight on to goal, only to be stopped by Myles Hogarth. The best chance though was when Scott McKenzie accidentally tripped up Graham Coughlin in the box to give Livi a penalty. Sadly, Marc Millar put it over the bar, sending with it any hopes the Lions' had of three points.

Milar had similar luck in the next game – against Raith Rovers – in a game that had no goals but plenty of action.

Millar was at it just two minutes in and his attacking efforts were followed up by Mark McCormick, Brian McPhee and Paul Deas all carving up the visiting team's defence. But Raith weren't taking this lying down and Ian McCaldon had to be at his best to stop Ansah Owusu from putting Rovers one up. Efforts by Paul Tosh and Jay Stein were either saved or just wide.

At the other end, Livi pulled off a few more chances – including a great one by Ray McKinnon – but half-time saw the game stay at a stalemate. It was a half-time result that no one could disagree with and the second half kicked off as passionately – if not a little more slow paced due to tiredness hitting the players for the first half exertions. Nothing came of it and most fans thought a draw was fair, even if both sides had desperately needed the full three points.

Only 684 people turned up at Cappielow for Livi's next game against Morton. It would probably have been more if the fans had known that after this, one of the top players would be gone and so would the manager.

As had been the case in so many recent games, Livi started the game attacking well with chance after chance. Ex-Scottish Cup Final hero Ally Maxwell was their foil here though, stopping a number of great shots, including a curling powerhouse of a shot by

David Bingham just before 20 minutes and then a low dig by Alan McManus.

Inspired by their keeper, the Greenock team tried for their own goal and Harry Curran, Andy Millen and John Anderson all went for broke, only for Ian McCaldon to hold the fort for the Lions'.

Just before the half-time oranges were handed out though, Livi nearly took the lead with some fantastic teamwork. After a crafty pass from David Bingham sent through Ray McKinnon, who had a fantastic dig from the edge of the box, but it just went wide.

The second half saw Morton pile on the pressure with Craig McKinnon having an excellent free-kick opportunity denied. Fans didn't have too long to talk about it though as two minutes would see the game change completely.

First up was when Marc Millar was subbed off for Paddy Kelly in the 72nd minute. There were some cheers as Kelly came on but what threw everyone was Millar making an obscene gesture to some of the fans. What no one had spotted was that Millar was doing it to a mate.

It landed Marc in real hot water. Dominic Keane had the player suspended and he was booted out rapidly, much to Millar's shock.

As he told the *Scottish Sun* afterwards: "The alleged gesture was not made to the supporters but to a friend involved with Morton who was giving me some stick. It was more of a joke than anything else but Livingston never gave me the opportunity to explain that to them.

"In my mind I know what happened and I am very surprised and disappointed with the way it has been handled."

In the end it worked out well for Millar as he ended up in the SPL quicker than the rest of the club, being snapped up by St Johnstone. To this day, it baffles so many that a player as talented was allowed to go for such a minor thing – and without being allowed to plead his case, but there may have been a sinister reason for letting him go.

According to a club insider at the time: "Getting rid of Marc the way they did was a way to get a name off the wage list. I'm not saying that was why he was let go – everyone knows that Dominic Keane was determined to make Livi a family club, so this sort of thing wasn't on – but a fine and a public apology/explanation would have been as good.

"Marc was too good a player – and liked about the place – to be let go for something like this and a lot of people were left cheesed off about it. Of course, given the circumstances at the time, no one knew what was coming next."

Back on the pitch, Morton took the lead – and sealed the game's fate just one minute later when Harry Curran ran on to a pass inside the box from David Murie that he had no hesitation in thumping between the sticks. The result left Livi 11 points behind St Mirren at the top of the table and also seven points behind Falkirk, who they needed to overtake to stand a chance of getting into the SPL, but having only taken one point from their last nine, it didn't look good.

And the board agreed. An emergency meeting was held and the next morning saw the statement confirming Stewart's future – or lack of it – with the club.

The statement said, "It is with regret that Livingston FC today announce that manager Raymond Stewart has parted company with the club. He has left by mutual consent, both parties agreeing a change of management at this stage of the season was in the best interests of the football club.

"We recognise the role which Raymond has played in the development of Livingston FC, particularly the winning of the Second Division championship last season. And we would like to thank him for his valuable contribution over the last season and a half."

Jim Leishman was appointed interim manager, but the club said the hunt for the new manager would not be a prolonged affair.

It was a harsh verdict for Stewart, having taken the club up a league, but also having lost less than a fifth of the games he managed.

Stewart was diplomatic in his departure – saving his venom for later – but wasn't too shy about letting the players know his feelings.

He said, "Some of the players deserve criticism. Some of them, and they know who they are, couldn't look me in the eye when I said I was leaving and I hope it lives with them for the rest of their lives."

"I believe I gave everything but some of the players haven't battled. It would have been different if the players had not given up without a fight. Now I hope they can go on and win promotion.

"People have got to understand that teams have been fired up against us and make life difficult because they see what Livingston is all about."

"If you speak to any manager, consolidation in your first year in a new division is satisfactory and obviously Livingston have achieved that, but now the club want promotion."

Stewart would go on to manage Stirling Albion, but was let go by them at the end of the 2001/2002 season after the club were relegated the previous year and failed to come back up right away.

But back at Almondvale, Stewart going would be the catalyst for a number of changes which would end up with Leishman become manager, director and chief executive of the Lions', with Davie Hay coming in as head coach. Off the pitch, Celtic fan and lottery millionaire John McGuinness was named as director and vice-chairman.

The appointment of ex-Celt Hay wasn't made official until after the club's next game – an away tie to Caley Thistle – and if had any illusions about the size of the task in front of him, they were blown away during the 4-1 hammering that saw the Lions' act more like pussy cats.

Hay was always well known for being able to spot good talent in the game, having found the likes of Paolo di Canio, Pierre van Hooijdonk and Jorge Cadete for Celtic, when he was their top scout, before leaving under a cloud.

But he didn't need his abilities that dark day in Inverness. Truth be told Stevie Wonder could have told you that Caley's Xausa was one to watch after he banged in a hat-trick.

Livi may have started the game with all the possession, but that meant nothing in the 11th minute as Canadian Xausa opened up his scoring account.

The rout continued in the 32nd minute when Dennis Wyness opened up his goal scoring account for the day, but Xausa played a large part in it, passing the ball between himself and Paul Sheerin, dragging the Livi defence that they were cutting up with them, letting Wyness run free to get the pass and put the ball away.

As the second half started there was still a thought that Livi – with so much to prove – could pull themselves back into the game and they did so just before the hour mark with a fine drive by Brian McPhee. Not even ten minutes later though, the game was buried beyond hope as Xausa grabbed his next goal. He nearly made it three another ten minutes later, but McCaldon got to that.

Hopes of even grabbing a draw evaporated with 11 minutes to go as Graham Coughlan was sent off for a second bookable offence and Xausa made it three for himself and four for the club five minutes from time after a staggering run to beat the Livi defence.

To make matters worse, Paul Deas being booked saw him go over the points limit and he ended up with a two-game ban.

Afterwards, it was obvious that Hay had learned from Jim Leishman the art of never giving up as far as Livi were concerned.

"Anything is possible," he said. "We've still to play Dunfermline, St Mirren and Raith Rovers, and they give us the chance to make up some ground."

Perhaps the Livi team had been waiting until Hay was officially given his position before impressing him because they managed to turn on the win for their next game against Morton.

Morton took the game to the home team but for once the Lions' showed something that had been missing for much of the season – the ability to just grind out a win. All too often during the season, fancy, attractive football had been great to watch – but the team had failed to finish off winning scoring opportunities. But just like at Kevin Keegan's Newcastle and Tommy Burns's Celtic it had proved for naught. With this game the Lions' showed that they could play the more pragmatic game as well. The more dismissive said it was just luck and the team were due a win, but others like George McIntosh said, "The team had obviously started to respond to the new regime. Most people thought it was too late to get promoted, but at least things could look positive for the next season."

Anyway, the game against Morton saw Livi make the better opportunities, even though Morton weren't afraid to have a go themselves. Livi narrowly deserved the win and the three points came to them in the 82nd minute when sub Mark McCormick got on the end of a cross by Jamie Smith.

Bouyed by that, the team ventured to Jim Leishman's old stomping ground of Dunfermline but there was no fairytale or Rocky-like tale of the underdog coming back as the Pars thumped the Lions' 4-1, prompting Ray Stewart to come out with the bitchiest – but also most accurate and some would say justified - comment of the season: "One thing that never happened when I was in charge was getting beaten 4-1 but that happened twice after I had gone."

Dunfermline were the hungrier team on the day and that showed from early on with Owen Coyle starting the hammering in the 16th minute. Neil Alexander was between the posts as Ian McCaldon was recovering from an op on his nose. Poor Alexander would need an op after this game to remove the blushes from his face. His worst blunder was at the opening goal as Coyle hit a poor shot which he got to, but the bobbling ball went over his hands and into the net.

The second goal wasn't as much his fault as it was caused by some terrible defending after the keeper managed to get to a close-range shot by Stevie Crawford but no one ran in to clear it, allowing Ian Ferguson to have a shot, which he managed to get to, but again he was left abandoned and it gave Eddie May all the time he needed to put away the rebound just before the ref blew for half time.

May obviously enjoyed the thrill of scoring because he was at it again seven minutes into the second half – except it was past his own keeper after David Bingham put the ball into the box. The cruel deflection gave Livi a fighting chance.

It took only six minutes after that for the game to go beyond the Lions' though as the Pars put forward a great piece of attacking football. A free-kick from Paddy Kelly went to Stevie Crawford by mistake who beat a few players to slot in the third.

With just 15 minutes to go, the Lions' misery was made complete when Lee Bullen put the fourth away from the edge of the box.

Afterwards, Jim Leishman said there was still a chance of going up but conceded it was difficult.

"We gave away sloppy goals and it was disappointing to concede the third one so soon after getting back into game. We haven't been playing well for a few weeks now and the players have got to take a good look at themselves after that display."

"Nothing is impossible and being in the run for promotion is still mathematically possible for us."

And while many felt for Neil Alexander, there's not a lot of room for sentimentality when fighting for promotion so he was out for the next game – against Airdrie – and Ian McCaldon was brought back in.

And if the Lions' needed any encouragement, they were given a reminder of their ambitions as the SPL said Almondvale was now ready for the big time of the SPL, though as fan Roger Marthson put it, "They were taking the piss as most of us knew we weren't seeing the SPL next season – except on telly – so there was no need for them to announce it."

The stadium was deemed SPL ready and only the superstitious would say that boosted the team, but they gave a performance worthy of the SPL against Airdrie.

Anyone arriving late for this game missed a treat, as the Lions' were three up in just five minutes. Celtic loan player Jamie Smith opening the scoring up in the 11th minute with a fantastic volley. Ray McKinnon nabbed the second in the 23rd minute with his specialty of a low shot and Brian McPhee nutted the third goal in just 120 seconds later.

That doesn't mean the rest of the game was without incident at all. Airdrie pulled two goals back in the second half – the first coming practically straight from kick off with Stewart Easton scoring from just a few yards out and Alex Neil then scoring with 11 minutes left.

Probably due to trying to get back into the game, Airdrie found themselves well fired up. Too fired up. Eddie Forrest was sent off in the 80th minute after fouling David Bingham. He then landed himself in more hot water as he tried to boot a bin in the Almondvale tunnel, missed and whacked the Livi groundsman.

Sub Paul Jack followed him off – but he left the bin alone – after an elbow on Craig Feroz, and the Lions' held on until the end to get the three points.

The next game, an away leg against Clydebank, saw the squad a player lighter than normal after Lee Richardson had his contract terminated.

Morton found themselves terminated as well thanks to two goals from two Davids – Bingham and Rowson – in the two halves.

The game wasn't the best of starters, but by the half hour mark, the Lions' were looking the more dominant team and shots and rebounds had gone everywhere for the team, except the net. That changed in the 34th minute when a shot from Fleming was blocked, but Bingham banged it in from 20 yards out.

Livi were quick to attack in the second half as well when Brian McPhee was one on one with the keeper but he blasted it over.

Morton had the odd attempt but most of the attacking was being done at their goalmouth and in the 62nd minute, goal two turned up courtesy of a cross from Jamie Smith found David Rowson and he put it away.

With seconds to go, Ian Cameron scored for Clydebank, but anything than three points going to the Lions' would have been a travesty.

This gave the Lions' a slim – but mathematically feasible – chance to still make the SPL, but it would take them beating league leaders and relying on a lot of luck with other results.

Lady luck obviously never got the message as the team crashed to St Mirren, who showed why they were top of the league.

It was a spirited performance by Livi though and if they had played like this all season, who knows what might have been? For the first 20 or so minutes of the game, it was all Livi as they looked determined to nab the first goal, but perhaps they were trying too hard because in the 23rd minute David Rowson – last week the goal scorer, now the goal setter-up, just at the wrong end – hit a poor back pass that Steve McGarry was able to get to before Ian McCaldon, who he cheekily lobbed.

Bingo Bingham brought the Lions' back into it in the second half, getting onto the end of a Brian McPhee cross. They battled on, even after Mark Yardley grabbed the Saints second with 15 minutes to go, but these saints weren't so Christian and there was no help coming for the Lions'.

While everyone at the club was disappointed, Jim Leishman still managed to find something positive to take from the game.

"I thought the boys' commitment was superb. We asked for passion from them and certainly got it. However, the game's all about scoring goals and St Mirren got more than us so they deserved to win."

"For us now though at Livingston, it's a case of going forward from here. I want to make sure it is us who are celebrating next season."

The Lions' used the last three games to remind everyone else in the league that they could be dangerous and that this extra year in the first division was nothing more than a temporary setback. A 3-1 result against Raith Rovers – thanks to goals from McPhee in the 60th and 89th minute and a goal from Gerry Britton in 87 – set up the same result against Ayr United with Bingham scoring from the spot in the 49th minute, McCormick getting number two in the 73rd minute and McPhee nabbing the last goal 10 minutes from time.

The final game of the season was against Airdrie and given that the club was in terrible condition with rumours of takeovers and the liquidators KPMG having been called in.

The Lions' took the three points from the game thanks to a volley from David Bingham in the 52nd minute and Brian McPhee scoring in injury time to give the club the final league placing of fourth.

But there was an optimism about the club that next season would provide something special and the club would achieve its destiny of reaching the SPL.

CHAPTER
8

DESTINY FULFILLED

And here it was, the season where the club fulfilled their destiny. Or a part of it anyway. It was also a season of a lot of red cards and penalties.

As the season started on August 5, many felt this would be the year, especially the bookies who had them favourites to be champions. And there were a bundle of new faces with Grant Smith from Hearts, David Hagen and Scott Crabbe from Falkirk, Mark McCulloch and Barry Wilson from Inverness Caley, and Bolton's Gordon Smith all joining before the kick off of the new season.

Some people also left, including John Millar and Lee Richardson, while Charlie King and Jim Sherry were put out on loan.

All of the new kids were in the squad for the first game of the season - a 2-0 away win against Morton. Scot Crabbe showed that he'd be a player to watch early on after working with Allan McManus to help set up Marino Keith for a quick attack, but his header wasn't to be.

It wasn't to be a one-sided battle though as Morton piled it on, Livi getting on the break when they could, but by half-time it was 0-0, though Crabbe could have scored in the dying seconds of the half but Cappielow keeper Matthew Boswell was able to stop the shot at close range, keeping the home side in with a shout.

The second half started off as even as the first but McCulloch made it a debut game to remember when he scored in the 51st minute when he managed to just get a touch of the head to a pass from Crabbe.

Morton didn't give up at this point, but their game did become a little rougher and Paul Dees was booked for fouling. While the 'ton might have thought they still had a chance, the game was put past them in the 83rd minute after Darren Davies tried to clear the ball out of a crowded penalty box. He hit it, but it thumped off the back off Bingham, and went straight into the net.

While the team got the points, there was a price to pay in that Marino Keith – who had been subbed in the 68th minute – was out for the next game, the first home tie of the season, against Caley Thistle. On a brighter note, Crabbe and Bingham were able to play.

And it would be an earlier chance to see if the Lions' had what it would take to beat the Highland team, who were their hoodoo the season before, being the only team that Livi couldn't beat.

It wasn't the most exciting start of games. Crabbe, just like the last game looked eager, and Wilson was getting pelters off the fans of his old team.

Things started to perk up after 17 minutes when Scott Crabbe was sent flying by Ross Tokey, who was booked for his efforts. Nothing came of the free-kick, but it showed there was some life in the game.

Things got even better for the Lions' just seven minutes later after ex-Stirling player Paul Deas opened the scoring with a shot from roughly 40 yards out.

Livi kept at it and nearly doubled their lead in 41 minutes from a Dollan attempt from 18-yards out crashed off the bar.

It was nearly 2-0 in the dying seconds of the half when Wilson was tripped up in the box by Robert Mann. Crabbe took the kick but 'keeper Les Fridge got to it, keeping Caley in the match.

Fan Peter Daley remembers the game well: "Once they saved that bloody penalty, I was convinced they were going to a jinx team again that year."

Peter's nerves would have been settled a little in the 51st minute after Crabbe scored from around ten yards out. Livi kept pushing though, hitting the woodwork a number of times, but their defence was starting to slacken and Caley punished them for it in the 75th minute when Iain Stewart took the ball round Neil Alexander before shooting and scoring to make it 2-1.

Caley pushed to get back into the game and it looked as if they could do it until three minutes from time when Wilson paid back the boo-boys by scoring against his old side to give the majority of the 4113 fans reason to leave the ground with a smile on their faces.

Then it was time for the cup and an early round against Partick Thistle.

The Jags had the best of the game pretty much up until the last eight minutes, but both sides had their chances, when the deadlock was broken by ex-Thistle star Gerry Britton, coming on after Crabbe was taken off, who headed home the opener.

And just before the blow of the whistle for full-time, fellow 73rd-minute sub Barry Wilson managed to put enough effort into a shot that 'keeper Michael Brown wasn't able to keep a hold of. It was a shame the Jags had to go out as it had been an entertaining match, but a match that had clearly taken toll on the east coast team as the next league game, against Clyde, saw them manage nothing more than a single goal draw.

Livi did have the bulk of play, but that didn't stop Clyde from taking the lead after 70 minutes when Andy Kane fired in a shot.

They didn't get to keep the lead for long – four minutes to be exact – as John Anderson levelled things for a sharing of the points, but for Livi it was more a case of two points lost than a point gained – especially when you considered that Clyde were new to the division.

Two players were also lost along with the two points – Barry Wilson and Scott Crabbe – and they had to sit out the cup game against Dumbarton, which the Lions' romped 4-0. Anyone who came late to the game though missed most of the excitement as Livi were three up within seven minutes (not that many people were at the game – just 357 was the official attendance).

The nightmare for Dumbarton started in the fourth minute with David Hagen getting onto the end of a rebound from 'keeper John Hillcoat.

If Hillcoat thought his day couldn't get any worse, he was proven wrong just two minutes later when he was humiliated by Hagen putting the ball through his legs to get the second.

Bingham's header in the next minute killed the game off and there was a fourth by Jamie Dolan not too long later, but that was ruled offside.

As superiority smugness set in, Livi did become a little lax, and Dumbarton had the odd chance. Kevin McCann probably had their best chance of the half in the 30th minute but he hit the post.

Stephen Jack caused the fourth goal when he brought down Bingham in the box. And while it was a soft challenge, he was red carded and strolled off as Bingham banged in the fourth goal.

The second half saw some attacking – and while Dumbarton did try and get back into the game, Livi casually defended to go through to the next round.

That win obviously had a good effect on team morale as the high-scoring continued with a 6-0 demolition of Alloa.

This time the goals were more evenly spread out with Bingo Bingham rattling home a rebound from his own header in the 35th minute.

Alloa probably didn't think 1-0 at half-time was too bad given that they were the underdogs, but the Lions' raised the tempo in the 53rd minute with McCulloch scoring. It was three just after the hour-mark thanks to Hagen. Fleming joined in to make it four, before McCulloch nabbed a hat-trick by scoring in the 78th and 83rd minutes.

But the drama wasn't confined to the pitch that day. John Alexander had to miss the game after his car – carrying Allan McManus, Grant Smith and Gordon Smith – hit the back of another one just outside Cumbernauld. No one was injured by John had to wait for the cops, while the others dashed to the ground and made it just 30 minutes before kick off.

August was wrapped up with another victory – this time against Ross County, but at first it looked as if Livi were going to be the cowards of the country, narrowly holding out against a determined home team. Indeed, the first half saw Livi only have one decent chance – Barry Wilson having a dig on the half hour – while Ross County could have been four up early on.

Whatever the team were told at half-time seemed to do the trick though as they came out fired up in the second half and the goals weren't long in coming. They started in 50 minutes after a Derek Fleming corner found that man Bingham, who scored with a header.

Three minutes later, the game looked to be all but over after Brian McPhee's classy run on the right finished with a cross to the left hand side of the box and half-time sub Britton nutting in a header past Nicky Walker.

And the super sub scored again in 80 minutes, to put the Lions' through to the next round.

There was more cup business next – this time against Hearts – and the game was a chance for pundits to see how the SPL - promotion favourites would actually fare against an SPL team.

The answer: not too great, especially when you consider that it was a weakened Jambo side due to an accumulation of injuries. Livi were also missing some players including Scott Crabbe, but Hearts were practically half a team down. Perhaps it was because they felt so weakened that they tried to compensate by going heavy on the attack, getting the first goal in the 15th minute. And while the goal may have belonged to Hearts, bizarrely it started with an attack at the other end of the park. Barry Wilson's free-kick failed to reach Mark McCulloch, allowing Juanjo to take the ball and race 70 yards down the left wing before passing to Colin Cameron who made no mistake in giving Hearts the lead.

Livi were pushing more up front after that though and while they had some decent attempts, Antti Niemi was never truly bothered and had even less to do in the second half – especially after Gary Naysmith scored a second in the 54th minute.

While some fans were upset at the scoreline, others felt it was a realistic reminder of how far the club had come – and had yet to go.

John Mabury said, "To be disappointed at being beat by Hearts showed that we thought we had a chance, which was the sort of spirit we needed at that stage. Also, it let us concentrate on winning the league, which was the priority. It was time to get the Hell out of the first division."

Davie Hay though so as well, saying, "The league has always been our priority."

And the next game – against second placed Ayr United would – if won – go a bit in helping that ambition, but they would have to do it without Crabbe, who was still crocked.

By five minutes in though, it seemed as if the team would get by just fine without him as Barry Wilson scored to give the Lions' the lead with a cracking 20 yard shot that took a little helping nudge from the crossbar.

Ayr had some chances, but the hungrier team by far was Livi and if it hadn't been for some good defending and a liberal dash of good luck, Ayr could have been three or four down at half-time.

The second half continued in the same fashion with Livi going two ahead in the 49th minute when Bingham scored. As the game went on, tempers flared and it came to a head with 11 minutes to full time after a challenge saw David Hagen stretchered off and Glynn Hurst red-carded for his antics in the subsequent multi-player scrap that transpired.

Next up was the next round of the Challenge Cup with a game against Brechin and for a while it looked as if they would be the giant killers of the round, grabbing the first goal of the game after 23 minutes after a Leask volley.

It stayed 1-0 until after half-time – though Barry Wilson was ruled offside in the 30th minute, not noticing that he was offside until after the ball was in the net – and there were worries that Livi could be out, especially as half-time saw Gerry Britton stretchered off.

Just like earlier in the season, it took a half-time pep talk for the Lions' to come back into it. And they came back into it quickly, Mark McCormick scoring in the 47th minute after a grand pass from Brian McPhee. Livi got another boost 10 minutes into the half after Kevin Bain was sent off for a foul on Gerry Britton.

A second goal added to the ten man team's misery with Britton getting the glory in the 66th minute and Marino Keith wrapped the game up 5 minutes from time after getting to a cross from Bingham, setting the Lions' up for a semi-final clash with East Stirling.

By now the fans were starting to enjoy the winning streak, some even taking it for granted. They were reminded that they wouldn't be getting things all their own way in the league game against Raith, being beat 4-0 at home.

This was just a horror of a game and about the only good thing Livi could take from it was the fact that it exposed certain weaknesses to the team – weaknesses that could then be worked on and eliminated.

The demolition started early as the Kirkcaldy side took the lead in the fourth minute after a whirlwind opening in which John Anderson, Brian McPhee and Paul Browne all had efforts on goal.

Two weeks after this game, he would be a Livi player, but on that day he was a Raith player and he was devastating - Marvin Andrews opening his scoring after diverting an Alex Burns cross into the goal.

Raith went two ahead 11 minutes later when Alex Burns classily rounded Neil Alexander and knocked the ball into the empty net from 14 yards out.

From the Livi fans' point of view it was a load of Tosh in the 39th minute when Paul Tosh got to an Andrews header to make it 3-0.

Unlike previous games there was no great transformation in the second half – unless you consider the fact that the team only let one goal in during the second 45 minutes as opposed to the three in the first half.

Andrews' second goal was merely the icing on the cake for Raith in the 69th minute. It barely registered on the Livi players, who by the point seemed as shell-shocked as any soldier had been at the Somme in World War One.

Obviously heads had to be lifted for the next game. In days gone by, the papers would have written wittily about Jim Leishman coming up with ditties and poems to inspire his teams, but now they reflected on the solid, professional graft that was being put together by the team.

And while the next game, an away match against Airdrie, wasn't pretty, it signalled a return to league wins.

The first half was a poor affair and Airdrie opened up the scoring with Martin Prest.

But Airdrie weren't to be denied and Martin Prest. fired the opener two minutes after the start of the second half, getting on to the end of a Darren Brady.

Their joy at taking the lead was short lived as Livi fired back in just under a minute when John Anderson headed home a Derek Fleming corner to haul the league leaders' level and they then grabbed the lead in the 59th minute.

Scott Crabbe had been brought down in the box by Miguel Alfonso and David Bingham rattled home the penalty.

That was it for goals, but there was still some drama to come as Graham Coughlan was sent off after throwing a punch at Stephen McKeown after he didn't pass the ball back when it was kicked off to allow David Bingham to get treatment.

Then it was back to the drama of the cups and Livi booked an appearance in the final of the Scottish League Challenge Cup after they beat East Stirling 2-1.

But it wasn't plain sailing – and that's not just a reference to the bad rain pour that nearly saw the game abandoned. In fact, the Lions' got a fright early on as East Stirling went one up in the fourth minute thanks to Gregor McKechnie.

Undeterred Livi pressed on and got a penalty in the 21st minute. Gordon Russell brought down Barry Wilson, David Bingham stepped up and fired the ball home. A second was grabbed just seconds before half-time when John Anderson got onto the end of a cross from Wilson, sending Livi to their first cup final.

September was rounded up by a reminder that the Lions' couldn't take anything for granted though after Falkirk beat them 3-2.

At half-time it all looked to be going well with the visiting Livi two up thanks to a header by Coughlan in the 17th minute and a 25th

minute strike by debutant Alex Burns getting on the end of a Barry Wilson deflected shot.

The Bairns dragged themselves right back into the game in the second half though with goals by Davie Nicholls, John Henry and Steven Craig in the 48th, 56th and 67th minutes.

While there was little criticism publicly of the team, the players were given some competition for places after the club swooped for three Raith Rovers – Marvin Andrews, Steve Tosh and Alex Burns.

The team picked up for the next game – against Ross County – with two goals from Marino Keith and a 70th minute penalty from David Bingham after Eddie Cunnington got a hand on a John Anderson header.

The performances weren't classics by any definition – critics would say they were grinding them out and it wasn't attractive football, but they were getting the results that would keep them at the top of the league. One game that definitely fitted that category was the mid-month 1-0 win against Morton. It was another penalty that gave the Lions' the win, coming on the stroke of half-time after Barry Wilson went down from what seemed to be a very light Derek Anderson challenge.

The day pessimistic fans had been dreading came on October 21 as the team were knocked off the top spot by Inverness Caley Thistle. The result was a 2-2 draw but that was enough for Falkirk to go top.

Ex-Caley captain Mark McCulloch opened the scoring for the Lions' just after the half-hour getting onto the end of corners by other ex-northern jag Barry Wilson. Obviously the Caley defence didn't learn anything from that as the duo did the exact same thing in the 58th minute.

Caley came back into just seconds later though as Roy McBain slid onto the end of Martin Bavidge cross. It was the same story just minutes later as Paul Sheerin got on the end of a Dennis Wyness cross from just six yards out.

The Wilson and McCulloch duo could have kept Livi at the top of the league with five minutes to go but McCulloch goofed at the end.

The club refused to let the heads go down though and picked back up for the next game against Alloa, but it took them two penalties and an own goal as well as a normal goal to get the three points. But that wasn't because of anything fancy that Alloa did, more a lack of attacking – rather, finishing – ability from the

Lions'. There was plenty of attacking, just not a lot of finishing chances from open play.

The scoring opened in the 29th minute after Frank Conway poorly chested the ball over his own goal line after trying to clear a Marvin Andrews header.

The first of the two Bingham-scored penalties came 3 minutes before half-time after Gregg Watson fouled Derek Fleming.

The two goals in the second half came from Alex Burns in the 75th minute and another Bingham penalty after Grant Johnston brought down Marino Keith five minutes from full-time.

A cracking game against Ayr was next. And while it may have been a 1-1 draw, it wasn't short of drama. Before the first 11 minutes were up, Pat McGinlay had a header saved by Neil Alexander while at the other end, David Bingham thumped the ball over the crossbar.

The two goals came in two minutes with Livi's Derek Fleming scoring first after some excellent work from Barry Wilson and David Bingham in the 34th minute. The 36th minute saw Hugh Robertson level the scoreline.

The second half was equally dramatic with the most notable moment being minutes from time when John 'Yogi' Hughes was sent off after jostling with Marino Keith – and then red carded again for protesting about the sending off.

The Scottish League Challenge Cup was still more than a week away, but fans were given a warm up for it as the Lions' and Airdrie faced off at Almondvale.

Livi, as had happened all too often in the season, took a two goal lead – Marino Keith in the 9th minute and Alex Burns in the 11th – but Airdrie didn't stay down for two long, starting their comeback in the 14th minute as Stuart Taylor went on a glorious run after a pass from Antonio Calderon and scoring.

It was nearly 2-2 not long after as John Anderson fouled Prest in the box, giving Airdrie a penalty. Fortunately Neil Alexander was on form to stop the Fabrice Moreau shot.

But Airdrie smelled blood and went for it big time, getting their deserve equaliser after 66 minutes when Calderon scored.

Livi had a chance with 13 minutes to go to equalise but when they were awarded a penalty, but Bingham's sure-fire spot-kicking touch deserted him and Airdrie held on for a share of the points.

The Lions' were given a boost before the November 19 cup final though as Motorola announced a new three year sponsorship deal with the club, bringing in a much-needed six figure sum.

And then it was time for the cup final. While the players were up for it, the fans didn't seem to be, with less than 2,000 Livi fans turning out to support the team, giving Airdrie a psychological advantage as they had twice that many fans there.

Like so much of the season, this wasn't a game of silky soccer.

Airdrie had the first best chance to go ahead with Antonio Calderon hitting the, but it was Livi who took the lead after just 18 minutes when Scott Crabbe scored thanks to a Paul Armstrong gaffe.

Airdrie refused to give up so early on though and it was 1-1 before the half hour had passed thanks to a Martin Prest header.

The second half saw John Anderson header Livi back in front just after 50 minutes, but the exertions were taking their toll on the Lions' and the defending became really slack, which was what allowed an unmarked David McGuire to score an equaliser from a corner 12 minutes from the end.

Extra time was unremarkable – if not turgid –as the players wilted and penalties loomed. Despite Livi's luck with penalties during the season, Airdrie were the better of the spot-kick teams, mostly thanks to some psychological warfare from Broto, who put off the Livi players with distractions as they ran up to take their kicks. Scott Crabbe and Mark McCulloch weren't put off but Michael Hart, Brian McPhee and Derek Fleming all were. There was no such problems for Airdrie though as they slotted their penalties in to win 3-2.

But while losing in the final was a blow, the fact that they had got there at all showed the club was still ambitious. Those ambitions now focused back on the league and a 2-0 win – with goals in the 12th minute from Burns and the 81st minute from Bingham – put the Lions' back on top as November drew to a close.

Livi kept pushing for the SPL with a 4-1 hammering of Falkirk. Barry Wilson opened the scoring after eight minutes, Graham Coughlan kept it going in the 23rd minute and Alex Burns had a great run three minutes from half-time to make it a comfortable 3-0 by the end of the first 45 minutes, which had seen Livi's attack do plenty of work, contrasted to the easy game that Neil Alexander had enjoyed at the other end of the park.

He had to graft a little in the second half but not by much. Bingham made it 4-0 with ten minutes left and Mark Roberts grabbed a consolation goal in the dying seconds of the match for Falkirk but it was far too little far too late.

Livi lost another 90th minute goal the following week, against Raith Rovers, but two Bingham goals in the 21st and 36th minutes made sure all three points went to Almondvale.

A 2-0 win against Clyde the following week saw the Lions' stretch their league lead to eight points, thanks to goals by Scott Crabbe and Steve Tosh.

Christmas joy was assured in Lothian thanks to a 2-1 win against Morton the week before Xmas and the New Year saw the winning ways continue with Raith Rovers being beat by goals from David Bingham and Alex Burns in the 5th and 22nd minutes.

The unbeaten run continued one more week with a 1-1 draw against Airdrie which kept the club ten points ahead of Ayr United and 11 in front of Falkirk – though they had a game in hand. The game was slightly soured by Steve Tosh being sent off for a second bookable offence after a collision with Antonio Calderon. It was a soft sending off and while a draw was a fair result, if he had stayed on, there was a good chance the Lions' could have taken all three points, especially as at that point they were in the lead thanks to a Scott Crabbe goal in the 44th minute. Tosh's sending off in the 64th minute helped Airdrie out and they equalised in the 77th minute.

The next game, against Falkirk, was on the 13th of January and it was certainly unlucky for the Lions' as they were beat 1-0. More worryingly for Jim Leishman and Davie Hay, there was another red card. This time for Alex Burns for trying to kick Davie Nicholls in the 29th minute. As the frantic and physical game went on, Livi toiled slightly and with 12 minutes left on the clock, Gareth Hutchison scored thanks to a header from a Kevin McAllister free-kick.

But then it was time for the last of the cups – the Tennents Scottish Cup –and while it ended in a 4-1 victory, it all started badly with East Fife taking the lead in the sixth minute thanks to a Barrie Moffat low shot.

Then Tosh was off again! Just ten minutes into the game, he carried out a late two-footed tackle on John Allison – who had to be taken to hospital because of it – and was shown the red card for it.

Ten man Livi carried on though and hauled themselves back into the game with a goal just after the half hour, thanks to David Bingham and they went ahead on the edge of half-time thanks to Barry Wilson.

The second half saw Wilson back on the score sheet in the 75th minute. He was then subbed, Gerry Britton came on in his place and he scored the fourth in the 77th minute to set the Lions' up with a game against Aberdeen.

Confidence boosted from that, Alloa were beaten 2-0 thanks to goals from Barry Wilson and John Anderson in the 20th and 52nd minutes.

The start of February saw Clyde fall 3-0 thanks to goals from Brian McPhee in the 18th minute, a Barry Wilson penalty in the injury time of the first half and then Wilson again with a fantastic volley with five minutes to go, setting the team up confidently for a cup game against Aberdeen.

The game was a draw but not without incident in the dying moments as Alex Burns was booked after a minor collision with David Rowson in the box. To ref Kenny Clark, it looked as if Alex had gone down for the dive to get the penalty. The player insisted that he hadn't been diving, he was just tired, but Clark was having none of it.

Marvin Andrews had a fantastic game and it says it all that afterwards Aberdeen were relieved to still be in the cup while Livi were disappointed at having to face a replay.

Before that game though there was league business to attend to and February was rounded out with Alloa being beat again – this time thanks to a Bingham goal in the 63rd minute.

The season of penalties lived up to its name in the March opener against Ayr. Not only did Livi take the lead thanks to a Brian Wilson spot-kick in the 16th minute, John Bradford equalised for Ayr just before full-time with one and while some would grumble, a draw was a fair result as it was one of Livi's poorer performances of the season. The fact that they held on for a point – and it was nearly three – showed though that they had the grit needed to tough games out when the inspirational football was lacking.

They may also have had their minds on the next game, the cup replay against Aberdeen and not for the first time in their short history, Livi gave Aberdeen another beating. The scoreline may only have been 1-0 thanks to a Scott Crabbe goal seven minutes from the end but Livi were the far more dominant team in both halves, earning themselves a quarter-final tie against Peterhead, which Livi won comfortably 3-1 just days after the Dons replay thanks to two goals from John Anderson in the first half and a Bingham strike in the 63rd minute.

The most notable thing about the game for Livi was the absence of Neil Alexander, who had been ruled out for the rest of the season after a double hand fracture the day before the game. Ian McCaldon took his place and he had a comfortable game.

The rest of March saw a hiccup on the road to SPL glory – losing 1-0 to Ayr, drawing 1-1 with Ross County and a 2-0 defeat on the last day of the month to Raith Rovers. The best thing that can be said for this period was that future club legend David Fernandez joined along with Javier Broto, both convinced that the Lions' were going to be a force to be reckoned with in the SPL in the next season.

April saw a return to form with a 4-1 win against Inverness Caley Thistle and a 1-0 win against Ross County thanks to a Barry Wilson goal.

Mid month saw the Scottish Cup semi-final against Hibs and while getting to a semi was a great achievement for the club, it says it all that there was great disappointment at the team being beat 3-0. Hibs started the scoring early – going up in the second minute and then cementing the result in the 69th and 76th minutes – and Livi were unlucky not to get a penalty in the 65th minute after the ball hit the arm of Hibs's Gary Smith.

The team didn't play badly, but Hibs had the rub of the green, but not having to worry about a second cup final in one season meant that the next five games would all be about making sure promotion took place.

The last three games in April saw Livi confidently beat all comers – 2-0 against Morton, 3-0 against Falkirk and a terrific 3-2 scrap with Caley Thistle which clinched the promotion spot.

Dominic Keane dedicated the win to the workers of Motorola in Bathgate. The firm had been the club's sponsors but had rocked the area with news that they were closing their mobile phone plant and making 3000 people redundant.

He said: "At a time when West Lothian is suffering I hope we have brought a bit of hope and happiness. It saddened me as much as anybody else to see Motorola pulling out of the area and I hope all these people can find new jobs."

The team continued the scoring run with a 5-0 thumping over Airdrie – Gerry Britton scoring a hat-trick – and the season ended on a slight downer with Clyde beating the Lions' 2-0 at Almondvale, but if truth be told, by that point everyone was already dreaming of the SPL.

And no one had an idea of just how good it was going to be.

CHAPTER 9

PLAYING WITH THE BIG BOYS

And there they were – playing with the big boys! And there was a lot of changes to the team and ground since the previous season.

One of the biggest surprise was that McCulloch, Deas, Dolan, Fleming and Britton all left for Partick Thistle to be replaced with Cherif Toure Maman, Javier Sanchez Broto, Massimiliano Caputo, Carlos Aurellio and Davide Xausa, which at one point prompted a joke that the club had run out of O's and other letters for its strips.

Leishman was very candid about the changes wrought by him and Davie Hay.

"It was easy because we were rebuilding, it was progress. We shook hands and thanked them for everything they'd achieved."

For Hay, it wasn't so easy: "I have never shied away from the truth," he reflects, "but it was painful for the players I had to tell."

Maman, especially, looked set to be a character with his number 91 strip. It was also a boost for fans when they learned that he had knocked back league runners-up Rangers to join Livi for four years.

He said, "I was training with Rangers and things went very well. I could have signed there but my agent George Wright told me to speak to Livingston and I decided coming here would be better for me."

And the mystery of the shirt number is no great mystery – for anyone from Maman's native Togo that is

"Like kids all over Togo I started playing football in the streets. One day when I was just eight, I bought a basketball top from the local market. It had No 91 on it and I wore it all the time when I played football with my friends."

"When I went to play in Germany I kept that number. I said that to the manager when I signed and he checked that it was okay with the officials."

And along with the large number he gave journalists and sub-editors across the country great joy with his decision to be known as Sheriff on the back of his jersey rather than Cherif, prompting many battles for good puns in copy and headlines.

110

There were also appointments off the pitch.

Former St Mirren chief Tony Fitzpartick quit his football academy Total Soccer Experience to take over from Tony Taylor as Livi's Director of Youth Football which was the end of a months-long chase for Dominic Keane, who used the signing as a chance to hit back at the club's critics, who pointed out that Livingston had brought in a lot of foreigners and had high player turnovers.

He said, "People talk about the players we have brought to this club but the board has never flinched when it comes to investing in youth."

Meanwhile off-pitch Livingston's director of operations Alistair Hood, who had worked at Rangers as security boss for 11 years and had been at Livingston for 3 years, was involved in making a number of changes to the stadium including increasing capacity from 10,005 to 10,030. That may not seem like much but the extra 25 spaces were so more disabled fans could get in to see games, reinforcing the club's position as being there for everyone in the community.

And more than 4,000 of the seats would be taken up by season book holders – an incredible rise from their first games where they were lucky to get 500 people at some of them.

Other changes included a new media centre built at the back of the west stand, an extension to the police control box and a relaying of the pitch after undersoil heating was installed to meet SPL criteria.

Hood also pointed out a new concern the club had, especially when dealing with fans from clubs with reputations like Aberdeen, Hearts and Rangers.

Hood said at the time: "We're aware that security has to be tightened this season, but we've held several meetings, both at the club and with the police and are confident we'll be ready.

"We also have the Old Firm games to contend with, but the police are aware of the influx of fans into the areas and things will be prepared - inside and outside the ground - for those matches."

The club prepared for the big season ahead with an unprecedented seven friendlies against a variety of clubs including Royal Antwerp on a Dutch tour, Berwick Rangers, Walsall and Raith Rovers, coming away with five victories and two draws, which bode well.

As the big day for the opening game against Hearts approached, newspapers slaughtered trees by the thousands to fill column inches with tales of the return of Jim Leishman and Davie Hay.

But one thing that did get to Leishman slightly was that a lot of the coverage was going over very old ground – specifically his poems from days gone by.

As he lamented after one game: "I haven't done anything like that in years, but it's still mentioned."

However none of it was in nastiness and Jim knew that the sports reporters were just looking for angles for their tales.

As one sports reporter put it: "What Livi did was incredible, but the SPL is where they had to prove what you're made of. The reason that Jim got so much stick for the poems was because it was a good angle and it was how people remembered him."

"I know it annoyed him a little, but it made the club a little more prominent and then as the club kept going, we were able to let that go and concentrate on what he was doing in the here and now."

"Jim is a lovely guy – a complete gent – and no-one would go out of their way to offend him or Davie Hay – and a lot of people were glad when he brought Livi up because regardless of anything else, Jim is a character and there's a lack of them in the top level of Scottish football. He's old school."

The day before the game saw some light-hearted banter between Jim Leishman and Dominic Keane. Keane ended up leaving after giving Jim three different versions of what he thought the line-up should be for the game and following it up by pointing to some rope hanging off a scaffolding and saying, "If the result goes the wrong way, that's where Jim will end up."

Just before the game starts, the First Division flag is unfurled and there's even a chant of, "Keano, Keano," along with the more regular tunes, which was a nice touch of praise for Keane and then the club gets down to business.

But it started with a panic as a lob by Hearts' Gary Wales in the opening seconds shows the home team what they are up against. Fortunately Gary Bollan, positioned on the goal line, was able to head it over the bar for a corner which saw the pressure continue as Adam tried to nudge the ball past Broto. This time it was Philippe Brinquin who cleared it off the line.

As Keane remembered: "I had to ask John McGuinness to take my heart out of my mouth."

As the game progressed, Livi found themselves able to pull themselves more into the game and both teams had some excellent chances. For Livi, Quino and Stuart Lovell had two excellent chances but both went wide. Fernandez was also making a pest of himself to the delight of the home fans and the first Premier goal came in the 34th minute when he knocked a cross along the six yard box to Quino at the back post, who slotted it past Niemi to make it 1-0.

For Keane, this was a moment of justification as well as pride. "It showed to me that David Fernandez was the star I knew he'd be."

The second half saw that very star – and future Celtic player – cause a lot of trouble for Hearts.

His first good chance saw him shoot wide of goal after some excellent passing and build-up play by Xausa and Wilson. His second chance came after he strolled through the defence to force a save from Niemi, who by now was starting to look like a man lost at sea.

Niemi's skill could only help him so much though with Fernandez's next effort in the 58th minute, a blazing rocket from 25 yards out which made it 2-0 to the SPL new kids on the block.

Hearts, to their credit, continued to play with some pride and effort but as frustration settled in, they looked more and more like the Dundee United of the mid-1980s with constant long balls. Unlike the Dundee United team of that time though, the Hearts' efforts posed no threats, but in the dying minutes they did manage to achieve a consolation goal in the closing minutes.

Keane was ecstatic at what had happened and Jim Leishman was cautiously happy and optimistic, but he also fired a warning shot to the rest of the teams in the SPL in the after-match press conference.

He said, "We played some good football and without sounding too big headed, we can get better."

Fan David Black: "Our first ever SPL game seen a victory for the new boys. Francesco Quino grabbed our first ever SPL goal in the first half and the legend that be David Fernandez twisted and turned and made it 2 not long into the second half with a strike from Colin Cameron making the score 2-1."

Then it was a game that everyone dreaded. Rangers. At Ibrox. Everyone knew this game would have to happen, but most fans agreed that it would have been nice to get a run against the smaller teams before being thrown in at the deep end. However as many a child has learned, sometimes when you are thrown in the deep end, that's when you learn what you are made of and if you can swim. And that's what happened at Ibrox on August 4.

The line-up of Broto, Brinquin, Bollan, Rubio, Andrews, Wilson, Fernandez, Bingham, Quino, Xausa and Lovell was the same as the opening week team, not that a lot of fans got the chance to work this out as they turned up late because of bad traffic. This worked to their favour in one way though. They missed a horrific challenge by Claudio Caniggia on Javier Broto in the 10th minute which left him with a swollen eye.

The lack of away support – still stuck in traffic – actually seemed to spur the Lions' on and at times they looked comfortable containing the Rangers' strike force of Flo and Caniggia.

The visitors' best chance came around the 30 minute mark when Fernandez fired a low shot in, but Klos was able to get down to it.

At half-time the score remained a draw and some Livi fans were pinching themselves. Others were expecting to be hammered by the Glasgow bears in the second half, but some confident types were starting to see that there were possibilities for the visiting eleven.

The second-half saw a changed line-up for Rangers with Michael Mols coming on for Flo and he quickly set about causing problems for the Lions', turning the defence and firing his trademark quick shots with only the lightning reactions of Broto keeping the team in it.

Rangers looked determined to score as wave after wave of pressure was mounted. Mols being joined in the shooting attempts by Stephen Hughes, and again, Broto being the main reason for the scoreline staying even.

Ten minutes into the bombardment of the second half, Livi managed to grab a break and go on the run with it, Barry Wilson tore down the right hand side of the pitch, firing the ball in, about eight yards from the goal-line which David Bingham headered towards goal, but it came off the inside of the post to the groans of eleven men on the pitch and hundreds in the stadium. They were drowned out by the sigh of relief from the thousands who were there to cheer on Rangers though.

After that, both teams had their chances, though Rangers did have the upper hand and seemed to get better as the game went on. Despite some last minute injury-time scares though, the game ended with both teams sharing the points.

Leishman was delighted with the result. "That was one of the best - if not the best - performance we have put in during our six-year existence," he said. "It's made all the better by the fact that this was an away game against Rangers.

"But it's not just the result that makes this so good. It's the way we played. We passed the ball well and it wasn't just a case of holding on."

Of course most of the papers said it was more a case of a poor Rangers' performance than credit to Livi for the result, but people were starting to take more notice of the team.

After a win and a draw, there was only one result left for the team to experience in the SPL and sadly that came against the next game on August 11, an away game against Dundee.

Just as Broto had been the man in the Rangers' game, this time it was all about the Dundee keeper, Jamie Langfield. The young Scotland keeper was just one of the highlights in a game which was a great advertisement for Scottish football (despite the actual lack of Scots on the pitch) but he – along with Juan Sara's scoring header in the 24th minute – were the main talking ones for Livi fans.

The goal actually fired up Livi and David Bingham came close to scoring when he managed the rare feat of beating Langfield with a chip, but it came off the crossbar.

The Lions' kept the pressure on and both Xausa and Quino had excellent chances but it wasn't one-ended because at the other side of the pitch

Fabian Cabellero and Barry Smith were having a go but Javier Broto more than earned his wages with a string of saves.

Stevie Tosh, Nathan Lowndes and Michael Hart all came on to try and help the visitors grab at least one point from the game and it almost worked apart form one person again – Langfield with a reflex save that defied belief to thwart Lowndes shot from a Tosh pass.

And just as the ref was about to blow for full time, Langfield denied Michael Hart.

After the game, Big Jim told reporters that he was deciding to look on the positive from the game.

He said, "We created a lot of good chances, possibly six or seven, and that is pleasing. I was disappointed with the result but not the performance."

Then it was time for the second of the first Old Firm clashes, with a home tie against Celtic on Saturday August 18.

This was a game that many thought would cause emotional problems and they were right. Dominic Keane was getting abuse in his own household.

As he pointed out: "My son Stephen is Livi-daft and Mark is entrenched in the Celtic tradition which until five years ago was not too dissimilar to his dad, so it was to make for an interesting game."

Of course, it would also prove to be an emotional time for Davie Hay, but he shrugged off snipes that he would be more for Celtic than Livi on the day.

He said at the time: "Livingston are the team who pay my wages now and that's all that counts. And from a professional point of view we all have to make sure the team strives to give their all in every match."

"The team we put out will go out there to give their all, and if they do there will be no criticism from me. What the result will be I don't know and I'd never predict it."

"That will apply to anyone who plays for Livingston whether they are playing against Celtic, who have always been my team, or someone else. When I was there I always gave it my best and I think when Celtic people see that, whether you are a player, manager or scout, they will respond to you."

"Celtic won't be treated any differently from any other club. I won't have a problem with that and I don't think the Celtic people will either."

"It's all in the past and I don't dwell on it."

One thing that Davie and Jim did dwell on was how to deal with Celtic and its fearsome attack. They came up with a tactic that, at the time, few had tried against Martin O'Neil's side – go at them.

When fans saw that they were playing with three up front, there was a lot of worry the back would be exposed, especially as Philippe Brinquin was injured and this would lead to Celtic's Larsson and Hartson scoring a barrowload.

But it didn't happen. The three men up front ran their legs off, causing all sorts of problems while at the back Andrews – later awarded man of the match - and Rubio kept the attack at bay.

Celtic did get one great chance though – a penalty after Gary Bollan was sent off – but Broto called it right to ensure that his foot was in place to block the shot.

Livingston also kept their former team-mate Rab Douglas busy up the other end with Bingham, Fernandez and Lovell all having great chances but the keeper kept a clean sheet. Sadly for Celtic fans, so did Broto at the other end of the stadium.

There may have been only one point for the team at the end of it, but the result gave them a fantastic boost. Within a matter of weeks they had taken points off three of the SPL old-timers, including the two big teams of the league.

Leishman wasn't going to let the players go crazy with it or anything, but he did note that it was having a unifying effect on confidence on people at the club, while the press were starting to ask if Livi were going to be a force in Scottish football or were just having a good start and would flounder later. Jim also pointed out that the next game against Motherwell would be where the league really started as he expected the Lanarkshire team to be one that they would be battling it out with over the campaign.

Paul Deas was given his debut for the season thanks to Bollan's red card from the previous game, while Hart covered for the still injured Brinquin.

And Motherwell showed no sign of the troubles that would hit them later in the season with a strong performance, fighting the Lions' for supremacy all over the pitch, especially after an early substitution and one at half-time.

Defensively, this was one of Livi's finest hours and a half, though there was a little touch of luck as well when a second-half chance by Pearson ended up being shot just wide of the post.

There was also an injury scare when Marvin Andrews, took a bad knock to the head which soaked both his shirt and his spare with blood and he ended the game looking even worse than Terry Butcher did in his infamous England pictures. He would miss the next two games thanks to the injury.

Leishman summed up the game quite fairly afterwards, pointing out that the result had been the right one.

"A draw was a fair result," he said. "I think the fact that we're a bit disappointed at taking a point away from home shows just how far we have come." But looking to keep everyone's feet on the ground he added, "perhaps that's a bit cheeky of us."

The next game saw a welcome return of three points after the two draws with a 2-0 win against Dundee United on September 8.

John Anderson made his SPL Livingston debut to cover for Andrews and he was soon in the thick of things as visitors Dundee United came out quick and fast against the Lothian side.

Broto was lucky to get to a thumping free-kick by Danny Griffin, but the home players managed to assert themselves with the highlights including Barry Wilson firing a shot in after a pass from David Fernandez which was just put over by keeper Paul Gallacher.

Gallacher was stretched again moments later after some excellent one touch football from a number of players including Quino, Bingham and Lowndes.

A scare for the home support was when Broto was beaten by a shot but it was cleared off the line and the halftime result was nothing each.

Livingston put Gallacher under pressure again from the early moments of the second half and he pulled off a string of saves to deny the home team the chance to break the deadlock.

But he eventually had to succumb to the overwhelming Livingston attack and did so in the 58th minute when Nathan Lowndes nabbed the ball after a Gallacher clearance from a corner - and claimed his first Livingston goal.

This fired up United, who were already starting to look as if they were going to have a poor season, but the defence shored up their attacks, while the midfield and attack pushed forward, probing and hoping for a break that could lead to a second goal to kill the game off.

It came in the 84th minute when a clearance from Lauchlan fell to Stuart Lovell who volleyed the ball in from around 25 yards, to guarantee the points and put the club fourth in the league.

The next game started on a sad note. The Saturday September 15 game against St Johnstone at McDiarmid Park started with a minute's silence for the victims of September 11.

After the silence both teams put on an entertaining game in an effort to take people's minds off the atrocities, and by and large they succeeded. Livi fans had thought this game might be a bit easier than some of their games to-date because the saints appeared to be struggling early on in the season. That wasn't the case and they nearly took the lead in the first minute with Broto being the saviour yet again.

But the attacks continued and in the 16th minute Livingston went a goal down after Peter Lovenkrands sent in a high ball for Willie

Falconer to head over Broto and into the net for the home team to take the league.

Livi responded to the goal by battling back and grabbing an equaliser in the 25th minute when David Fernandez squared the ball across the 18-yard line to David Bingham, who fooled everyone by leaving the ball for Francisco Quino, to whack a low shot past Saints' keeper Kevin Cuthbert.

Boosted by this, the visitors kept on the pressure and were rewarded on the half hour with Bingham hitting a goal home after some fancy footwork from Fernandez.

It was Fernandez who had the chance to make it three just five minutes later with a free-kick, but Cuthbert managed to get to it.

The second half started just like the first – fast and furious and it took just four minutes for an equaliser which was partially caused by too many people being in the box as Peter MacDonald's shot went through and past a number of legs before going in the net for it to be two-each.

Things got worse for Livi when Quino – who had a fantastic match – was sent off for a challenge with McBride, forcing Livingston to play more defensively which they did for the last 25 minutes, managing to hold on to a share of the points.

Marvin Andrews returned for the next game – an away tie against Dunfermline – but missing because of injury were Fernandez and Brinquin, and Quino was suspended because of his red card, giving Dario Aurellio and Steven Tosh their SPL debuts.

And it didn't take long for them to realise how hectic it was as the Pars; Steve Crawford grabbed an early opening goal, which whizzed by Broto.

Stevie Tosh came close to equalising just minutes later, but it went wide of Scott Thomson's goal.

The home team had a chance to double their lead on the half hour when Jack De Gier volleyed a shot towards the goal, but an amazing dive by Broto let him to get to the ball to tip it to safety and for the defence to clear away.

Max Caputo was then brought on for Nathan Lowndes and Bingham was put into a more forward role as the Lions' fought back and one of their best chances came just before half time when a Marvin Andrews header was ruined by Davide Xausa and a powerful Stuart Lovell shot was well held by Thomson.

Livi looked even sharper in the second half but the pars were not up for giving anything away and Leishman started considering making changes to see if the team could get a breakthrough

Barry Wilson came on in the 67th minute and it worked well because just minutes later the two teams were level, even though Wilson wasn't directly involved in the goal. The kudos for that belonged to Caputo passing to Bingham who was running into the box. He drew Thomson out the box and then fired in the equaliser.

The Pars pushed hard for a winner but Broto frustrated them time and time again and that frustration started to show because Livi managed to get up front and this time it was Wilson who grabbed the goal – after some clever play by Caputo.

Then it was time for a break from the trials of the league as Livi faced up to East Fife for a home game in the second round of the CIS Insurance Cup.

The starting line-up caused some concern for the fans as Oscar Rubio was rested and Captain Stuart Lovell started the game on the bench but acting skipper David Bingham had the team fire forward, and the first goal came in just two minutes as he passed the ball to Caputo who clipped the ball over keeper Ross Godfrey.

The striker added his second in the 17th minute, this time heading home a pass by Dario Aurellio.

In the 21st minute Livi scored again but Bingham's header was ruled offside.

East Fife's Paul McManus tested Broto near half time with a superb chip but Livi showed why the team were now doing so well with an excellent stretching tip over the bar.

The third goal came in the 85th minute when a powerful dig by Tosh took a wicked deflection off East Fife sub Ross Graham and hit the back of the net after coming off the post.

The win set them up for a game against Aberdeen at Pittodrie on October 9th but before that there was the business of a league game against Hibs, a game that would end in tragedy for one of the club's players.

The home game, on the last Saturday in September, was – so the home fans hoped – a chance to avenge the cup defeat of the previous season.

The game started strongly with a Quino 25-yard shot in the second minute which ended up just past.

Hibs replied with a Matthias Jack shot from the edge of the area in the 18th minute but Broto comfortably dealt with the effort.

Minutes later Tom McManus could have done better when he failed to connect properly with a Laursen knock down in the box.

The Lions' fans screamed for a penalty in the 24th minute when Barry Wilson raced onto a Michael Hart pass and seemed to be impeded by Laursen as he was about to shoot but referee Bobby Orr wrongly waved away the appeals.

Close to the half hour mark a short corner by Max Caputo was fed into skipper Lovell by Quino and his chip from 12 yards beat Colgan but struck the cross bar. Barry Wilson headed the rebound goal wards but it was cleared off the line.

After half-time a string of corners kept the pressure on Hibs and certainly caused goalmouth panic. Livi built on this pressure to get the goal in the 63rd minute when Hart put a low cross into the area which was met by a perfectly timed run by Quino who put it in the net.

Livi kept the pressure on but the game looked to be heading to a 1-0 win and some fans had already starting leaving when tragedy struck.

Broto dived for a long ball and came down awkwardly.

As he was taken off – and taken to hospital - David McEwan came on and took his place, managing to take care of a Hibs corner in his first moments on the park.

The defence tightened ranks to ensure that Hibs didn't get to put too much pressure on the young keeper and the game ended with the three points going Livi's way.

At the after-game conference, Leishman revealed that Broto had broken a leg and it looked more than likely that he would be out until the New Year.

Then it was time for the cup game against Aberdeen and if anyone hadn't been paying attention to Livi before this, they certainly were afterwards as the team walloped their way through to the CIS Cup quarterfinals.

The game was really over before it even started as two goals were sent in the space of two minutes during the opening 12 minutes.

The first one came in the 10th minute and owed much to the talents of David Bingham. His clever ball behind the Dons' defence allowed Barry Wilson to race in on goal and score from 18 yards out.

The score went to two just seconds later as Max Caputo humiliated Derek Whyte before running on to score the goal.

The Dons were clearly struggling under the Livi onslaught and it was not a case of if Livingston would score another goal, but when.

That question was answered in the 28th minute when a shot by Caputo deflected off of McGuire and flew into the goal.

The fourth went in just minutes later as a nutmeg by Michael Hart set up a cross which he covered to make it 4-0, which is where the score stayed until half-time.

A fired-up Aberdeen came out in the second half looking to start pulling the game back and it didn't take them long to do so with Darren Mackie scoring in the 50th minte from a rebound.

After a few more attacks by the Dons, Livingston pulled themselves back into taking control of the game with captain Stuart Lovell scoring the fifth after some lovely set-up and build-up by almost half the team.

David Bingham powerfully headed home the sixth goal just yards from the goal-line and Aberdeen looked relieved when full-time was blown – and they were blown out of the cup.

But revenge wouldn't be long in coming for the northerners as they were playing them just days later in the SPL and while October 13 wasn't on a Friday, it wasn't the luckiest event for Livi either.

It was obvious from the start that Aberdeen were not going to allow for the game to be a repeat of their previous shambles with a number of hard tackles and close shots, but they were trying too hard and Livi found themselves with an opening goal after Barry Wilson scored from the penalty spot – a penalty that had been caused by Esson bringing down David Bingham.

The next best effort came just minutes from half-time and it was an Aberdeen dig at goal, only for Culkin to tip it away with a magnificent save and dive.

Aberdeen started the second half like the first half – on the attack – but again it was Livi who took the goal, this time with a powerful crack from Stevie Tosh.

At two-nil the Livi fans were starting to think the game – and the three points - had a good chance of going their way but no-one told Aberdeen this and they sullied the premature celebrations with a Mackie goal just before the hour-long mark.

Mackie was in definite party pooper mood as he then grabbed a second just minutes later.

Both sides then battled it out with both having chances – and Mackie nearly grabbing a hat-trick near the death of the game – but it ended up a draw, which most people accepted was a fair result.

The following game, against Kilmarnock, saw the return of the high-scoring Livi and a result which lodged them firmly in third place in the SPL. But just minutes into the game, fans found it hard to believe this was going to be a good day for them.

Didier Santini had the start from Hell, scoring an own goal in the fifth minute as he attempted to clear the ball from a free-kick and then setting up a second moments later, only for the skill of Livi's loan keeper Nick Culkin to manage to get to it to save red faces all round.

Then it was a game against Kilmarnock and the team's confidence in going into this game was proven to be well justified as they ripped the Rugby Park team to shreds with a final result of 5-1.

But it was all change at the next game as Livingston were torn to shreds on satellite television for the first SPL home defeat of the season against Rangers.

The Lions' started well with a number of attacking moves, but Rangers found them on the break and were able to take on the home team and while Livingston had some chances, it always looked as if Rangers would score first and they did, in the 23rd minute, with Reyna scoring from a Cannigia pass and, despite some great playing from both sides, the score stayed that way for the first half.

The second-half saw Livi, complete with Fernandez on for Quino, but it seemed to have little effect as Rangers continued pushing for a second goal and nabbed it in the 58th minute with Reyna hitting it home again.

Livi were then fired up and Stuart Lovell almost made it 2-1 just after the hour mark when he whacked a shot at goal, only for Klos to narrowly put it by the post.

It looked certain to be 3-0 when Marvin Andrews was sent off for causing a penalty, which many fans thought was a dubious call, but Culkin managed to save it.

The only piece of good news from the day was that Livingston managed to stay third thanks to a mixture of results from elsewhere in the league.

Then it was time for an away game with Hearts and they showed their hunger to make up for the Rangers' defeat by trashing the capital city team 3-1, but it started with the Jambos looking the more dangerous team.

Kevin McKenna's header in the opening minutes was well saved by Culkin and minutes later he had to do it again as McKenna kept harassing the player with excellent efforts that would have beaten many a keeper.

But there were moments of panic for Hearts as well in the opening phase as the three front men took the game to the normally defensive Hearts and they were not to be denied when, in the 21st minute, Fernandez knocked one in past Niemi.

From there on, the pressure continued and Fernandez grabbed his second of the day within minutes of the first one, headering this one in from seven yards out.

As the second half started, Hearts pushed up yet again, but Culkin was well on form, doing especially well to reach another attempt by McKenna, who had fired a blistering free-kick at goal.

Livi recovered from the early frights to regain their composure and they started to mount a new challenge on the goalmouth and the third came in the 72nd minute when Barry Wilson fired a shot in from just in the penalty box.

There was still one more goal to come, but it wasn't anything that would put a smile on the Livi fans, though it was a consolation to the hard-working Kevin McKenna, who finally got a goal 13 minutes from time.

The next home game, against Dundee on November 17, was nowhere near as exciting; but after recent games the fans had little to moan about as they still managed to grab three points and stay in third place in the league.

Livingston attacked from the opening minutes with Fernandez looking hungry to add to his goal tally and Bingham setting up some good shots, but it came to nothing.

Dundee tried to cause trouble, but Lovell and Tosh were earning their pay-packets with solid shifts in the midfield and all too often the visiting Dundonians found themselves getting beaten by the home midfield and then scrambling back to their goal to try and stop Livi going one forward.

Disaster struck for Livi five minutes from half-time when Fernandez and Dundee's Barry Smith went to the ground after some argy-bargy.

Dario Aurelio was of the opinion that Smith had played up the fall and told referee John Rowbotham his opinion. Rowbotham obviously did not agree and took umbrage at being told how to run the game as the player was sent off, giving Dundee a one-man advantage for the second half.

It proved useless though as the second half saw Livi come out and hammer the Dundee goalmouth and get a goal in the 57th minute with a Barry Wilson header from about seven yards out.

Dundee fought back and a number of players, especially Ketsbaia, had a number of good shots but Culkin and the defence held strong.

Livi kept pressing for a second goal to finish the game off and despite a number of great attempts, nothing came of it and then Dundee handed the home team some help when Del Rio was sent off after being booked a second time in the 75th minute.

With the sides even, both went for goal with great abandon and it became a battle of goalkeepers.

Dundee's Fabian Cabellero had a sublime chip look set to beat Culkin but it came off the post and Gavin Rae hoofed the rebound over the crossbar.

Then it was time for another trip to Edinburgh, this time to face off against Hibs, a team that Livi were facing many comparisons to.

In the previous year in the SPL, Hibs had been third for long periods but ultimately faded away. Many pundits expected Livingston to do the same after their excellent start to the season.

Livi were boosted for the game by the news that Franck Sauzee was unable to play, meaning Hibs would be without a key player for the game.

Again, Livi went at it from kick-off with the up-front three of Fernandez, Santini and Wilson putting 'keeper Tony Caig under constant pressure.

The first goal came early. Santini took the opportunity from a free-kick to pass to Fernandez who put it over for Xausa who thumped in a drive from 18 yards out. For a moment it looked as if it was going to bounce off the post but it glanced just the right way and went in to give Livi the lead in just eight minutes.

But Hibs did not lay down and die and more or less after the game started again, they caught the Livi defence sleeping when Paco Luna passed to Matthias Jack and he fired a rocket in, but Culkin managed to get to it to save the moment.

A second goal before half-time made things relaxed in the Livi dressing room.

Fernandez went on a run, passing to Xausa who tore down the defence, beating Gary Smith and firing a rocket past Tony Caig to make it 2-0 for half-time.

Nick Culkin was the man of the second half as time after time he stopped Hibs from getting back into the game. Craig Brewster in particular must have been cursing the Manchester United 'keeper as he saved not one, but two, really good efforts in the opening minutes of the second half.

This was followed up by pressure and shots by Ulises de la Cruz and Zitelli.

But as the game went on, Hibs began to tire and a new sheriff came to town to further tire them out.

Cherif Toure-Maman came on and started ripping down the left wing, causing all sort of trouble and he was unlucky not to have assisted in the creation of a third goal when he put the ball into the box for Nathan Lowndes but Laursen beat him to it and punted the ball away for a corner, which the sheriff took and this time Lowndes got to it before Laursen, firing a shot in, which Caig got away. But the danger wasn't over yet as Caputo got Caig's weak clearing away, had a shot, but Caig got to it and this time it went over the bar to give the Hibs defence a breather before the next corner.

Hibs were on the ropes, tiring heavily as the second half took its toll and Livi managed to take a third goal off them in the 86th minute.

Lowandes – who had been hungry for goal all throughout the game – ran down the right, beating the leaden legs of Hibs players to get to the edge of the goalmouth and he fired in a curling shot that went by Caig and found itself in the back of the net to make it three-nil and a total of six points that the new East Coast team had taken from the old-timers. When the Hearts points were added, Livi were the top team in the East Coast having taken all the points from all of their neighbours.

As December started, a game against Motherwell loomed and despite the time of year there was no festive goodwill towards the Fir Parkers by the home team.

The visitors put up a good fight for around 11 minutes before the home team, roared on by the fans, started to make inroads and pressure Steelmen 'keeper Mark Brown and Fernandez was at the front of it.

Xuasa grabbed the opener in the 20th minute with some excellent team playing. Quino shook off a bundle of challenges and passed the ball down the right wing to Barry Wilson who fired a high ball into the box where Xausa rose leaped up to header it into the net.

The second goal looked to be a certainty just seconds later when Fernandez went for a chip just eight yards out but Brown managed to get to it to keep them from going too far behind.

But the second was not to be denied, though no-one could have predicted how it was going to turn out as it was an own goal as the ball came off of Steven Hammell before going in, much to the anguish of the visitors.

Brown tried to keep his team in it, pulling off a number of great saves but he was the only one trying and he couldn't do much to stop the third goal going in on the 40th minute as Fernandez headered across a clearance from the Livi goal, which Xausa nipped between two 'Well players to get. He then brought Brown out of goal, rounded him and slotted the ball in the net.

The second half saw more of the same – without the goals – as Livingston stuck to the philosophy of attack being the best form of defence, but in the 78th minute Livi slipped up and a Motherwell free-kick ended up going in to give Motherwell a consolation goal

The next game was a far tougher 90 minutes for the SPL newcomers, an away game taking on Dundee United.

The Tangerines piled on wave of pressure after pressure but thanks to some great teamwork and solid defending at the back, United were unable to break down the Lions' and most of there shots were forced in from long ranges.

That's not to say Livingston sat back and took the pounding. Barry Wilson had a chance that was blocked by United keeper Paul Gallacher, while a Quino shot at goal came off David Fernandez and went by the goal.

The second half saw more of the same with both defences holding out firm against strong attackers. Fernandez was instrumental a few times in the second half – when he curled a free-kick round the wall and when he tore through three challengers in a run for goal – but both of these amounted to nothing. Barry Wilson also had a few good attempts that might have worked in other games, but the exiting moments were few and far between.

Of course it was an indication of how far the club had come in such a short space of time that the fans and players were disappointed from getting a draw off a team that had once been the terror of Europe and Jim Leishman was quite happy to point that out when he said, "At the very start of this season we would have been absolutely delighted to have taken home a point from Tannadice."

The good news for fans after this game though was that Barry Wilson was gearing up to sign a new contract to stay at the club. The main reason he hadn't beforehand was because he wanted to know that he had the ability to play in the SPL and not feel out of depth – something which had now proven to himself, and to the club as he was at that time the top scorer.

He said, "A lot of the boys who helped the team get to the SPL were moved on without getting a chance to show they could do it at that level, so I will always be grateful that Jim Leishman and David Hay stuck with me.

"To be honest the first thing I had to do was prove to myself that I could play at that level again because there is a nagging doubt that you weren't good enough anyway when you drop down the divisions."

"To be honest after the first five games or so I thought it might not happen as the team in general were struggling to score and other boys were arriving nearly every week."

"But the bosses were patient and I would like to think I have repaid them with a few goals now although I know that I could have had a few more."

The club hoped to put the Motherwell game behind them with a win against St Johnstone, but from the start it looked as if the club could be heading for a defeat instead of anything resembling Christmas cheer.

St Johnstone had done their homework against the home team and their defending showed this, with Livi finding it hard to get any efforts at goal and a frustrated Livi started throwing more and more players up front to try and get a goal, with Marvin Andrews coming up and trying a few times. He came close twice but close wasn't close enough, even though he did force a fantastic save from St Johnstone keeper Alan Miller.

The first half ended nothing each and the more optimistic fans were saying they would be happy with a draw from the tight game, but within the opening minutes of the second half they realised they weren't going to be that lucky when a Paul Kane free-kick was passed to Paul Hartley, who fired in a 30 yard screamer.

To their credit, Livi came back just minutes later when Xuasa passed a ball over to Fernandez who beat Darren Dodds, dragged Miller out of his goal and then fired a shot across goal, to make it one each.

Livingston pressed forward for the winner and Stuart Lovell had an excellent chance to take the team ahead but Miller produced another fantastic save.

Livi brought on Dario Aurellio and Nathan Lowndes for Quino and Xausa - in an attempt to try and nab the three points - and it seemed to work as the pair teamed up with Aurellio passing the ball to Lowndes, who pulled off a cheeky header over the keeper and into goal to make it 2-1.

As the game went on, St Johnstone appeared to flag and Livi turned up the heat with Fernandez, Bingham, Lowandes and others all having a go at goal but the score ended up 2-1.

Then it was time for a break from the league as Livi played the first of two games they would play against Celtic in one week. The first one was the C.I.S Cup quarter final. The match was a re-arranged one following floodlight failure at Almondvale in November.

Some people thought Livi were in with a good chance but Barry Wilson was a bit more realistic about the club's hopes.

He said, "People think they won't worry too much about the CIS Cup but they have won every domestic trophy since the new manager took over and I don't think he will see it that way."

"Despite that, we have a real chance to get through but with Rangers waiting in the semi-final for the winners of this game we will have to win the trophy the hard way.

"I think we have done well enough this season not to be overawed by the occasion of playing Celtic in the cup."

The game was doubly important for Wilson because he had already played the giant killer against the club before – when he scored in the famous defeat of Celtic by Inverness Caledonian Thistle.

It was a boost for the Livi home fans when they learned that Henrik Larsson was to sit on the bench for the start of the game, but that was tempered by the fact that Livi would be without Stuart Lovell.

The game was an excellent advert for football with both teams Living up to their attacking philosophies. Celtic had first go with Steve Guppy sending the ball over to John Hartson, but it was a bad pass and by the time Hartson got to it, Didier Santini had cleared the ball away.

Livi then went on the attack as Bingham and Fernandez had shots, both of which were blocked by Rab Douglas and cleared by Bobo Balde when the Celtic number one was found wanting.

Neither side enjoyed superiority with both attacking and being forced to defend in equal measures.

A great pass from Rubio to Fernandez ended sadly as the player was called for offside while minutes later Wilson had a close call as a shot went just by the left-hand post.

The Celtic defence did at times appear overwhelmed with the attacking of Xuasa, Fernandez and Bingham – along with the others – while Andrews, Rubio and Culkin kept Livi in at the other end, especially as players like Petrov flew at the goalmouth.

It was only a matter of time before a goal was scored. The only question was which team would score it. That question was answered in the 35th minute when Moravcik showed why he is regarded as one of Europe's best free-kick takers.

He took the kick from the left hand side of the pitch and into the box. Chris Sutton put it to the back post and Bobo Balde thumped the ball into the back of the neck with an incredibly powered header and the game ended up 1-0 to the Scottish champions at half-time, but the hooped fans weren't celebrating yet as they knew Livi were more than capable of coming at them in the second half and getting an equaliser.

The second half saw more of the same with Livi taking the game to Celtic, looking determined to pull something back.

Indecision by Joos Valgaeren and Bob Douglas gave Wilson the chance to cause trouble from a David Bingham pass but Balde yet again thwarted the club's efforts, just like he had been doing all afternoon.

A lazy pass gave Livi their next great effort with future team-mate David Fernandez nabbing it, leaving Jackie McNamara for dust but Stillian Petrov covered for McNamara's weakness, tackling Fernandez and keeping the Celts in the lead.

Big Bobo Balde then became the target of some booing – and later criticism in the press – when Bingo Bingham had to leave the pitch because of a strong – but fair – tackle from the big man, as did Fernandez. They were replaced by Steven Tosh and Nathan Lowndes and as the players got into the game, Celtic pushed forward hunting for a second goal.

Sutton especially pushed for a goal but it never seemed to happen for the Englishman despite a number of skilful attempts and manoeuvres, and a goal in injury time was disallowed because he fired it home from a free-kick which was indirect, not direct.

Minutes before that though, Celtic grabbed a second goal as Hartson headed in a corner from Guppy.

That didn't stop Livingston trying to get goals but they never managed it and were put out by Celtic, who would be put out by Rangers in the next game, yet again showing that Livingston were always just behind the Old Firm, champing at the bit.

It was a slightly different line-up for the last game before Christmas, against Dunfermline, because as Jim Leishman put it: "Some of the lads are knackered. They are playing hard, training hard and that's what we expect, but the constant amount of games – and the effort they are putting in, does take an eventual toll on them and of course some of the lads are injured from knocks and injuries.

"The good thing is here the squad is big enough for other boys to come and take their place and that spirit of competition is always healthy in a club."

Nonetheless Livingston looked up for the game, running frantically around – although as one wag put it, "That may have been something to do with the freezing cold weather."

Lowndes, Quino, Aurellio and the Sheriff all had a number of attempts in the opening minutes, and the number 91 especially showed why Leishman had been so impressed by the player, as he carved up the defence on a number of occasions, only to be thwarted by the posts or the keeper. Sadly he never got a chance to show off for too long, going down after a tackle with Stewart Petrie that saw him come off and be replaced with David Bingham and the Sheriff wouldn't be the last player to take a knock in the very physical game. Petrie himself would come off after taking a head-knock later in the first-half.

Nick Culkin again earned his wages, having to pull off a combination of excellent point-blank saves and long balls.

The game ended at half-time at a draw and the second half saw more hard battling by both sides but little to excite the cold crowd.

The second Livi substitution came in the 63rd minute when Caputo came on for Fernandez, who was injured after colliding with Gus MacPherson.

The third substitution was when Barry Wilson came on for Quino as Livi tried everything legal to try and win the game but it came to naught.

And while the rest of the country was winding down for the festive period, there was no such joy for the Lions' who had to face Celtic on Boxing Day and while they didn't get three points, the game was even better than the previous clash and was an excellent present to anyone wondering if the SPL could still provide exciting football, and even Celtic fans had to concede that Livi were unlucky to lose a share of the points with an extra-time goal courtesy of goal machine Henrik Larsson.

The first goal of the game came in the 11th minute after Lubo Moravcik scored from a free-kick about 20 yards away from the goal line.

Celtic showed they were up for the game with constant attacking, but Livi were no slouches either and they kept at it with a couple of good attempts. They were given a boost in the 34th minute when Chris Sutton was taken off after falling badly on his ankle after a challenge with Marvin Andrews. John Hartson came on in his place and quickly had a shot at goal that Culkin was lucky to get to.

After that the goalmouth action was at the other end of the pitch as Livingston pulled themselves right back into the game with an equaliser when Rubio headed home free-kick from Barry Wilson.

The next 10 minutes were the Barry Wilson show as he ran from one end of the pitch, stopping Moravcik from almost certainly scoring and then tearing back up to the other end of the pitch to almost score before being brought down by Valgaeren.

The first-half ended at one-each, leaving both sets of fans expecting an exciting second half and they certainly weren't disappointed.

Celtic started the half more on the attack than the visitors with Lubo having a great chance from 25 yards and then Hartson having a shot, but both times the Hoops were denied by Culkin, who was in no mood to give away late Christmas presents.

Celtic regained the lead in the 50th minute when Larsson turned inside of John Anderson and ran to about 12 yards out before putting in a low shot for goal number two.

It is to Livi's credit that at this point – and every other time during the season when they played Celtic – that they never stopped attacking. They were one of the few teams to constantly take a game to Celtic. That attacking spirit saw them level the game just before the 60th minute when Barry Wilson tore down the wing and fired a shot at goal, which Rab Douglas was able to parry away, but Quino volleyed in the rebound.

Livi were then given a boost as Celtic went down to ten men after Valgaeren was shown his second yellow for a tug on Lowndes, giving the Lions' the chance to snatch three points with only minutes remaining on the clock.

And while one team did snatch the points in the dying seconds, it wasn't Livi.

Henrik Larsson was on the receiving end of a threatening cross from Alan Thompson and the super Swede made no mistakes with it, just before the referee blew for full-time.

Afterwards Big Leish was upset at not getting a share of the points but he added that he could have no fault with the players for the effort they had put on – or with the thousand or so fans that turned up and at times drowned out the massive Celtic support.

However the Paradise performance, which would have won anywhere else in the country, was lacking in the next game as Kilmarnock came looking for revenge after their 5-1 trouncing earlier in the season.

To say Livingston weren't in the game for the first half would be cruel but not completely inaccurate, as even Jim Leishman conceded after the game, as Killie piled on the pressure with only the posts and crossbar saving Livi a few times.

Killie took the only goal of the game in the 35th minute after a cross from Kris Boyd took a cruel deflection off Steven Tosh to fall to Canero. His shot seemed to be covered by Brinquin and Rubio but an awkward bounce saw it come off Rubio's ankle and into the net.

As with all Killie games, there was plenty of work for the physio afterwards with Nathan Lowndes being looked at for a head knock while Quino came off at half-time because of an inflammation to a blood clot on his lower back.

The second half saw Livi try harder – with four men up front at one point – but Gordon Marshall and his defence held on to make sure that three points from this game wouldn't be first footing Livi.

A New Year brought the chance for the team to forget the last few defeats and concentrate on winning again with the first challenge being an away game against Aberdeen on January 2.

The youngsters of Aberdeen showed that, like Livi, they were determined to get the year off to a winning start and the opening half hour was all about the Dons as they piled pressure after pressure on the visitors, who handles the attacks magnificently, though there were some frightening moments.

After the 30 minute mark, Livi started to pull themselves back into the attacking end of the game a bit more.

Fernandez in particular had a fantastic chance in the 31st minute, teaming up David Bingham as he had done so often through the season, to fire a shot at Kjaer who managed to get to it and then seconds later was at it again, this time saving a Bingham shot.

But he couldn't stop the shot in the 39th minute which gave Livi the lead and again it was Fernandez and Bingham casing trouble.

Fernandez took the ball off Russell Anderson, passed it to Bingham in the area and Steven Tosh raced after getting the ball from Bingo to put it past Kjaer, who would go off at half-time with a knee injury, being replaced by Ryan Esson.

The 1-0 half-time lead gave Livi a boost for the second half and one of the best goals of the year – despite the fact that it was only two days into it –was scored just before the hour mark.

Fernandez, Tosh and Bingham went on a run down the pitch, with Bingham then passing to Brinquin who thumped in a 22-yard screamer into the top right goal, giving him his opener for the Lions'.

Aberdeen seemed to fade after the goal – and who can blame them – and a third was not long in coming as Marvin Andrews took a Barry Wilson cross and headed it home.

He nearly nabbed a second just minutes later in an identical set-up but it went wide, but nonetheless the team were fired up for the next game – against Rangers at Ibrox in ten days' time.

Livi were shoved on the defensive more or less from the word go and Culkin stopped the bluenoses from getting an early goal with a diving save of a shot from Shota Arveladze.

But the action quickly moved to the other end of the pitch with a Barry Wilson corner being headed just past the goal by Marvin Andrews.

Livi's best effort of the first half could have changed the game completely as Fernandez passed to Bingham but Bingham couldn't get to it in time to beat Klos.

Rangers, sensing the danger, upped the ante a little and their improved effort paid off in the 30th minute with Flo went by Culkin to score the opener. Caniggia made it 2-0 just minutes later after taking delivery of a pass from Ronald de Boer. Culkin went down for the ball but it was not enough.

Rangers defended solidly in the second half and despite Michael Hart and Davide Xausa being brought on, the scoreline didn't change until the dying minutes when Caniggia grabbed his second after a pass from Neil McCann, making the 3-0 defeat Livingston's largest in the league to date.

The Lions' recovered some of their roar for the third round Tennents Scottish Cup tie against Albion Rovers – another cup replay as the original leg had been cancelled because of floodlight failure – with some fans getting in for free, thanks to Dominic Keane's kind free ticket offer.

Anyone arriving late for the game missed the first goal as Barry Wilson grabbed the opener in just 30 seconds with a powerful 18-yard drive.

It took the Lions' another half hour to get another goal as Fernandez crossed the ball from the line for David Bingham to nod home for two.

Albion came back into it just before half time though as Charlie McLean ran onto a loose ball on the edge of the area and thumped it into the net.

While during the second half, Livingston never looked under any real pressure, Rover's defence – and a little luck it has to be said - held out, denying a number of efforts from Livingston, including Barry Wilson.

The inevitable third goal came in the 83rd minute when Fernandez and Nathan Lowndes teamed up to cause problems for Rovers' defence and the Spaniard did a little bit of showing off to round the keeper before putting the ball into the net.

Sub Richard Brittain came on as the game wound down but he played a pivotal part in the fourth and final goal of the game, taking the free-kick which Bingham was able to jump up for and put over the keeper to guarantee the club were in the next round of the cup and a game against Aberdeen later on in January. Before that though, there was the matter of a home game against Hearts.

Before the game Hearts' boss Craig Levein admitted later that he was an admirer of Fernandez, though God alone knows how as he had scored in every game against the Jambos and this game was no exception, but the first main incident involving the player had nothing to do with scoring.

Fernandez was also involved in a controversial 33rd-minute incident with Alan Maybury, which saw the forward pulled down before the former Leeds United defender was dismissed for kicking Fernandez on the ground and the whistle had been blown.

The ten men of Hearts held out for as long as they could but after David Bingham netted his seventh goal of the season with a 53rd-minute header from Philippe Brinquin's cross.

The loss of a goal put a bit of blood into Hearts and they shoved up the park looking for an equaliser and a 20-yard curling shot from Fuller brought out a good stop from Nick Culkin in the 55th minute to remind the small travelling the support that the game wasn't over.

There was sighs of relief from that support just minutes later when Fuller was booked for diving in the box. Livi fans couldn't gloat too much though as the exact same thing happened at the other end of the pitch later on the game in the 88th minute when Wilson was booked for it.

A second goal from – who else - Fernandez, getting his seventh of the season, in the 64th minute more or less wrapped up the game but Hearts had a chance at the death to pull one back when they had a penalty, but Nick Culkin saved the shot and the game ended with third-place Livi nine points ahead of Hearts.

After the game Livi coach and ex-Hearts player John Robertson who admitted that while a UEFA Cup place was a possibility, former Deportivo La Coruna striker Fernandez may not be there for it, which was proven to be uncannily accurate.

He said: "We want to keep David as long as possible, but if he continues to show the talent he has, it is only a matter of time until someone bigger comes in for him."

"We have a real chance of qualifying for Europe now and it is up to us to consolidate our place in the last 14 games. That would turn a fantastic season into a great one."

Then it was cup duty time for the Lions' and a game against Aberdeen. Hopes were high given results earlier in the season but it was not to be and the Lions' went out two-nil after losing two first-half goals, leaving the Dons to face a financial boost from a tie against Celtic, who were Livi's next opponents at home on the second last day of January.

For the first hour, this game was more or less all one way as Livi set out determined to make up for being kicked out the cup and the Boxing Day injustice when these two teams met the last time.

The first goal came in four minutes with Andrews firing the ball down the left wing which eventually ended up with Barry Wilson who passed to Quino 25 yards out who volleyed it in off the crossbar.

A second goal nearly came in the 20th minute through a similar set-up, this time with Barry Wilson in the Quino position, but Douglas was alert for it this time and managed to prevent a repeat event.

Wilson had to come off just ten minutes later though as a knock picked up in a fair challenge with Bobo Balde earlier in the game continued to niggle at him.

Fernandez threatened his future employers a couple of times before half-time with Bingham and Hart helping him out, but he was unable to finish any of them off, but the team went in at half-time one-up against the champions.

It was a different Celtic who came out in the second half though, with everyone bar Rab Douglas pushing forward to get the goals. It was to Livi's credit that they held Celtic off until almost the hour mark.

The equaliser came in the 58th minute as Lubo Moravcik – who had come on for an injured Jackie McNamara in the first half – fired a free-kick from the edge of the box into the net.

Two minutes later it was two to Celtic as young Jamie Smith passed to Larsson who made no mistake from such a close range.

Celtic's third came in the 73rd minute as Hartson put it in. The game ended 3-1 but the result flattered Celtic who had been given one of their toughest games of the season by the east coasters.

The midweek game looked to have taken its toll on Livi as they flagged on the next weekend game against Motherwell.

The Steelmen gave the Lions' a tough game that wasn't helped for Livi by referee Mike McCurry disallowing a goal by David Fernandez in the sixth minute for offside.

Six minutes later a free standing Stuart Elliot almost put the Fir Parkers one-up with a whack from a long ball pass but Culkin managed to get to it time.

As the first half developed, the battle went from end to end, though the long season did look as if it was starting to tire some players out.

Livi had a great chance to go ahead in the 30th minute when David Bingham fired one in and the 'keeper was nowhere but Scott Leitch managed to head it off the line.

After soaking up some attacks from Livi, the home team decided to have a go and it put them ahead after Soloy hit the ball through the legs of Culkin and into the net in the 38th minute.

The score didn't stay static for long though and the first half ended as a draw after Marvin Andrews scored from a Fernandez corner.

'Well put Livi back under the cosh in the second half with only some great defending and team play keeping the scoreline level but Quino took the opportunity to put the team ahead in the 71st minute when he took a pass from Lowndes to put it in and for the last 20 minutes of the game Livi were able to hold on to keep the three points, though at times it did look as if the team were riding their luck.

Culkin was able to be philosophical about the mistake in the first half afterwards, though he did concede that getting the three points made that a lot easier.

He said, "If we had went in one nil down at half time I think I'd probably got a taxi home. I made a few good saves to keep us in the match but that goal was a once in a lifetime - hopefully."

Leishman added, "Nicky was disappointed at half time but the whole dressing room got behind him. He kept us in the game before and after the goal with some good saves. We showed bottle and great team spirit to come back from a goal down."

However it would be the last three points Livingston would see for a while as the club entered one of its darker periods in its short history and a lot of critics were all too happy to mention it, saying that the club was just like Hibs in the previous year and that no club could really compete with the SPL regulars, especially in their first season up with the big boys and so on.

The bad run started on Saturday February 9 with a home leg against Dundee United.

It all started well enough with Livi taking the game to United, Fernandez especially having an inspired game but goalkeeper Paul Gallacher kept frustrating the classy Spaniard.

Gallacher's best moment though was in the 23rd minute when Quino fired off an incredible overhead kick but the 'keeper managed to block it.

The rest of the defence helped out as well with Jim Lauchlan blocking a Fernandez rocket in the 37th minute.

The first half ended in a draw with Livi having had the vast majority of the action and it looked as if it would only be a matter of time before they would grab a goal and it came in the 51st minute with three excellent touches from the team.

Fernandez took a corner and fired it over to Marvin Andrews who deftly knocked it to Bingo Bingham, who gave the ball a glancing touch to put it in the net and make it one-nil.

This fired the team up and they kept putting on the pressure with Steven Tosh and Fernandez having a number of chances, keeping Gallacher and his defence under pressure.

As the game looked to be heading to a cosy one-nil win, it was all turned upside down in the 85th minute when Derek Lilley headed in a cross to equalise.

United then spent the last few minutes making life very uncomfortable for Livi, almost snatching all three points but a combination of luck and determination kept them in the game and it ended a draw – a result which certainly did not tell the true story of the game.

A draw wasn't the end of the world but the next game nearly was. An away game against St Johnstone was not expected to pose any problems, but it did. Big time. In fact if it had been two days earlier, it could have been Livingston's version of the St Valentines Day massacre.

Just like the previous game, Livingston did all the work for most of the first half, being unlucky not to score but a combination of great saves from Kevin Cuthbert and shots coming off the post, or just going over them.

And also just like the previous game, the danger came just as things were winding down.

Nick Culkin's view was obscured in the 43rd minute due to there being a large number of players in and near the goalmouth. Paul Hartley took advantage of this to fire in a shot from around 20 yards out to make it 1-0.

Despite going a goal down, most Livi fans felt an equaliser was in the offing in the second half, judging by the run of play in the first 45 minutes.

A change in tactics by St Johnstone saw the game change completely though as Livingston were thwarted in their attempts to get near the goalmouth. The Saints managed to nab a second goal in the 80th minute and the misery was made complete right on full time as Graeme Jones knocked in a third, making Livingston's day of misery complete.

The defeats continued in March with another away game, this time against Dunfermline.

Unlike the previous two games where Livi had done all the work in the first half, this was a bit more balanced out with both sides having great chances.

Livingston's best effort was when Fernandez fired in a cross which Steven Tosh headed just over the bar. Meanwhile at the other end of the pitch Barry Nicholson had a great header put over by Culkin just as the ref blew to call half-time.

The second half was equally action-packed and the Dunfermline goal came in the 51st minute when Lee Bullen volleyed in a high shot.

Livi tried to pull themselves back into the game, and had a number of good chances, but failed to make anything of them and the three points went to Dunfermline.

The bad run continued the following week against Hibs and their new manager Bobby Williamson.

Just over 8100 people turned out for the game which was certainly full of excitement – over 30 free-kicks, two bookings, ten corners, 19 attempts on goal and 11 off sides.

The third goal came courtesy of unfortunate Livi substitute Morten Petersen, who headed into his goal late in the game.

Marvin Andrews's attempt at a pass-back was poorly dealt with by Nick Culkin and he spilled the ball into the path of Garry O'Connor. The young striker duly fired home from close range to give the Edinburgh side the advantage.

The Almondvale side had a great chance to equalise after 35 minutes when skipper Stuart Lovell squared the ball into the path of the onrushing David Bingham but he failed to connect properly and sent the ball past the post from just a couple of yards out.

David Fernandez went even closer four minutes later when he met a long kick from the goalkeeper before taking the ball past goalkeeper Nick Colgan but the Spaniard somehow managed to volley over the crossbar.

With just seconds of the first half remaining, Hibs doubled their advantage. O'Neil's close range effort was blocked by the goalkeeper but the ball fell kindly to the skipper and he lobbed Culkin with his second attempt.

Hibs were still hungry for goals and they could have added to their tally just four minutes after the restart.

Ulises de la Cruz flighted a long cross into the area, picking out O'Connor at the far post, but the striker was denied his second goal of the day by the vigilant Michael Hart who headed clear for a corner kick.

O'Connor was threatening again after 54 minutes when Frederic Arpinon fed the ball through to the young striker but Culkin pounced from his line to block before O'Connor could pull the trigger.

Although Livingston were looking dangerous at times, Hibs were creating the better chances.

O'Neil touched the ball on to Brewster to set up the shot for the former Lonikis hitman after 59 minutes but he bulleted just over the crossbar.

Brewster went close again after 65 minutes when Alen Orman was hauled down by Lovell on the edge of the box and he stepped up for the free-kick. He sliced the effort through the Livi wall but Culkin managed the save.

De la Cruz had been looking dangerous out on the right wing and he sent another cross into the box after 77 minutes but, in his haste to clear, substitute Petersen misdirected his header.

A comeback from Livingston at that stage looked highly unlikely and the home supporters started pouring out of the ground with more than 10 minutes remaining.

And while he was disappointed afterwards, Leishman took the philosophical route when asked about it.

"How can you criticise guys who have given you 102 per cent all season?" he said

"People are now saying 'Livingston might not make Europe this year and that shows how expectation levels have risen as people had us written off at the start of the season."

There were a lot of changes for the next game – a midweek away leg against Dundee – and the team were fired up for it, but sadly the three points went elsewhere again.

Poor discipline cost Livingston the next game – a 2-0 loss at Dundee.

Both Massimiliano Caputo and Stevie Tosh were red-carded and Jim Leishman was ordered to the stand for protesting the former's red card.

The first real chance of the game fell to Dundee's Georgian star Temuri Ketsbaia who powered an Enrique Torres free-kick just over the crossbar after nine minutes.

Livingston's first chance fell to Francisco Quino who rattled an effort off the upright before the danger was eventually cleared by goalkeeper Julian Speroni.

The Dundee goalkeeper was called into action again after 24 minutes when he did well to tip over David Fernandez's shot.

But the game turned in Dundee's favour after 32 minutes when Caputo appeared to raise his hands to Massimo Beghetto and referee John Rowbotham showed the Livingston player a straight red card.

Leishman was handed his own punishment for his protestations when he was ordered to the stand - but not before receiving a friendly arm around the shoulder from Dens Park boss Ivano Bonetti.

For one horrible second after the restart Livingston thought their numbers were to be reduced even further when Fernandez was shown the red card for dissent after arguing about the direction of a free-kick - but Rowbotham hastily retracted the card and replaced it with the yellow.

Dundee eventually made the extra man count after 56 minutes when Javier Artero flighted a perfectly weighted cross into the path of Juan Sara who nodded home the opener, leaving Broto helpless.

The home side could have added to their lead three minutes later when a beautifully-worked move between Rae and Fabian Caballero allowed the Argentinean a chance at goal but his effort was off-target from just a few yards out.

The home side were looking impressive again after 65 minutes. This time Ketsbaia fed the ball to Enrique Torres and he squared into the path of Caballero.

The striker unleashed a long, low effort that looked goal bound but the ball went just wide of the post.

Livingston tried to force their way back into the game two minutes later when Lee Makel picked out Fernandez for a shot but the Spaniard watched as his effort deflected wide.

Tosh had replaced Stuart Lovell after 68 minutes and – just six minutes later - he was dismissed as Livingston found themselves down to nine men.

The Almondvale player showed his studs as he went for a tackle with Ketsbaia and the official was left with no option but to show the red card for the second time.

As the game entered the final minutes Dundee should have added to their lead when Ketsbaia exchanged a neat one-two with Sara before racing into the box, but Broto blocked before the Georgian could pull the trigger.

Livingston could have snatched a draw with just three minutes remaining when a Barry Wilson free-kick forced Speroni into a superb save and he was called upon again to block the rebound effort from Fernandez.

But Dundee sealed the win in injury-time when Ketsbaia squared the ball into the path of Sara and he fired home his second of the night.

Fortunately the misery came to an end with a draw against Kilmarnock.

Livi gained an advantage in the 15th minute when Gordon Marshall was stretchered off. Proof of how vital the experienced keeper was shown in the 24th minute when Barry Wilson scored to make it one-nil to the Lions'.

It didn't stay that way for long though as Craig Dargo pulled one back in the 35th minute

Both sides created chances in the second half but the points were shared at the end and Livi fans were happy to have a point after the recent run of results. It also boosted confidence for the game against Aberdeen – a game that could decide who would be in third place.

Just one point from their last five league games meant Aberdeen's aspirations of leapfrogging Livingston became a reality and they headed into the game at the West Lothian Courier Stadium two points ahead of their hosts.

For Livingston, the game provided the ideal opportunity to reclaim third place in the league but a win for the Dons could mean Livi praying for an Old Firm Scottish Cup final to ensure the remaining European place goes to the fourth-placed team in the league.

As though to emphasise the importance of this clash, the pace of the game was fast and furious right from the outset in front of a packed house, which included a large number of travelling supporters who had made the long trip from the north east.

The game also had its fair share of heated moments and the Dons found themselves down to 10 men after 33 minutes when Darren Young picked up his second yellow card for his second challenge on Spanish striker David Fernandez.

The sending-off proved to be the main talking point of a first half which lacked goals from either side.

The home side could have taken the lead after just four minutes when a Francisco Quino cross was expertly met by Barry Wilson but the Livi player nodded straight into the hands of Dons goalkeeper Peter Kjaer.

At the other end of the park Robbie Winters had two decent opportunities to give Aberdeen the lead.

His first, after 30 minutes, was an unsuccessful attempt to chip the ball over goalkeeper Broto.

The second was a weak effort that was easily blocked by the Livi defence and it was left to Darren Young before his dismissal to prompt the Livingston goalkeeper to break into a sweat with a rebound effort that fell just inches wide of the upright.

The home side enjoyed the first chance of the second half when Fernandez produced an impressive shot just two minutes after the restart but Kjaer managed to conjure up an equally impressive save to keep the scoreline level.

The Dons should have taken the lead when the ball broke to Leon Mike just outside the six-yard box after 53 minutes but Broto who had raced off his line stood his ground and managed to block the shot with his arm.

Tempers flared as the game progressed and the referee was called upon to prevent Derek Young confronting Fernandez after an initial challenge by the Dons player.

His name was added to Clark's book to bring the crime count for the game to seven yellow cards and a dismissal.

The best chance of the game so far fell to Livingston after 73 minutes when the Sheriff touched the ball on to Fernandez and he unleashed a powerful shot which smacked off the crossbar to deny the home side the opener.

Livingston were unlucky to have a penalty claim ignored just minutes later.

Fernandez played a corner kick out to Oscar Rubio on the 18-yard line his shot was blocked but Didier Santini tried to follow up inside the six-yard box.

He appeared to be brought down by the Aberdeen goalkeeper but the referee opted not to give the spot kick.

The home side were screaming for a penalty again with just six minutes remaining when Bingham claimed he was pushed in the box by Phil McGuire but once again Clark was not impressed.

The next game – against Celtic – can only be politely described as a rout with Celtic wanting the points to wrap up the league.

Livi had threatened to turn party-poopers in the opening seconds of the game but Wilson's cross from the right was too strong for Davide Xausa.

But the Hoops were desperate to retain the SPL title at the first time of asking and Larsson was up first to start the party in the 3rd minute.

Lambert's throw-in was shielded from two Livi defenders by Hartson before the Welshman laid the ball back to the Scotland captain.

Lambert looked up once inside the box to see Larsson waiting unmarked in the area and the Swede slotted home the opener.

Then, in the 19th minute, Hartson got in on the act with his 20th goal of the season.

The former Arsenal, West Ham and Coventry forward pushed the ball wide to Didier Agathe and then drilled home the return cross from the Frenchman.

Minutes later, Hartson added his second when he rose above former Rangers player Gary Bollan to power home a Guppy cross.

Larsson clearly had no intention of playing in the shadows of his strike partner and, when Guppy deceived Morten Petersen on the edge of the area, the forward seized his chance.

One-time England winger Guppy floated the ball across the area where Larsson pinched a yard on Oscar Rubio to head home Celtic's fourth.

Larsson completed his hat-trick on the hour with credit to referee Willie Young.

The match official played the advantage for the Hoops after Cherif Toure-Maman felled Petrov.

Midfielder Neil Lennon delivered a great ball into the area for Lambert to collect and he squared the ball to an unmarked Larsson who stroked it home.

Wilson stole a consolation strike for the visitors with 17 minutes remaining after a great through ball from substitute Nocko Jokovic.

Fans feared it would be a similar result the following week against the other half of the Old Firm when Rangers visited. Instead, it was one of Livi's best games.

It got off to a bad start though when Neil McCann won a corner, Andrei Kanchelskis floated it in to a crowded six-yard box and there was Amoruso to head it into the net.

The Livi defence, and the giant Marvin Andrews in particular, had been static and allowed the Italian a free header.

Javier Sanchez Broto was required to prevent Michael Mols from doubling that lead when he produced one of his trademark turns to fool Andrews and set up a low drive. The Spaniard could only parry but defender Didier Santini was there to mop up.

Rangers appeared to be in control but their domination was challenged by the pace and skill of David Fernandez and Wilson's desire to get on the score sheet.

Bob Malcolm had to get in the way of his header when Cherif Toure Maman floated in a free-kick and not long afterwards Amoruso was only fractionally the better man in two penalty box challenges.

Wilson went to ground on both occasions but referee Stuart Dougal appeared to be doubly correct when he ruled "play on."

But those incidents were proof that the home side was beginning to come back into the game and it needed a fine save from Stefan Klos in the Rangers goal to preserve the lead.

The Sheriff gained control of the ball just outside the area to feed Wilson in the box and when the ball was fired into the danger zone Cherif was there to get a close-range connection only for the German to parry.

Klos was behind a Stevie Tosh volley soon afterwards but was given no chance with Wilson's equaliser.

Rangers had been forced to regroup at the back when Tony Vidmar limped off to be replaced by Arthur Numan, and the entire defence were spectators when Wilson received the ball from Santini some 25 yards from goal and turned to smash it past Klos into the top corner.

The second half began in similar fashion to the first, with Rangers taking the early initiative only to be pegged back later.

Livi saw Cherif stretchered off to be replaced by Lovell before Fernandez twice troubled the Rangers defence.

The first occasion saw him fire across goal and wide with Amoruso in hot pursuit and the second saw Quino's flying bicycle kick fall to him in the box.

But the ball was travelling just too fast and ended up bouncing off him and away to safety.

Andrews was just wide with a header from a Wilson free-kick from the left touchline but Lee Makel was way off target with a rising long ranger.

Fernandez was still keen to make an impression however and when he got the better of Amoruso chasing a Lee Makel long ball he was able to find Wilson with a cross.

Wilson could not find the target on that occasion but Fernandez was still able to set up a winning goal for a team-mate.

Lovell was the man who provided it, launching himself into the air to fire a bicycle kick past Klos with just 2 minutes left on the clock

The three points from the game meant that the team only needed three points from the three games left to grab a UEFA cup slot.

Of course, in true Livi style, they did it the hard way, starting with a three-nil hammering by Aberdeen, who were still wanting that third place in the league for themselves.

The Dons raced into an early two-goal lead, the first coming in the seventh minute after a lucky break in front of goal

Darren Mackie raced down the right and swung his cross into the Livi six yard box.

Keeper Javier Broto appeared to have it covered but only succeeded in punching the ball into defender Marvin Andrews.

When the ball broke to Leon Mike the Dons striker had the easiest of tasks to score from inside the six yard box.

Three minutes later, with the visitors still shocked, Aberdeen doubled their lead.

A Robbie Winters free-kick was headed towards goal by Mackie and, although Broto pulled off a good save, Philip McGuire was on hand to blast the ball into the corner of the net.

The Dons then had a good penalty claim turned down moments later when Mackie was sandwiched between Andrews and Philippe Brinquin, but referee Douglas McDonald opted to give the corner.

Andrews recovered from his earlier mishap and looked solid in defence, repelling the Dons' threat.

On the half hour he had to clear off the line after Broto had failed to cut out a Kevin McNaughton cross which was then guided towards goal by Robbie Winters.

Moments later David Fernandez had the ball in the net for the visitors after he followed up a Lee Makel shot but was controversially ruled offside.

But in the 37th minute Aberdeen scored a third when a Winters' through ball fell kindly to Mackie racing in on goal.

The youngster held off Livi defender Oscar Rubio all too easily then hammered the ball past Broto from 15 yards.

The visitors needed a quick goal after the break if they were to have any chance of rescuing anything from the game and brought on David Bingham for Stevie Tosh to give them three forwards.

Bingham nearly made an immediate impact after two minutes of the restart when he clipped a 20-yard free-kick off Kjaer's left hand post.

The Danish keeper, who had almost nothing to do in the first 45 minutes, was rooted to the spot and gladly watched the ball eventually being cleared to safety.

Livingston still could not make an impact on the Dons goal and as the second half wore on it was the home side who looked to improve on their lead, and Winters was guilty of missing a couple of decent chances.

In the 58th minute Dons defender McNaughton crossed into the box and Andrews poor defensive header, under no real pressure, fell to Mackie inside the box.

Despite having plenty of time the youngster snatched at his angled shot and it hit the side netting.

As the game threatened to boil over at times frustrated Livingston manager Jim Leishman was warned by referee McDonald.

And then it was that game against Dunfermline which helped complete the fairy tale.

The game started off at a frantic pace and a scare for Livi when the Fifers' Stevie Crawford had a great chance at goal. Fortunately he headed wide, but it gave the visitors encouragement to take the game to the euro-chasers.

But as Dunfermline tried to break down Livi, Lovell controlled the midfield, prompting action from his strikers with long passes that made sure the Dunfermline didn't have the whole game to themselves.

At this point Javier Broto was the hardest-working player on the park though, constantly dealing with trouble in or near the goalmouth.

While Broto was busy, it was the goalkeeper at the other end who provided the first controversial moment of the game. Marco Ruitenbeek picked up the ball when he shouldn't have and even though it was well spotted, referee Mike McCurry took ages to react before finally blowing for a free-kick.

However that came to nothing – though Fernandez's free-kick was powerful – as Ruitenbeek got to it, determined to make up for his stupid mistake in causing the free-kick in the first place.

Quino then had a chance at the far post but it shot straight into the arms of Ruitenbeek.

But then an opener came in the 28th minute in the shape of the midfield general Lovell after Barry Wilson sent in a corner from the left of the post and Lovell got up to it and nutted it into the net.

And while this fired the crowd up, it seemed to have the opposite effect on the home players while Dunfermline charged forward time after time with only Broto managing to keep the score at 1-0.

And while his defence didn't seem much help to him, one thing that was useful was the shocking finishing by Dunfermline, who were squandering chances left, right and centre.

Jason Dair powered a close-range drive past the despairing hands of Javier Broto in the Livingston goal after the home defence had failed to deal with a Sean Kilgannon attempt at levelling the scoreline.

Kilgannon then ran on to a short ball from Stevie Crawford to unleash a shot that forced a fine diving one-handed save from Broto before Lee Makel cleared the loose ball.

Broto also proved he was the day's saviour when he brilliantly beat out a Scott Thomson header and then had to rely on Phillipe Brinquin to make a goal-line clearance from a mistimed header from Marvin Andrews.

As half-time approached, it was looking as if the home team could hang on, but in the 41st minute, all the plans were changed and again, Kilgannon – who had been causing problems throughout the whole game – when he sent a long cross to the far post where Barry Nicholson headed the ball back across the face of the goalmouth where a lurking Jason Dair thumped it into the net to make it 1-1, which it stayed it going into half-time.

As the second-half kicked off, Dunfermline still looked like the more inspired team, pushing forward, but this was to the detriment of their defence.

Barry Wilson exploited this to try and restore the home lead. His first chance came in the 48th minute when Fernandez took the ball from Crawford to set up Wilson inside the area, but the attempt came to nothing as it shot into the side netting. Two minutes later, Fernandez again slid the ball through to Wilson, who from a similar position, fired his shot across the face of the goal.

Minutes later, Dunfermline broke free and Crawford fired in a great cross from the right with only Broto to beat. It was one of those goals that looked harder to miss than score, but Nish managed it, putting the ball past the far post instead of tapping it into the empty net.

Ten minutes later, as the game turned into the hour-long mark Barry Wilson took a corner that he hit low for Davide Xausa to slot home and make it 2-1 for Livi against Dunfermline, who were down to 10 men after new signing Karnebeek limped off.

Livingston's Wilson came off in the 72nd minute to be replaced by Tosh and he was thrown into the thick of it as battling Dunfermline refused to give in though and hunted for a second goal, coming close in the 73rd minute when they had a free-kick 20 yards out in front of goal.

Broto was the man of the moment with a fantastic save of a Barry Nicholson shot.

Realising the threat Dunfermline still posed, Livi started to up the gears to show why they were the team challenging for Europe and they started to show it quickly.

The score became three-one when Xausa fired in his second goal – an 18-yard belter – after a set-up from Fernandez in the 75th minute.

That was Xausa's last contribution to the game as he was replaced by Bingham in the 78th minute.

And while that had the fans starting to chant about going to Europe, the club's apotheosis to the European elite was confirmed in the 83rd minute with some dramatic work by Fernandez and Quino.

Fernandez had beaten three defenders to force a save from Marco Ruitenbeek, who could only clear it as far as Francisco Quino, who got the ball in the air and volleyed it in from inside the penalty box to make it 4-1.

For Leishman the fourth goal was when he let himself believe that he had helped guide a club into Europe for the first time in his career.

"It wasn't until Quino's goal went in that we could relax because we knew Dunfermline wouldn't score three so that was when it all began to sink in," he said.

Fernandez then came off for the ending moments for an eager Caputo.

And in the dying seconds an incredible chip by Lee Makel wowed the crowd but it came off the Dunfermline crossbar instead of making it five.

This left only the game against Hearts, which if the club won, they could seal third place, topping off an incredible season.

Hearts didn't make it easy for them though, nearly taking the lead as early as the third minute when striker Ricardo Fuller made a run deep into the visitors' defence before cutting the ball back for Stephane Adam whose flick sent the ball goal wards. However, Livingston defender Marvin Andrews popped up and cleared the ball.

Moments later at the other end, Livingston striker Barry Wilson went on a run before firing in a shot from 20 yards which Hearts keeper Roddy McKenzie saved comfortably.

In the 12th minute Hearts keeper McKenzie pulled off a great save from David Xausa after the Canadian had powerfully volleyed a Lee Makel cross towards the top corner.

The West Lothian side looked dangerous going forward and should have taken the lead after 19 minutes.

Fernandez broke clear on the right and squared the ball to Francisco Quino who looked to have the easiest of tasks but the Spaniard miskicked from 12 yards out, allowing McKenzie to recover and save.

But the game was flowing back and forth and Flogel, making his last appearance for the Edinburgh side, tried his luck with a 25-yard effort but the ball flew well over the visitors' crossbar.

Livingston came out for the second half determined to turn their neat passing and good midfield play into goals.

But the opening stages were rather sedate with neither keeper being troubled.

That was to change quite dramatically when the Tynecastle men increased their work-rate and took the lead in the 50th minute after Livingston keeper Broto had flapped at a corner from Joe Hammill.

The ball was cleared off the line by Quino but Ricardo Fuller was on hand to force the ball into the net from close range.

But barely two minutes later the visitors equalised and once again it was due to a goalkeeper's error.

Quino shot at McKenzie from 12 yards and the keeper somehow managed to let the ball go over his head and then tried in vain to claw it back.

The game then stepped up a bit in its intensity as both sides went for goal although too often it was via route one.

There was plenty of brawn and commitment on show and consequently the deft touches of Fernandez shone like a beacon.

On the hour mark Adam, who had made little impact, made a good run into the heart of the visitors' defence but his clever, chipped shot from outside the box was just too high to beat Broto.

It looked as if the next goal would be the winner and it was the visitors who grabbed it in the 72nd minute.

Makel cut the ball back from the by-line and the grateful substitute David Bingham, on for Xausa seven minutes earlier, had a simple tap-in to an empty goal.

As the game drew to a close it was the visitors who looked more dangerous on the break and almost inevitably Wilson added a third in the 87th minute with the aid of a wicked deflection off Hearts midfielder Scot Severin.

With seconds remaining of the 90 minutes, the home side pulled one back with a penalty from substitute Stevie Fulton who had come on for Tommy Gronlund, but it didn't matter as news came in of Aberdeen's defeat by Celtic, meaning when the whistle blew – and it did just seconds later – Livi were third – and in Europe – in their first season with the big boys.

Davie Hay was delighted afterwards, saying, "It's a strange feeling but I think that you could say that we won the secondary championship - the one without the Old Firm."

"We never expected to win the championship, so qualifying for Europe is a fantastic achievement in our first season."

"Finishing third was the icing on the cake because, to be honest, just qualifying for the UEFA Cup surpassed our targets."

"What we achieved proves that it's not all gloom and doom around in Scottish football."

"No one here wants to be smug about how we fared but I think that other teams can look at Livingston and see what a provincial club can achieve."

But he warned that there would be no resting on laurels.

"This club never stands still. It will be difficult to finish third again next term, but we will be doing everything we possibly can to try and build on the success that we enjoyed last season."

"It will be tough, but everyone at this club is looking forward to it."

CHAPTER
10

HOW DO YOU TOP IT?

Now how do you top a year like that?

Another season, but some things never changed, including naysayers writing the team off before a ball had been even kicked. Some pundits said the club had been lucky to do what it did the previous year, while others said that they would be doing well if they managed to stay in the top six. Some even said that the team which ended third, normally had a terrible following season, to which Stuart Lovell said, "We can learn lessons from the other teams who finished third and then had a bad next season."

"I finished third with Hibs the season before I joined Livingston and then watched them struggle with relegation last year."

"I would probably have stayed at Easter Road but the contract offer forced me out of the door."

"Mixu Paatelainen also left and there's no question Hibs made mistakes and failed to build on their success."

"I don't know whether the board weren't backing the manager but something was definitely wrong."

"We have a strong squad of more than 20 players which should see us through the season."

Certainly, the loss of David Fernandez to Celtic for £1.2million was a blow to the club on the pitch, but just as good players had been released before, management said the club would survive the release of this latest talented player.

While the rational said it was a bad move, the superstitious fans saw the change in strip as a worse omen. The *Edinburgh Evening News* reported that the club had decided to change from the traditional black and amber home strip to a white strip in a decision to shake things up.

It seemed to be a lucky omen at the start of the season when Livingston won a European cup. Sadly it wasn't The Cup or even the UEFA Cup but the VDH trophy, which the club won after taking part in a mini tournament.

As always, there were a number of changes at the club for the new season, with a lot of free transfers. Amongst the new faces was Emmanuel Dorado from Malaga, Juanjo Camacho from Real Zaragoza, Sergio Berti from Barcelona de Guayaquil, Rolando Zarate from Velez Sarsfield, Eugene Dadi from Aberdeen, Gustave Bahoken from Coton Sport and Fernando Lopez, also from Real Zaragoza.

As well as Fernandez, other players who left included John Anderson to Hull City, Nathan Lowndes to Plymouth, Steve Tosh to Falkirk, Morten Petersen to Aarhus as well as Didier Santini and Nocko Jokovic.

Everything looked to be going well for the club's opening game against Motherwell - and there were rumours of a new £1million bonus deal with bank Intelligent Finance but one last piece of transfer movement took the shine off that.

Sergio Berti was booted out for spitting on teenager Richard Brittain during a friendly win over Morecambe.

Dominic Keane explained quite simply that this sort of behaviour was not to be tolerated at Livi.

He said, "We've ended the contract of Sergio Berti on the grounds of gross misconduct. This follows an incident which took place during the friendly against Morecambe on Sunday.

"It's a sad state of affairs but we do not feel this is a harsh decision. An incident like this is totally unacceptable. We preferred not to keep this quiet. We could not allow this to go unpunished for the sake of the rest of our squad."

Berti wasn't missed in the opening game anyway as Livi won 3-2 in an excellent advert for the Scottish game.

It took Livingston less than ten minutes to open the scoring. Lee Makel was the provider, swinging in a corner in the 8th minute which eluded the away defence, and fell to Spanish defender Rubio who controlled the ball on his thigh before smashing it high in to the roof of the net.

Livingston's second goal on 34 minutes came after the ball went to the edge of the box, and Dadi rose to guide it into the path of Zarate who eased it in.

Livingston then stunned their opponents inside a minute of the restart with two simple passes. Dadi fed Camacho on the edge of the box. The little winger spun his marker before spotting Quino overlapping on the left-hand side of the penalty area. The midfielder could have shot himself but unselfishly rolled the ball to the back post where Zarate slid in to tuck it away.

Motherwell's reply was instant, bringing their vast travelling support to their feet. Steven Hammell crossed into Keith Lasley who laid it off to Scott Leitch who lobbed the ball over Broto.

Butcher's young side launched attack after attack. Livingston, it seemed, had won the battle, but Well's players kept pressing and were back in the match on 63 minutes. McFadden again turned the Livingston defence inside the box, picked out Dirk Lehmann at the back past, who nodded home.

Livingston were in all sorts of trouble. Motherwell's players flooded their defence from every area of the field until the last whistle. And by this stage Butcher had become so animated that he had been sent by Rowbotham to the stand, where he joined Jim Leishman as Jim had 11 games left from a 12 game ban from the previous season to work through. And while he hated that, he managed to salvage one tradition, as he told reporters afterwards.

He said, "I've maintained throughout my career that it's important not to lose on the first day and that applied to today as well."

Sadly, the winning run didn't continue as the Lions' first game away to Dunfermline ended in a 2-1 defeat, a game that was the opposite of the previous week's excellent advert for the game and Livi. Only Broto, Livingston's best performer on the day, could hold his head up high as he stopped the scoreline from being nearer 5-1.

Davie Hay sent his side out in a typically positive fashion, even though it was missing injured skipper Stuart Lovell.

Livingston were unable to mount any real attacks of their own and never really tested home keeper Marco Ruitenbeek, except in the opening minutes.

Broto, on the other hand, was forced to earn his keep with some fine stops.

Crawford, Sean Kilgannon and Steven Hampshire were all denied by the towering Spaniard who was eventually beaten by an exquisite Crawford finish in the 28th minute. Brewster was the architect of the goal, stepping off his marker before splitting the defence with a wonderful reverse pass which Crawford met first time with the outside of his right boot to thrash the ball into the net.

Crawford returned the favour just five minutes after half-time when he squared for Brewster to net from inside the six-yard box.

Livingston's hopes of coming back into the match had taken a dent minutes prior to the interval when striker Eugene Dadi was substituted after breaking a finger. Davide Xausa was his replacement and the Canadian grabbed a consolation in injury-time when he netted from close range.

Afterwards, Leishman was brutally honest about what had gone wrong.

He said, "We've set standards for ourselves through our performances last season and we didn't live up to those standards."

"That's the best I've seen a Dunfermline side play for many years - they created a lot of chances and caused us plenty of problems."

"Against Motherwell we created seven or eight opportunities but we hardly tested Dunfermline at all. We don't want to make any excuses - we simply didn't do the things we were supposed to do and we were punished for it."

But then it was the game that everyone had been waiting for - the European game against Swiss second division minnows FC Vaduz!

Andrews was out with chickenpox, but one person who was there was Bill Hunter, after Dominic Keane insisted that his predecessor be there for Livi's night of glory.

And he loved it.

"I said it would take seven years to reach the SPL and Dominic did it in six," he said. "I also said it would take the best part of 15 years to take the old Meadowbank into Europe under their new guise - but he has done it at the first time of asking."

Around 350 fans travelled for the game and saw a brave, battling performance by Livi, which ended in a 1-1 draw

There had been a pre-match doubt over the inclusion of Broto who suffered a muscle spasm in his back during training but the Spaniard was passed fit to play and proved his fitness by making some smart saves after suffering one rocky moment in the first period when he missed a cross ball, allowing Moreno Merenda a free header at goal which fortunately looped over the bar.

Quino tested Broto's opposite number, Romuald Peiser, with a rasping 25-yard effort, while striker Eugene Dadi missed a golden chance to open the scoring when put clear by Barry Wilson.

Broto denied Marius Zarn a headed goal before the break, during which Leishman and Davie Hay decided to replace the ineffective Juanjo Camacho with David Bingham.

The Lions' took the lead in the 51st minute when Gary Bollan thumped in a free-kick from just outside the area which Peiser was unable to hold. The rebound fell to stand-in skipper Rubio who lashed the ball into the net - his second goal of the season.

That, in theory, should have been the start of a deluge of goals for the Scots side, but it did not materialise.

The equaliser was a well-worked affair, with Franz Burmeier running at the heart of the shaky Livingston defence and playing a one-two with Merenda before slotting the ball home.

It could have been two soon after when Rubio dithered under a high ball before eventually electing to head it back to Broto.

The keeper had decided to react to the indecision of his centre-back and had charged off his line to collect. Rubio's header took the ball towards goal, but Broto recovered well to scramble back and claw it away.

Broto made a final save when he held a deflected shot from Lithuanian playmaker Validotas Slekys.

Philippe Brinquin showed a touch missing in many of today's footballers - humility - when he praised the fans who made the journey, including those who travelled by bus.

He said: "Most of our fans aren't rich but they give up so much time and effort to follow us. We need to give them so much respect for that. We aren't happy with how we played for them, but at least the result was not terrible. We got an away goal and that could be important for us."

Those words would prove prophetic, but Jim Leishman felt the players could have done better.

He said, "We're a bit disappointed in the way we played, but we should still go through."

"We're disappointed in the way we performed but the scoreline is still a good one for an away European tie. However, the players wanted to go out and put on a good show for the fans in the club's first European game and that didn't happen."

"We sat down after the game and each and every player was asked how they felt. A lot of positives came out of those discussions and we know the problems are not unsolvable."

"The expectation levels surrounding the club are very high and there's no doubt we're suffering a bit of a reaction to last season."

The disappointment continued in the next game with a 2-2 draw against newly-promoted Partick Thistle, but the conviction the players showed, left people in no doubt that Livi would be battling all the way throughout the season.

Stuart Lovell and Barry Wilson started the game, having shown progress from their injuries and it was the Lions' who nabbed the first goal.

The first half was a scrappy affair, with little football played and possession squandered on both sides. The Almondvale men had a claim for a penalty turned down when David Bingham collided with Thistle keeper Kenny Arthur after knocking the ball towards goal.

While the collision seemed accidental, it sent Bingham to the ground denying the forward the opportunity to score and allowing Stephen Craigan to nip in and clear the ball.

The opening goal came just after the half-hour mark when Rubio rose at the back post to bullet Philippe Brinquin's right-wing free-kick in off the bar with his head.

The lead lasted barely two minutes as former Livingston forward Alex Burns sent over a corner which keeper Javier Sanchez Broto failed to deal with properly.

The Spaniard rose to punch the ball but succeeded only in pushing it into the path of Mitchell who nodded home from close range.

Thistle took the lead in the 64th minute when Bahoken misjudged a high ball which bounced off the back of his head towards his own goal. Burns beat Rubio for pace and as he bore down goal, the defender brought him down.

Referee David Somers pointed to the spot and Mitchell stepped forward to ram the ball straight down the middle of the goal.

That setback did not dishearten the Lions' and they continued to mount wave after wave of attack.

The introduction of substitute Dadi to the forward line brought a physical presence and Brinquin's raids down the right flank were causing all sorts of problems for the Glasgow side.

Zarate saw a shot blocked on the line from a Dadi knockdown and then the Argentinean was denied by a fine save from Arthur.

The resultant corner saw the ball laid back by Camacho to Brinquin who again planted the ball on Rubio's head at the back post for the equaliser. The goal was Rubio's fourth in as many games - and four times his amount the previous year.

Marvin Andrews brushed off the chickenpox to be ready in time for the next game - against Kilmarnock, but while he might have been able to fight off chickenpox, fighting off the attacking Killie was another problem.

Kilmarnock's goal came via the simple route with a move worked right through the heart of the home defence three minutes before half-time. Craig Dargo managed to recover possession after being tackled by Brinquin and ran at Andrews before threading a pass into the penalty area.

Kris Boyd had managed to sneak goal-side of Bollan and required only to stretch out a toe and prod the ball past Javier Sanchez Broto from 12 yards.

Apart from that moment, neither goalkeeper was seriously tested, although two excellent first-half runs from Bingham brought chances for Quino and Zarate who both saw their efforts blocked.

Dadi and Zarate were withdrawn in favour of Juanjo Camacho and Davide Xausa on the hour. The two substitutes provided a bit more impetus to the attack but the former was rightly booked for diving as he tried to win a penalty.

The Lions'' best chance of an equaliser came four minutes from time when Camacho found Xausa with a fine pass down the left flank. The Canadian invited Freddy Dindeleux towards him before slotting the ball across goal. Bingham slid in to connect from close range but Gordon Marshall thwarted him with a fine block.

The longer the match went on, the more Livingston committed men forward and Killie nearly caught them on the break in injury-time when substitute Jose Quitongo hit the post.

After the game, Leishman said he knew where the team had to improve and he had every faith that it would.

He said, "We've been working hard on our fitness levels in training but I feel the forwards need to be a bit quicker to get on the end of things. In saying that I felt that the quality of the balls we were putting into the box from the wide areas could have been better."

"It's not a worry at this stage because we know these players can improve. It's only a worry when you can't improve any further and things aren't going well for you."

"We have a few problems but everything we are doing at the moment is focused on solving those problems."

"The expectation levels have risen because of what we achieved last season and we have to rise to that challenge."

It's often said that in life it can be as beneficial to be lucky instead of skilful and while no-one is suggesting that Livi have been lucky all the way - no one could be that lucky - the first professional European game at Almondvale ended so luckily for the club that no-one would have been surprised to learn that the players had all ran out and bought lottery tickets.

Livi toiled to take a stranglehold on the game and were careless in the middle of the park, with the resultant effect that the supply to the front line lacked quality.

Indeed, it took a brilliant diving save from Broto to deny Zarn a shock opener after fine work from Telser had opened up the home defence.

The best the West Lothian outfit had to offer was a weak header from Cherif straight into the arms of Vaduz goalkeeper Romouald Peiser, who then excelled by fisting clear a raking 22-yard free-kick from Rolando Zarate.

It was a most unconvincing first-half performance from Livi, who never managed any spell of dominance in front of a crowd almost stunned into silence.

The build-up lacked drive and pace and the eventual use of the high ball into the box caused little serious concern to the well organised men from Liechtenstein.

A spark of encouragement did come from some good work from Jose Camacho, but the young Spaniard's shot on the turn from inside the box flew wide of the far post.

There was little sign after the break of it getting any better for Livingston in terms of creating scoring opportunities, despite a significant rise in the tempo of the game.

At the other end, Broto had to scramble from his line to dive at the feet of Moreno Merenda as he darted through the middle. Quino produced some magic with a mazy run through the middle, but his shot from just outside the box skidded wide.

Livi could not even score when Vaduz were reduced to 10 men for the last 15 minutes after Marius Telser was dismissed for a second booking.

Wilson missed an absolute cinch when he slammed a cut-back from Bingham wide with the goal at his mercy.

Then with seconds remaining and the tie level at 1-1 from the first leg, Marco Perez fired in a corner from the right and Marius Zarn slammed the ball into the roof of the net from the edge of the box, but Croatian referee Ivan Novak indicated that he had blown for full-time before the ball hit the net.

Sadly the European celebration was dampened down within a matter of days as the Lions' had to go and play Celtic.

The Lions'' were boosted by the news of the signings of Burton O'Brien and David McNamee just hours before the closing of the transfer deadline, but while that was good news, most football fans were looking forward to a repeat of some of the wide open, attacking football that had characterised the games between these two clubs. But unlike the previous season's cracking clashes between the two, both clubs seemed as if they had a Euro hangover, which was worse for Livi though as they were beaten 2-0.

Celtic had initially threatened to rip the Lions' apart in the opening minutes as the tried and trusted partnership of Chris Sutton and Henrik Larsson caused problems Livingston were unable to deal with. Sutton drove wide in the 4th minute, with Marvin Andrews then having to make a brilliant challenge to deny the Swede who had surged on goal as the defender misjudged a high through ball.

And Larsson then saw a header deflected over the crossbar by Oscar Rubio, then a free-kick come off the outside of Javier Sanchez Broto's right hand post after 14 minutes as the pressure continued.

But it would take until the 26th minute for the breakthrough to arrive, Celtic moving in front with the simplest of goals, and one that will have had both Jim Leishman and David Hay pulling their hair out.

Steve Guppy picked up the ball on the left hand touchline and then swung in an inviting back post cross.

Andrews and Rubio appeared to leave the ball to each other, and Larsson took full advantage, rising unchallenged to power a header down into the bottom left hand corner of Broto's net.

The Swede then saw another free-kick tipped over the bar by the keeper as Celtic looked for a quick kill.

But the Lions' instead then enjoyed their best period of the half, with Lee Makel and Stuart Lovell, booked for pulling down Larsson, knocking the ball about freely in the middle of the park.

Gustavo Bahoken drove over Magnus Hedman's bar in the 32nd minute, with Francisco Quino going even closer just minutes later.

But all that good work was undone when the Lions' failed to perform the simple task of clearing a Guppy free-kick in the 38th minute.

Broto came for the winger's cross, only to see Rubio beat him to it, the defender only managing to head the ball straight up in the air.

Joos Valgaeren barged in to head the loose ball forward, and although Bahoken was on the goal line he could only drive the ball off Balde and watch on in horror as the ball nestled in his own net.

Livingston should have found themselves back in the game two minutes later, David Bingham failing to even hit the target with his header after being picked out by a Makel cross.

Celtic replaced Larsson and Sutton with Shaun Maloney and John Hartson in the 68th minute, and both subs immediately saw shots blocked by Rubio as the Hoops tried to step things up again.

Lions' sub Ronado Zarate had Hedman - who did not actually have a save to make throughout the 90 minutes, scrambling across his goal in the 73rd minute to make sure the striker's shot trickled wide.

Dadi contrived to miss the best chance of the game, scooping the ball over the Swedish international's bar after Bingham's cutback appeared to hand the former Aberdeen man an easy chance.

And as Celtic temporarily slackened off Bingham then chipped narrowly wide from ten yards out, although Hedman was again not required to actually make a save.

Petrov drove wide in the 78th minute, although at the other end Balde did well to get to the ball before Dadi as Livingston continued to push numbers forward, but it was all for nothing as the game ended in defeat for the Lions'.

The results kept going against the Lions' with the game against Dundee. Stuart Lovell and Philppe Brinquin were out for the clash, but it looked as if Lady Luck was on the team when the club took the lead after an own goal by Giorgi Nemsadze just after 30 minutes. It could have been 1-0 thanks to more conventional methods though as Burton O'Brien, making his SPL debut for Livi, had a fantastic chance just before Giorgi's goal, getting to a Eugene Dadi cross, but having a woeful first touch.

While Livi were having opportunities, the home team were having the majority of play and in the second half and it paid off in the 51st minute when they nabbed the equaliser thanks to Nacho Novo.

Novo was the danger man for the game but Rae got in on the scoring act with 13 minutes left on the clock after some nifty passing work from Nemsadze, Wilkie and Novo.

A win before going into their European game would have been the perfect tonic for the Lions'; sadly it wasn't to be as the club faced Rangers. The one consolation Livi had is that they weren't that different from Rangers. They may have been separated by most of the teams in the league but Rangers put in a scrappy performance, that while not pretty to watch, was enough to grab the three points.

However Livi fans were right to feel aggrieved when Toure-Maman was sent off after 60 minutes for a second bookable offence on Fernando Ricksen in the second half. Not that he didn't deserve to go off, it was a bad foul, but Kevin Muscat should also have been off, especially after an elbow strike, that could only be described as vicious, on the face of Juanjo Camacho.

The most worrying thing for Livi was the lack of competent finishing by Rolando Zarate who seemed to be struggling with the pressure he was under and every miss seemed to add to his agony.

The loss of Toure-Maman was the incident that turned the game though as Rangers were able to use the extra man to dominate the game, their first goal coming just minutes after the player was off as Maurice Ross, shrugged off David McNamee to fire a low shot under Broto.

Livi's frustration at the way things were going against them boiled over in the 87th minute when Marvin Andrews brought down Peter Lovenkrands and Barry Ferguson made no mistake in putting it away, getting the heads down.

There was some good news for the team in the run-up to their Euro game as Sturm Graz's manager Ivica Osim resigned after the team were beaten in the league.

Perhaps the Graz players had decided that they had to win for their ex-gaffer because win they certainly did, reminding Livi that they had come so far at home, but had a lot to learn if they wanted to progress at the Euro level.

Perhaps it was nerves, but the Lions'' passing was amongst the most casual - or jittery - that it ever had and while the team played OK, there was never any sense of them putting Graz under much pressure.

Marvin Andrews was one of the better Lions' performers, making two timely interventions to break up dangerous attacking moves from Graz.

The game could have changed for the better for Livi when Ekrem Dag nudged Barry Wilson off the ball just inside the penalty box, but Ukranian referee Shebek Sergey gave a free-kick right on the line, instead of the penalty that many thought it deserved.

Andrews failed to get on the end of the Camacho free-kick, leaving the diehard travelling fans wondering what would have been.

Just moments later the drama was at the other end of the pitch as Alain Masudi was sent down by Gary Bollan. Broto saved the kick though, but had to stretch right out to get to it.

It looked as if the first half was going to end in a nil nil draw, but a complacent defence paid the price in the 37th minute.

Graz's Imre Szabics ran down the left - and looked offside to many - but while the Lions' screamed for offside, instead of trying to get the ball back, he got the ball over to Arnold Wetl who put it away.

One nil at half time in an away European leg is not a bad result. Losing four goals in the space of eight minutes in the second half is another story altogether.

Livi fans may have many highlights to pick from as their best memory - getting to the SPL, winning trophies, even getting into Europe, the thumping of Queen of the South - but there's no contender for the worst on pitch moment. This was it.

Between the 51st and 59th minutes, Graz put four past the Lions', starting with Szabics. Then the goals came every two minutes with Dag scoring in the 53rd and Mudjiri scoring the next two.

It wasn't a case of the Lions' suddenly collapsing. Graz just made the most of some poor defending and had some luck as well. In most games of football, one or two moves would have paid off: here they all did, though the last goal was a howler and Mudjiri will be lucky if he ever scores another goal that easy in his career.

Somehow though, Livi didn't collapse even further and they fired back two goals against Graz, who had, admittedly, taken their foot off the gas after their goal-grabbing spree.

Zarate managed to grab Livi's first European goal in the game and in the 92nd minute Lovell fired in a shot from 25 yards out.

In contrast Celtic beat FK Suduva from Lithuania 8-1 at Celtic Park showing the Lions' that they may be playing with the big boys, but still had some distance to go.

The Euro hangover continued into the league game against Aberdeen. In fact, the team must have had jet lag as Aberdeen rattled in their first goal as most people were still getting into their seats in the first minute.

And while it wasn't a particularly bad tempered game, Eugene Dadi seemed to have a grudge against his old North-east club, throwing in some shocking tackles early on and it was no surprise that he was pulled off 25 minutes in. As Jim Leishman put it: "I felt the crowd were getting to him after the yellow card and felt he may get a red as well. I did not want us to be playing with ten men, so he had to come off."

Davide Xausa replacing him turned out to be an inspired move because - after a campaign of sustained pressure in the first half - he brought Livi back into the game with a six yard strike in the 56th minute.

Instead of firing Livi up though, the goal invigorated Aberdeen more and they put Livi under heavy fire and no one was surprised when they grabbed a winner with 15 minutes to go, McNaughton grabbing the winner.

Perhaps the team's minds were on the next European game, but against Hibs they were lacklustre with pundits summing the game up as a midfield battle. And as had happened so often before, a slight lapse in concentration saw Livi pay the price just before half-time as Brebner passed to Murray who beat Broto.

The second half saw Livi attack time and time again, but it wasn't to be and their only consolation as that they were only beaten by one goal.

Throughout their short existence, Livi have had many people put the boot in, from fans of other clubs and high profile fans of other teams (Brilliant satirist and author Christopher Brookmyre once remarked that Livingston weren't a real team). A lot of this animosity seems to have come from the fact that Livingston have had money to spend in the lower leagues when others have not. Whether this is a reflection of the Scottish psyche and the belief that the only way up is through hard graft or is something more simple like jealousy, it is hard to say. One thing was certain though, only the hardest of the hard would not have been impressed by the club's efforts in their second game against Sturm Graz.

Being three goals down made it look as if Livi were doomed from the start, but full credit to the team, they went out there and showed a real pride.

Graz sat back for the opening of the game, which suited Livi, allowing them to surge forward. Livi got an early break though when an over-enthusiastic Davide Xausa hard-thumped Gerald Strafner but the ref never spotted it. It may also be that he did see it but decided to ignore it as the Graz team were, in the words of fan Alan Peterson "going down rather easily" or as fellow fan Peter Dickson eloquently put it: "diving bastards."

At the other end, Broto was alert when he needed to be and pulled off a few fine saves.

And then Livi pulled into the lead just after the half hour mark with Gunther Neukirchner bringing down Bingham. Wilson made no mistake from the spot, letting Graz know that they may just have a game on their hands.

Graz responded just on the mark of half time with Szabics getting on to the end of a cross to put the away team on the score sheet.

But it wasn't over for that half just yet. Wilson almost restored Livingston's lead in stoppage time with a clever direct free-kick from 40 yards, when everyone was expecting a cross, which forced Hoffman to scramble back and paw it clear.

The game looked as if it was put beyond Livi just three minutes into the second half though as David Mudjiri got onto a pass from Masudi to give Graz a 2-1 lead.

Just seven minutes later, nightmare memories of the first leg were starting to come back as Szabics made it 3-1 for Graz.

Livi refused to go quietly though as just over 60 seconds later Xausa made it 3-2 after he got on to the end of a cross and volleyed it home.

An equaliser was grabbed with 13 minutes still on the clock, giving some fans a chance to wonder 'what if...' as Andrews put one past the keeper.

The seconds ticked down and as the 90th minute dawned, the Livi faithful realised that they next time they would see Europe would be on their holidays, but Barry Wilson showed them a touch of what could have been with a spectacular far out shot to make it 4-3. It was a gutsy win, but Graz still went through 8-6 on penalties.

After that, you would think that Graz would be gracious winners. Oh no. Despite the fact that Livi played down their players spitting on the home team, Sturm Graz president Hannes Kartnig told reporters: "The referee was a catastrophe. What the Scots played had nothing to do with football - that was rugby."

"My players were clearly the better ones. However, the referee let them be treated as if they were hunted game.

"For the first half an hour of the game we were totally up against it because the referee played on as Livingston's 12th man. He was very, very bad. I don't believe that it was a fair decision to award them a penalty for a start.

"I saw several Livingston players chasing Alain through the game and putting in bad tackles.

"We could have won the game having taken a deserved 3-1 lead, but if you get most of the decisions going against you lose interest."

Livi boss Jim Leishman was not happy with the rant.

He said, "This is a classic case of sour grapes. They came over here 5-2 up expecting to win again easily and we gave them a real fright."

At 1-0 down they were scared and their players started rolling about all over the place and play-acting. And if he wants to talk about discipline then he should look at the Sky TV pictures and see his player clearly spitting on Gary Bollan.

"We kicked a player out of the club for doing that earlier this year - but if he wants to condone that sort of thing then that's his problem.

"I think blaming the referee for the defeat is very poor. Look at the quality of our goals. Do you think the referee caused them?"

"Why can't he just accept that we played better and deserved what we got? We did the people of West Lothian proud.

"If he wants someone to blame then perhaps he could start with his defence. They lost six goals to a side playing European football for the first time.

"I can't wait to get a chance to play this side again after these remarks. Then we will see how far we've come."

With Europe over, Livi looked to the league for some comfort.

Didn't happen and the SPL curse of doing well one season, doing bad the next seemed to be staying true to form.

There was a decent turn out for the game and Livi tried to lift themselves from the Euro defeat. And by half-time it seemed to be working. The Lions' had enjoyed the best run of play and went one up just four minutes from the break thanks to a goal from Barry Wilson, but he did have some help from Jambo Kevin McKenna.

The defender had been trying to get on the end of a Broto punt up the park, but messed it up and sent the ball to Wilson, who rounded keeper Craig Gordon and scored. And unlike an earlier goal by David Bingham which was ruled out, this one stood.

Hearts didn't waste too much time in the second half though, bring the equaliser in just two minutes after the game restarted. Phil Stamp scored with a quality shot straight into the corner.

The second half was fairly even matched but Livi squandered two great chances to win the game with Xausa hitting the bar, and then Quino sending the ball deep into the stand.

A point was good, but the team needed to discover it's winning ways in the league again and they started a seven game unbeaten run with a 3-2 battle against Dundee United.

Despite having five goals in it, this game was a slow starter, the first goal - a United strike - not coming until Derek Lilley put one past Broto in the 45th minute.

United kept the scoring going just shy of the hour mark when Jim Mcintyre gave the home team a serious advantage.

But Livi came back into the game just shy of 70 minutes when Gary Bollan scored. Barry Wilson made it all even in 74 minutes to silence the home fans after a one-two with Roly Zarate. And the home fans silence turned to jeers of rage when Eugene Dadi tapped home the winner for Livi just 4 minutes later.

From three goal to five goals. That was what the Lions' put by Motherwell in the next league game. Unlike the last game, the scoring opened early on this one with Lee Makel scoring in the ninth minute with a peach of a left footer goal from 30 yards out, easily beating Fir Park keeper Stevie Woods.

The half-time score was 1-0, giving no indication of the goal deluge that was to follow and it started with Cherif Toure Maman nabbing the first of his two goals with a cheeky chip in the 48th minute and his second following ten minutes later after a Motherwell defensive mishap.

Khelad Kemas gave the home team some inspiration and brief hope when he pulled one back for the Fir Parkers in 79 minutes, but it was not to be long lasting as David Bingham made it 4-1 with a chip from the left hand edge of the box.

Stevie Woods's day of hell was made complete after Xausa scored Livi's fifth right on 90 minutes with a tight shot.

The team stayed unbeaten, but only managed a draw, against Dunfermline as November started, and they rode their luck for that point. In truth the Pars should have cleaned up in this game. Craig Brewster opened the scoring after a goal-free first half, putting the ball past Broto in the 47th minute.

But it was Lee Bullen who was pretty much the unofficial man of the match after he did a fantastic run from his own end of the pitch, looking for goal number two, covered about 60 yards, was in the Livi box and then sklumfed it right off the park. That run pretty much summed up the Pars's day as they had a good few attacking chances but never finished them off.

At the other end, Barry Wilson had a great chance to level the scoring but Ruitenbeek pulled off a great save. There was no such save in the 79th minute though when Cherif Toure Mann scored to bring the Lions' back into the game.

The third round game against St Johnstone was finally going ahead - after a couple of cancellations - and it wasn't a great tie by any stretch of the imagination. Not to say it was dull - there was certainly some decent attacking football - but it wasn't a classic.

Livi nearly found their cup run grinding to a halt from the first minute with Chris Hay firing over the bar for the Saints. Hay was a consistent threat in the first half for Livi and only a busy box and some excellent goalkeeping from Broto kept Livi in it.

It could have been a nine-man Livi in the second half as well after Brinquin and Xausa were both booked in the first half. Jim Leishman decided to rest both players for the second half, putting on Bingham and McNamee. And it was an inspired idea as McNamee was instrumental in the game's only goal, coming on the 60th minute. He pushed forward with the ball, passed to Eugene Dadi, who shot for goal, Toure Maman Cherif got in the road, but happily it came off him and went into the net and set up a game later in the month against Dundee United.

The winning streak continued with a 3-0 thumping of Partick Thistle at Almondvale, but the result doesn't tell the full story. In fact, based on the first half performance, Thistle were unlucky not to be three goals up.

Livi old boy Alex Burns had a chance to score against his old team mates after Gerry Britton sent him on his way just 13 minutes into the game. And he wasn't shy for the rest of the half either, with Broto being called on time and time again to make magnificent saves.

Quino was brought off at half-time and Barry Wilson put on in his place and it transformed the team.

The difference was noticeable almost immediately with Dadi putting in the first goal just two minutes after kick-off. The fans didn't have to wait long for the second either - just five minutes later - as Marvin Andrews put one in after a corner and then David Bingham made it three six minutes after that to put the game out of sight for the visiting Jags.

"Nothing lasts forever," as the old saying goes, and the seven game undefeated run was extinguished by Dundee United in a game that was full of incident.

David McNamee and Eugene Dadi threatened early on with a series of efforts on goal, but United retaliated with Charlie Miller unlucky not to score from a free-kick - David Bingham saving the day there - and it looked as if the fans were in for a treat of a game.

Sadly, it turned more into a scrap than a treat as Rubio clashed hard with Lilley and he then tackled Thompson late, leading to a warning from the ref. Thompson got his revenge though on Rubio, resulting in him being warned by ref Mike McCurry.

On the ball, both sides had their chances but as the game passed 30 minutes, it looked as if it would be a no-scoring first half.

But that all changed in the 37th minute after Broto punched the ball clear, but a miss-hit saw it coming right back as Derek Lilley got to it and headed it past Broto.

Just like the Thistle game, the second half saw the team come out fired up, Toure Maman Cherif nearly getting an equaliser early on.

The hot point of the game though came 20 minutes later after McCurry blew for a penalty.

The ref believed that Rubio had elbowed United sub Allan Smart as they both fell after chasing the ball. Rubio was red carded for it, but Smart followed him off the pitch as the referee believed Smart had swung at Rubio while he lay on the ground.

Lilley had no hesitations in stepping up and thumping the penalty home to make it 2-0, giving United the money-spinning tie in the next round against Celtic.

It was back to the league for Livi - and an away game against Killie - but failure from the cup followed them there.

It was a poor performance from the Lions' - though admittedly Killie weren't exactly world beaters on the day either - and the team did have some chances, notably a fantastic run by Toure Maman Cherif, where he beat three players and had a go at goal, only for Gordon Marshall's legs to stop the ball going in. The rebound had possibilities but Dadi put it wide.

At the other end, Paul Di Giacomo scored first for Killie just after the half hour mark while Gary McSwegan killed the game in injury time. Jim Leishman was reflective about how it had gone: "Football is all about scoring goals and we certainly had the chances, but it just didn't happen for us."

The Lions' could have done with a pick-me-up after that. Sadly all they got was another put-down. This time at the hands of Celtic and specifically the club's super Swede Henrik Larsson.

Celtic needed the result to be top of the league, while the Lions' needed it to bounce back and while the points went the way of the Glasgow side, the scoreline wasn't actually a proper reflection of the game.

Celtic gaffer Martin O'Neill said after the match that he thought the Hoops played poorly; that may be the case but it fails to give Livi the credit they deserve.

Celtic took the lead from a penalty after six minutes. It started with a poor clearance by Broto which ended up back in the box. Stillian Petrov was looking dangerous when he collided with Marvin Andrews, going down hard and eventually needing nearly 20 stitches.

A chunk of the 10,000 crowd weren't impressed with the penalty call from the incident and they were even more displeased seconds later as Larsson slotted the ball away for the visitors to take the lead.

Livi took the game to Celtic in an effort to try and get back into the game. Toure-Maman, teamed up with David Bingham, only for their efforts to be in vain as he sent the ball over the crossbar.

Half-time saw the scoreline stay the same and there was a feeling that Livi could still get a goal and efforts from a number of players including Zarate, Andres and Toure-Maman reminded Celtic that this wasn't going to be their easiest game of the season.

But Livi's hopes of getting anything from this match were dashed with seven minutes to go as Larsson went on a fantastic run, beating Rubio and Brinquin and scoring the second from the edge of the box.

Livingston paid the penalty again in the next game as they shared the points with Dundee.

It had all started so well with Juanjo Camacho scoring in 80 seconds to put the Lions' one up after a David Bingham assist.

Dundee didn't take that lying down though and battle commenced with both teams attacking, looking to dominate the

171

game. And the Lions' could have had it all if it hadn't been for Rubio being involved in another penalty incident, this time tripping up Steve Lovell in the 71st minute.

And while Broto had pulled off a number of fantastic saves, the penalty wasn't one of them, giving the management team concern at how the Lions'' were letting these happen.

And the red cards reappeared in the next game - a seven goal smasher against Rangers at Ibrox.

It may have been a cold December, but no one in the ground felt the chill for the 90 minutes as this was a Christmas cracker - even if it was three weeks early.

Any Rangers fan turning up 20 minutes for the game missed their team rout Livi by three goals, the scoring account opened by Barry Ferguson and a well-taken free-kick after just eight minutes. Shota Arveladze started his hat trick just two minutes later after getting his head onto a cross from Neil McCann.

You would have hoped that Livi had seen the weakness in their defence after that, but sadly they didn't and the lesson was handed to them again in the 17th minute, this time the high ball coming from Fernando Ricksen.

Livi spent the rest of the first half under siege, with chances at the other end being practically non-existent except for a miss by Bollan after a Lee Makel corner.

The second half pretty much started as the first had - with Rangers scoring. It became 4-0 after Shota grabbed a fourth, this time from a shot next to the penalty spot.

More or less in reply to that, Livi fired on Roly Zarate, but many feared it was too late for the ex-Real Madrid striker to do anything to influence the game.

Rangers fans feel that after that, the team relaxed a bit, while Lions' supporters feel that Rangers stuck at it, but Livi resurfaced with their pride. The truth is somewhere inbetween probably, but what cannot be denied is that just minutes after going four-up, Rangers found their goal lead slashed.

It started with Fernando Ricksen bringing down Burton O'Brien 25 yards out. Zarate took the free-kick and rattled it between the posts to make it 4-1.

Rangers weren't overly concerned by the goal, but they were by the second in the 72nd minute as Wilson pulled another back, thanks to a pass from David Bingham.

The Gers were given a boost with Gary Bollan being sent off for his second bookable offence in the 75th minute, but they failed to capitalise on it. The Ibrox stiff upper lip certainly quivered with just three minutes left as Zarate managed to make it 4-3, but the bluenoses were able to cling onto their one-goal advantage to take the three points.

Not that the drama was over. Philippe Brinquin found himself red-carded for comments to a linesman after the full-time whistle was blown.

Both red carded players were out for the next game, just three days later, against Hearts.

And again, it went badly for the Lions' from early on, Andy Kirk starting the scoring for the Jambos in just the fifth minute after he was able to easily beat Rubio to get the ball from a Scott Severin pass and then beat Broto to give the home support something to cheer about.

The goal acted as a splash of cold water across the face of the Livi players and they wasted no time in taking the game to their east coast cousins, and while half time saw the visiting Lions' a goal down, it looked as if that was just a matter of time.

And indeed it was. The game was squared up in the 63rd minute with Zarate heading home a Barry Wilson header.

From that it looked as if Livi were going to romp the game. Someone forgot to point that out to Rubio though, who gave away a penalty with 20 minutes left on the clock after he brought down Mark de Vries. Andy Kirk duly obliged to make it 2-1.

And while many people were fuming at Rubio for costing them the game, it was quickly forgotten as tragedy hit the club.

The day before the club's game with Hibs, Eugene Dadi returned home to find his girlfriend had committed suicide.

Lydia Pritelli, 41, had been visiting Dadi for a month when she decided to hang herself. The couple had got together after Dadi's dad had passed away and Lydia had been a comfort to the player for many years.

She had been suffering from depression before her death.

Eugene wanted to throw himself back into football and play against Hibs, but he was talked out of it and the club held a minute's silence for her and also former director Bob Clark, who died the same week in December.

The game was muted, some believe out of respect for Dadi in the stands as if most of the players' hearts and thoughts were elsewhere.

Livi had most of the play in the first half with Zarate and Colgan putting a lot of pressure onto Nick Colgan with shots inside the box, but Hibs held on for a draw at half-time.

The Edinburgh team picked up the pace in the second half and took the lead in the 55th minute after Tom McManus flicked the ball on to Ian Murray, who wasted no time in volleying a shot in.

This fired up the Hibees, but was too much for Livi, who capitulated easily, a second goal being given away just 11 minutes later with Craig James taking advantage of a Broto deflection to get the second.

Livi did manage to get one back, but it was way too late, coming in as one of the last kicks of the ball with Philippe Brinquin scoring after Colgan parried away a Zarate free-kick.

The next game might have taken place just four days before Christmas but there was no festive cheer at it - and there certainly wasn't a Christmas card going to linesman Tom Murphy after he cost the Lions' three points.

Eugene Dadi was a last-minute addition to the team - Jim Leishman letting him run out against his old club because he felt it would help and due to the amount of well-wishing cards he had received - and he nearly put the Lions' up after 11 minutes but for a good save from David Preece.

The first half was entertaining enough and the Dons nearly nabbed a goal just before half-time after an Eric Deloumeaux free-kick was powerfully headed down towards the bottom corner by Russell Anderson. But Broto was able to get to it to keep the Lions' in the game.

In the 48th minute the Lions' took the lead - unless you were Tom Murphy - after Barry Wilson sent in a fantastically strong cross that Andrews got on the end of to score. Darren Young cleared the ball, but it was clearly over.

Murphy was at it again after David Bingham put the ball through to sub Colin McMenamin and he shot at goal. But before it could cross the line, Murphy had his flag up for offside - a decision that not many people agreed with.

But Livi stuck at it and were unlucky in the dying seconds of the game after the ball took a crazy deflection off Davide Xausa, but it went over the bar.

174

Christmas came a day late for Livi with their home game against Dundee United but the three points - and three goals were certainly welcome, putting the Arabs at the bottom of the league.

The Lions' wasted no time in showing their supremacy in the game, with the first goal coming after eight minutes with Juanjo Camacho scoring from a Philippe Brinquin cross.

The second was rattled in five minutes after half time when Marvin Andrews got on the end of a Lee Makel cross and Bingham cemented the result with a cheeky chip after a one-two with Xausa.

Late Christmas presents also came for John Robertson and Allan Preston. Robbo decided to go and manage Inverness Caledonian Thistle, ending his four and a half years with Livi. His departure meant Preston was promoted up from coaching the under-21s to coaching the first team. The move was prompted not only by his ability but also as a reward for his loyalty to the club, after he turned down the chance to join Robbo up north.

With the changes in place, Livi set about winning their last game of the year, a home leg against Motherwell.

The Fir Park side didn't make it easy for the Lions' though, but it was a cracking game of football to end the year with.

Motherwell opened the attacking with James McFadden snatching a chance early on, but Philippe Brinquin managed to keep the ball out of the net.

Livi then upped the offensive and 15 minutes in, Francisco Quino had a great chance, but he squandered it, shooting wide.

The Zarate had a great chance less than 60 seconds later with a freekick that bounced off the post. And moments later he had another chance after being set up by Xausa.

Every member of the Lions' was kept busy though and Broto had to earn his paypacket to beat off a great shot by Derek Adams.

The second half saw more of the same, with one side attacking and then the other going on the counter attack.

Marvin Andrews had a number of great chances, all foiled, but the Trinidadian's biggest contribution to the game was playing a part in a David Bingham goal getting chopped off.

It was just before the 55th minute when Lee Makel cross the ball in and Bingham got to the end of it, but ref Craig Thompson felt that Marvin had hindered 'Well's Dubourdeau in trying to get to the ball and chopped off the strike.

The Steelmen kept themselves in the game, but with three minutes to go, Michael Hart bolted down the wing and put the cross over to Zarate who managed to slide in and get a touch to it to grab a goal and three points.

It had been an eventful year for Livi - unpredictable as ever - and that uncertainty seemed to first foot the club as their January 2 game saw them crash 2-0 away to Dunfermline.

To be fair, the Lions' had eight players out, Broto was fighting a back injury and the pitch was in a terrible condition.

None of that stopped them from trying to take the lead just eight minutes in with Gary Bollan putting in a good cross to the end of Marvin Andrew's head, but it was directed more or less straight at Derek Stillie.

Ref Garry Mitchell must have still be feeling cheery from the festive season after he let Stillie stay on the park after he brought down Xausa outside the box.

Dunfermline had a few decent chances in the first half, but the terrible state of the pitch thwarted them and it looked as if it was going to be a deserved draw at the half-way mark before Stevie Crawford got on the end of a Jason Dair ball, ducked past Andrews and thumped the ball past Broto from the edge of the box.

The second half got off to a bad start for the Lions' as Broto was taken off just four minutes in after his back injury flared up and he was subbed for David McEwan.

Sadly, one of his first action was to pick the ball out the back of the net after a rebound from a saved Craig Brewster shot fell to Crawford and he slotted in his second of the game.

Both sides had scrappy chances after that, but the first three points of the year went to the Pars instead of the Lions', and the team had a few weeks to reflect on what they had to do to improve their season as that was the last game before the winter shutdown which ran until January 25 and when the Lions' would meet again, it would be a changed team as Broto followed David Fernandez and moved on to Celtic.

This left McEwan as the team number one 'keeper and no one could fault his first game – a cup tie against Dunfermline.

The drama was at the opposite end of the pitch from him at first though with Quino scoring in the 26th minute after a Gary Bollan free-kick came off him. Bollan, for some reason was noted as the official scorer, but the ball definitely came off Quino, who had good cause to feel aggrieved at not getting a goal bonus. Perhaps it was a form of farewell gift for Bollan who would join Dundee United just days later.

Livi kept the pressure up for the rest of the first half, Zarate having a good chance with a header and Rubio also threatening to score.

Livi did a lot of attacking from cross balls in the first half and the Pars seem to pick up some tips for the second 45 minutes. If imitation is the sincerest form of flattery then the Lions' should have been overjoyed at the compliment being paid to them. Instead they were worried as McEwan seemed to struggle at times with the ball coming in, unsure of where he should be.

His confidence took a dip in the 62nd minute though as Dunfermline pulled themselves back into the game – and it came from a cross. Barry Nicholson put the ball over, McEwan did well to get a palm to it and stop it going in, but he was powerless to stop Steven Hampshire getting the ball from there, putting it to Stevie Crawford at the back post, who elegantly tapped it in to equalise.

Dunfermline were fired up from that and had some good chances, but the Livi defence held on and McEwan redeemed himself in the 88th minute when he bravely threw himself at the feet of Crawford to stop him thumping in another goal.

Livi also tried for a last-gasp winner with a Rubio header, but it was cleared from the line and the teams had to settle for meeting a week later in a cup replay.

But first there were a few league games to take care of, the starting one being an away leg against Partick Thistle.

The first 30 minutes of the game were a relatively quiet affair with Livi having the upper hand thanks to some superior attacking, but Thistle 'keeper Kenny Arthur keep the home team in it.

Nothing could have stopped the opener in the 33rd minute though as Marvin Andrews got his head onto the end of a Lee Makel corner.

It only took the Jags five minutes to recover though with ex-Livi Sandy Burns thumping in a low 25-yard free-kick.

Thistle tried to capitalise on this in the second half and McEwan was feeling the pressure, which was all too evident when he gaffed with a corner, forcing a goalmouth scramble before danger was averted.

It was looking as if the Glasgow team would be the first ones to get a second goal, but Livi surprised the 3541 fans as Zarate got on the end of a ball from Marvin Andrews and snapped it into the net from 14 yards out.

Colin McMenamin came on in the 76th minute for the Lions' to replace Xausa who had been booked for an off-the-ball incident and within minutes, he showed why the club had picked him up the previous summer, curling in a beautiful shot to make it 3-1.

The next bit of club business took place off the pitch as the Lions' signed Julian Maidana, Fernando Pasquinelli, Alan Main and Tom English.

Not that they were any use in the next game, a 4-0 drubbing by Kilmarnock.

Warning signs were posted by Killie just six minutes into the game as they attacked with Kris Boyd having a dig after a defensive gaffe, but David McEwan managed to get to this one.

Boyd was instrumental in Killie's opener in the 21st minute. He was fouled, leading Stevie Fulton to fire over a free-kick into the box that Andy McLaren got onto the end of.

At this point Livi were still in the game and Davide Xausa could have made it 1-1 not long afterwards after some passing work from Makel and Bingham, but Colin Meldrum managed to put the shot past the post.

The second of the two goals in the first half came from Peter Canero in the 34th minute with a header at the edge of the six-yard box.

You started to sense that things weren't going Livi's way when Makel was taken off to be replaced by Cherif Toure Maman, but some fans felt they still had a chance, especially after McEwan made a decent save just before half time, thwarting Boyd.

Within four minutes of the second half starting, the game was put beyond Livi with Boyd thumping in a 25-yard smash that cracked off the underside of the bar to go over the line.

Completing the woe for the Lions' and their fans was the fourth goal in the 70th minute when Mahood put over a left-wing free-kick which Marvin Andrews accidentally headed into the path of McLaren, allowing him to volley the ball in from just eight yards out.

Afterwards Jim Leishman was philosophical, saying, "It's easy to say it was a bad day at the office but rather than jump in just now and criticise we will need to sit down and discuss just what went wrong."

Obviously whatever time and date that meeting was set for wasn't before the next game, the cup replay with Dunfermline.

Both sides were already quids in to the tune of £165,000 as the match was being shown on Sky – and the winner would be facing Hibs in another televised clash.

And perhaps it was TV nerves for David McEwan – or stage fright – but he cost the team the game and the cup fortunes after two gaffes.

The team were boosted running out though with the very welcome return of Stuart Lovell.

Dunfermline showed they were determined to win from the first minute with Crawford and Brewster combining to tear Livi apart, but the latter put it wide.

Twenty minutes later Jason Dair had a fantastic shot after some great passing to and from Brewster.

Livi didn't stay down and out for too long though with Zarate putting Derek Stillie under immense pressure for a spell, including a fantastic effort after beating Scott Wilson and a great free-kick that Stillie was lucky to get to.

But even though there were no goals in it, the first half belonged to Livi and they were unlucky not to grab the opener in the 43rd minute as Sean Kilgannon rattled in a great free-kick that McEwan managed to get to.

The onslaught continued in the second half and David McEwan was having a great game with a number of saves until the 68th minute.

He stopped Mason from scoring, leading to a corner which ended up at the feet of Brewster about 18 yards from goal. He whacked it. But the Livi fans weren't too worried as McEwan appeared to have it covered. No one could have predicted that it would slip right through his hands though - every 'keepers nightmare.

The lad's confidence took a knock after that, especially in kicking out the ball, but Livi tried to stay in it, exposing themselves at the back.

As injury time started, the die-hards were still hopeful but Brewster killed that off after McEwan tried to clear the ball, but it ended up with Brewster who then lobbed him from about 35 yards out to kill the game and Livi's cup hopes.

Afterwards, it was reported that the young player burst into tears in the changing room, but Jim Leishman refused to put the boot in.

He said, "It was a reality check for him. We threw him in at the deep end when Javier Broto left for Celtic, but he is a young lad and he will learn."

179

The last thing the Lions' needed after that was a game against an on-form team like Celtic, but that was what they got and it was a game that gave Celtic fans heart palpitations.

Livi took the game to Celtic and had their first attempt on goal in the third minute with Zarate taking a free-kick, but after that Celtic fired up - especially their super Swede Henrik Larsson.

He missed two great chances but Marvin Andrews and in-goal Alan Main held him off on each occassion.

But he looked a cert to score in the 14th minute as he jumped up to get on to the end of a Chris Sutton cross which Alan Main did well to get to.

However in getting to the ball he walloped into Gus Bahoken and had to come off with a badly-gashed mouth, which was a shattered jaw.

Larsson coming off would be a worry for Celtic fans but it was a boost and a half for the Lions' as Stuart Lovell and Burton O'Brien pushed the advantage, thwarting Celtic from getting the lead goal.

However stopping the Hoops came at the cost of Livi not doing much at the opposing goalmouth and come half-time the game was still at a draw, a scoreline neither side could really argue about.

And Livi got the second half off to a sensational start in the 52nd minute when a pass-back to Hedman from Joss Valgaeren was too short. As Hedman came to get the ball, Zarate sneaked round the Swede and put the ball in the empty goal.

The game upped a notch after that and Marvin Andrews was an inspiration in holding off the Celts, but it was one of his tackles in the 76th minute that lead to the equaliser.

A foul on Sutton by Marvin lead to Shaun Maloney having a crack at goal that came off the bar, but Momo Sylla was able to get it in the net to make it 1-1.

The last 15 minutes saw Livi well and truly under siege but they hung on for grim life and a point, but in the 85th minute that was taken away from them after Bahoken set in event a course of action that would lead to a Celtic goal.

He tripped up Valgaeren on the edge of the box leading to another Maloney free-kick, which Main was able to get to, but he couldn't hold it and Sutton was able to knock the rebound into the net to grab the Glasgow team all three points.

The other half of the Old Firm was up next for the first game in March and the result was the same with Livi crashing 2-1 again, this time at home.

It was a different sort of line-up for the game against Rangers with Dadi on the bench, Rubio out and Lee Makel and Barry Wilson brought back in.

The team got off to a great start with Burton O'Brien having a great chance from eight yards out, but in the hustle and bustle of the goalmouth, he managed to sky it over the bar.

Rangers, realising that they had a game on their hands, started to pick up and in the eighth minute Amoruso nabbed the opener, getting onto the end of a Mikel Arteta corner and putting it past Alan Main.

There were fears that it was 2-0 just five minutes later when Shota Arveladze scored, but it was ruled offside.

But there was no such call just two minutes later when Neil McCann raced down the left-hand wing of Livi's half, crossed the ball over to Arveladze at the back post who headed it into goal.

There were two more blows for Livi in the first half. First was when Burton O'Brien collided with Barry Ferguson and had to leave the pitch to get stitches and then Rangers' Arteta kicking Brinquin after a fair, but spirited, challenge.

Livi still hoped to get something out of the game and that was evident by the bringing on of Dadi for the second half, but Rangers looked the more dangerous team, having another goal chalked off for offside.

With just 20 minutes to go though, Livi were thrown a lifeline after Fernando Ricksen tripped Zarate inside the box, giving the Lions' a penalty. Zarate took the kick, but Klos was able to get to it with his feet.

The Lions' did get on the scoresheet in the dying seconds of the game, but it was too little too late, giving Rangers a six-point lead at the top and leaving Livi fighting relegation at the other end.

The following week, things picked up with Livi netting £70,000 from Livingston's Almondvale Shopping Centre and a point from a lively away game with Dundee.

The final result may have been nothing each, but it certainly wasn't a dull game.

Dundee were the more attacking of the two teams, but Livi - playing quite aggresively - soaked up the attacks and Cherif Toure-Maman and Julian Maidana were making sure no one got through, but the Dundee fans felt they should have been booked for some of their challenges.

The first booking fell to Gustave Bahoken after he ruthlessly brought down Steve Lovell in the 35th minute. Fortunately, nothing came of it and it was just one of numerous free-kick opportunities squandered by Dundee during the first 45 minutes.

Livi's best chance came in the 43rd minute after a Stuart Lovell free-kick found the head of Dadi but 'keeper Julian Speroni was able to get it just past the post.

Dundee kept on the pressure for the second half and as the Livi defence tired, Alan Main was all that kept the score sheet clean, particularly against a frisky Nacho Novo.

Novo did find the net at one point though around the 50th minute, netting the ball after a pass from Fabian Caballero. And while Dundee getting a goal at that point would have been a fair reflection of the game, it was ruled off side to the relief of the Livi fans.

Livi came more into the attacking side of the game in the last 30 minutes - Lee Makel in particular having a great shot - but when ref Willie Young blew for full time, it was still an empty scoresheet and a share of the points.

A point was better than none, was the reflection of many fans and it was an attitude that carried them through to the next game, a home clash against Hearts.

While it may have ended a 1-1 draw, the first half saw Hearts stomp all over the Lions'. Phil Stamp, well, stamped all over Livi, scoring in the eight minute with a fantastic 24-yard shot after Gus Bahoken screwed up a header to clear a ball from Jean Louis Valois.

Hearts kept up the pressure, but were thwarted by Main on a regular basis, while Livi had a chance in the 26th minute when Dadi was on goal, but he goofed it.

Bahoken's terrible first half was noticed by the management and he was pulled off at half time with Oscar Rubio coming on in his place.

He may just be one man, but bringing him on made all the difference to the team and just after the hour mark, the super sub nabbed the equaliser, getting his head on to the end of a Lee Makel pass.

The pressure was kept on the Lions' though and while it was Rubio who brought them back into the game, it was Alan Main who made sure they stayed in the game, pulling off a number of saves. Even Hearts gaffer Craig Levein had to concede that after the match, saying, "It was the goalkeeper who kept Livingston going. At a critical period in the first half when we were a goal ahead Alan made two really outstanding saves."

Boosted by the good team performance - though finishing had been a problem - the Lions' were in good shape for the away clash with Dundee United.

The Lions' walked away with the three points - mostly thanks to Marvin Andrews - but any fan thinking that a corner had been turned for the team after some average performances would be deluding themselves because, in truth, Livi were decent, but United were fairly dire. In fact, apart from a 15 minute spell, the game was Livi all the way, having the majority of possession and attacks by far.

It was only one goal that won it and the fans had to wait for it as it wasn't delivered until three minutes from the end, but the three points were welcome in the still-tight relegation battle of that season.

Before the next game there was a blow to the squad as Marvin Andrews picked up a thigh strain while on international duty with Trinidad & Tobago. He limped out of a Gold Cup qualifier against Antigua and then made it worse a few days later during a 3-1 loss to Cuba.

Missing Andrews may have been one of the reasons the Lions' threw away the good work at their next game. Aberdeen were a team Livi always stood a chance with and the omens looked good just two minutes into this clash as Stuart Lovell headed in a corner from Camacho.

But it started to turn sour 20 minutes later after a tough tackle between Bahoken and Derek Young, which lead to the Livi South African being taken off, Barry Wilson coming on for him.

Nine minutes later the Dons managed to equalise when Young beat Alan Main to get to the end of a Chris Clark corner.

And while heads didn't go down then, the spirits were dampened just minutes later as Paul Sheerin had what was the jammiest, flukiest goal of that season as he screwed up a cross which somehow ended up past Main.

The second half saw a perked up Livi go right at the Dons, particularly from the 70th minute onwards. There was an urgency and uptempo spirit about the side as they pushed to get back into the game, but the ball went everywhere except between the sticks and the game ended up 2-1.

Another loss looked on the cards just before the splitting of the league to the top six and bottom six with the game against Hibs. It was the debut first-team game for Argentinean striker Fernando Pasquinelli and he certainly was keen to impress, helping to give Livi an early dominance in the game.

Not everyone was so sharp though and Davide Xausa not being alert enough to notice that he was offside cost the Lions' a goal. A silly lunge by Hibs Yannick Zambernardi ended up in the back of the Hibs's net and it would have counted if Xausa hadn't been spotted offside.

As the game went on though, Livi seemed to tire and as they looked forward to half-time, Hibs managed to get a goal as Alen Orman headed in a cross.

Livi thought they were getting a tactical boost in the second half as Tam McManus was stretchered off after a challenge with Stuart Lovell.

It turned out to be anything but though as just five minutes after coming on, he curled in a great free-kick after Marvin Andrews brought down Derek Townsley on the edge of the box.

It was looking as if the Lions' would be empty-handed from this match, but that all changed in the 87th minute. Pasquinelli showed some pace to get the ball off of Townsley and the ball ended up with Barry Wilson, who slotted it home.

Hibs's three points were chopped to one just two minutes later as Burton O'Brien fired home a shot.

The next game, an away leg with Aberdeen, may have been the signal for the run-in to the end of the season, but there was nothing dour about this one.

The home Dons cried for a penalty in the 12th minute after Phil McGuire went down after a soft challenge from Lee Makel, but ref John Underhill blanked the requests.

Livi had a decent change in the 21st minute with a shot by Barry Wilson, but it came off the post.

And just minutes later Hinds scored to put the Dons one up after skinning Julian Maidana and putting the ball between Alan Main's legs.

Livi tried to pull themselves back in. Stuart Lovell had a great chance with a 25-yard blast that Dons 'keeper Peter Kjaer was lucky to get to. He was beat by a Zarate 30 yard free-kick, but that came off the woodwork.

The game entered a lull until the 70th minute when it heated up again. First, Maidana thumped a great shot in that was unlucky to come off the bar. Then, just over 60 seconds later, Barry Wilson was harshly red carded - a yellow would have done - after verbal jousting with McGuire over a possible Livi penalty. McGuire was pushed by Wilson and that was enough for John Underhill to send him packing.

To make matters worse, no penalty was blown for. Fired up - by justified anger as much as anything - Livi pushed to try and get back in the game, but it ended with Aberdeen getting all the points.

It was a happier - and scrappier - tale the following week with a home leg against Partick Thistle, a game which winning would mean the Lions' being safe from any possible relegation.

The best description for this one would be foul - not because of the weather, but because it was a heavily battled match.

Livi took the lead with a Xausa strike in the 25th minute which was nicely set up for him by a cross from Stuart Lovell.

The game was relatively quiet after that until a minute before half-time as Zarate thumped in a great free-kick.

Thistle's David Lilley gave the Firhill men some hope in injury-time when he headed in a Gerry Britton's cross.

The second-half had scarecely started when Juanjo Camacho gave Livi the two-goal lead again.

Apart from a flurry of substitutions - Milne on for Ross in the 56th minute, Andy Gibson for Burns in the 70th, Quino for Xausa in the 74th and Bingham for Pasquinelli - and some more fouling, there was little else in the match, but the three points that came at the end meant that Livi had theoretically manage to defy the naysayers who said that the club would be one-season wonders and go back to the first division.

Just as well that they saved their league campaign with that game because it all went to hell after that, starting with a game against Dundee United, which was a sore one for the Lions' to lose as they completely dominated the game.

Right from the start it was obvious that the omens weren't good with United going one up just two minutes in after Jim McIntyre headed home Derek Lilley's cross.

After that the game was more or less Livi all the way, with numerous efforts to try and score, but at half-time it was still 1-0 to the Arabs.

The second half saw more of the same - and fresh legs in the form of Brittain for Makel in the 51st minute, Quino for Xausa in the 68th and Bingham for Zarate at the same time - until David Bingham headed in a cross from Phillipe Brinquin to make it 1-1 with 12 minutes left on the clock.

It looked as if the points were going to shared - which would have been a travesty given Livingston's dominance, but better than nothing - until the dying seconds when Charlie Miller managed to get his foot to the ball, which also deflected off a number of Livi players - to give them a very late lead and three points.

The last game of the season at Almondvale against Hibs should have been a joyful affair. As it was, there was happiness, but the strongest feeling was more a general sense of relief of having survived the season than anything else. It was also emotional for David Bingham who, having played more than 200 games in his five years at the club, was rewarded with a trophy to go with an incredible amount of memories.

But before that presentation - witnessed by just over 5000 fans - there was a lacklustre game where Scott Brown scored two goals, in the 38th and 69th minutes, and Pasquinelli pulled one back with minutes to go.

As the season looked forward to its last weekend, Dominic Keane told the *Edinburgh Evening News* that he was planning some changes to the management structure of the club with hints that Jim Leishman would be going off-pitch and upstairs full time.

The good news about the next game was that the winning streak came to an end with an away game against Motherwell - but that's only because it was the last game of the season and it was a helluva downbeat note to go out on, being walloped 6-2.

The result was actually unfair to the Lions' as they didn't lie down and die. In fact, they were the first scorers with Lee Makel grabbing the opener in the 16th minute with a cheeky low shot.

The Steelmen pulled back into it just 15 minutes later when Keith Lasley headed a Steven Craig cross past Alan Main.

The second half start all square, but Livi made it 2-1 in the 54th minute when McMenamin shot inside a cluttered box.

The lead didn't last long though as James McFadden took the ball from Scott McLaughlin, passed to Steven Craig who beat Main and smacked the ball in.

Livingston were nearly brought back into the game - not once, but twice - by McMenamin and Makel, but 'Well keeper Francois Dubourdeau was on form.

The Motherwell romp really kicked in just after the hour mark with McFadden tapping in the first of his hat-trick, the second of which came from a penalty in the 74th minute after Julian Maidana fouled David Clarkson.

His third goal, just one minute later, was a thing of beauty, starting from the halfway line, beating four players - five if you include Alan Main - to score.

The hammering wasn't over, though some of the Livi fans didn't hang around to see the sixth go in, with an easy touch-in by Keith Lasley.

Despite the goals, Motherwell still ended up bottom of the league on 28 points. Livi fared a little better, coming in ninth on 35 points, beating same-points Partick Thistle on goal difference.

As the Lions' had reflected on the season, it had certainly fallen short of the glories of the previous year - but at the same time, the club had managed to survive in the SPL and go onwards, playing in Europe, so there were positive things to take from it.

What came next though just showed that Livi were unlikely to ever have a quiet season. The dramas just never stopped. If the club was a soap opera on the telly, the viewing figures would have been higher than the bums on seats at games.

CHAPTER
11

THE HIGHS AND LOWS

You would think that after coming from the lower leagues to third place, taking points off the Old Firm, going into Europe and beating off relegation that the club would be given a chance in the SPL. Not so. There were still pundits saying that the club would go down - The Sunday Times prediction was for the club to be 11th at the end of the 2003-2004 season - and the 2003-2004 and 2004-2005 seasons nearly gave them the chance to be right (though to be honest, even a stopped clock is right twice a day).

This was when Livi hit the footballing heights and also plumbed the depths in two seasons that were quite possibly the most bizarre in the club's history. And given how bizarre that history had been, that was saying something.

The first notable change was that Jim Leishman wasn't in charge any more. Brazillian Marcio Maximo was the new man in charge, joining the club just days after the end of the last season, giving himself plenty of time to see his new team and get an idea of what they could do. He was head coach to Davie Hays general manager. As for Leish, he was off back to Dunfermline as Chief Executive.

On the pitch though, things were a bit different as well – for all the wrong reasons. Out of the four games in August, the club only managed four points – one of which was from the opening game against Partick Thistle, which ended in a 1-1 draw. Fernado Pasquinelli grabbing an equaliser for the club with 15 minutes to go after the Jags took the lead in 14 minutes. It was a far cry from the pre-season friendlies where the club had beaten Newcastle and Fulham. The Lions' were slow to start in the Jags game but came into with a force by the end and Marvin Andrews had a number of chances to nab the Lions' the three points.

For the next game, it was £10 and £5 to get in and those who turned up got an entertaining but not high-scoring game of football as Livi beat Motherwell 1-0. The game was so evenly matched that a draw would have been a fair result, but football can be cruel – especially as Motherwell were denied a decent penalty claim after

Oscar Rubio elbowed one of the steelmen - and Derek Lilley snatched the only goal in the 77th minute after getting onto the end of a Pasquinelli corner.

But off the pitch things weren't looking as good. Marvin Andrews had been attracting a lot of attention and it was revealed that he could go for the right price. That right price came along, but to the relief of Livi fans everywhere, the player turned down a £400,000 move to Dundee United after he claimed that God had spoken to him and convinced him to stay at Almondvale.

Any thoughts that the Big Man was looking out for the club were dashed just days later though as Dundee beat them 2-1. The game was a tie going into the last seven minutes – Dundee getting the goal scoring started in the first half thanks to Nacho Novo, Livi equalising through Burton O'Brien. The most bizarre moment of the game happened just after half time when Jamie McAllister was taken off suffering from sunburn.

It looked as if it was going to be a draw until Oscar Rubio was blown against for bringing down Fabian Caballero. Novo took the spot kick for his second goal and the three points.

The worst was yet to come for the Lions' that month though. August ended with a 5-1 hammering by Celtic at Parkhead. Five was the number of the day as Dominic Keane helped make sure that the fans got a fiver off the high ticket price of £24 being charged for the visitors that day, but anyone who went along might have been tempted to ask for the other £19 back as well. At least David Fernandez didn't have to pay, but for the Livi fans there, it was a sad sight to see this great player sitting in the stands. His great move to Celtic having turned into a bit of a nightmare. Larsson and Maloney – who seemed to have trouble staying on his feet that day – opened the scoring for Celtic in the first half, the Swede made it a hat-trick after scoring in the 56th and 77th minutes. Derek Lilley grabbed a consolation goal in the 85th minute, but Alan Thompson made it 5-1 in the dying seconds of the game.

The only good thing from the day was the news that a Dominic Keane-instigated move to get Fernandez back at the club on a loan basis was potentially going ahead.

Celts' boss Martin O'Neill said: "David wants games, he needs to play and it may well be a year, although we would have to look at the possibility of bringing him back at the next window at Christmas.

"I'm not sure of it will be part of the agreement that he doesn't play against us but that would make sense, wouldn't it?"

And just a few days later it was all signed, sealed and Spanish delivered. The bad news though was that Barry Wilson had left to join Inverness Caley Thistle after ex-Lion John Robertson put in an offer. Xausa also decided it was time to leave.

But the main attention was on the skilful Spaniard's return. And he was glad to be back, saying: He said: "It's going to be hard. Everyone expects a lot from me and I don't want to disappoint them.

"I have been with Celtic for 14 months but when I returned to training this morning it was as if I had never been away.

"The welcome I received from everyone at the club was amazing and I am very happy to be back. I don't think I have anything to prove to anyone. The people at Livingston know what I can do."

The proof that people were glad to see him was in the fact that 1229 turned out to see him at a reserve game – more than the first team often got in terms of attendance!

Six points in September didn't do anything to reassure the fans that this was going to be a good season. It was hardly terrible, but neither was it terrific.

To make matters worse, rumours were coming out the club that there were communication problems between players and the gaffer.

Davie Hay was diplomatic about any such problems the club may be having saying: "I'm back seat. He can pick the team and dictate tactics."

The first of those six points came from a draw against an on-form Dundee United. Livi had some chances but were unable to get them on target. United had the better chances though. David Fernandez showed his commitment to his team though after it was revealed he needed a toenail removed at halftime after his sock was found to be covered in blood. The big Spaniard just got on with it, playing through the pain barrier.

The game was sullied though by allegations of Fernando Pasquinelli having spat at United defender Chris Innes. Dominic Keane dealt with the matter himself, but unlike the Sergio Berti incident, this Argentinian got to stay at the club.

Fernandez and Pasquinelli didn't even miss the next game, against Kilmarnock, but the Lions' did miss out on three points as, despite having the vast majority of play and possession, they were beat 2-1. Hessey and Boyd nabbed the goals for the Ayrshire team and a goal by Makel in between them wasn't enough for the Lions'. To make matters worse, Marvin Andrews picked up a shoulder injury that should have seen him ruled out for six weeks.

What no one knew at the time though was that after the game Marcio Maximo, who was fairly miserable and frustrated in West Lothian, told Dominic Keane that he wanted to leave. Keane thought he had managed to convince the coach to stay and everyone focused on the cup and a game against Queen of the South, the result of which was never really in any doubt, Livi winning 3-1 thanks to two penalty goals from Makel in the ninth and 79th minutes while Quino scored in the 40th minute. Clark scored for the home team in the dying seconds, but it was more a consolation goal than a sign of a late challenge by the team.

God showed that he's an East Coast kind of guy by curing Marvin Andrew's injury five weeks ahead of schedule and he – Andrews, not God, played a part in the 3-0 romping over Aberdeen. Quino, Rubio and Pasquinelli nabbed the goals in a 25 minute period that ended in the 70th minute – pretty much at the same time the boos and jeers for Dons boss Steve Paterson reached a crescendo.

October started with a 0-0 draw against Dunfermline that was deadly dull with the most exciting events being the insults being thrown from the stand. That got so bad that newspapers pointed out there was a tannoy announcement asking people to stop swearing.

There was more swearing after that as it was revealed that Maximo still wanted away.

The Scottish Daily Mirror spoke to Maximo's pal Marcos Tinico who told them: "I have spoken to him several times recently and he told me he was working hard to try and get the players to understand his methods.

"He was concentrating on tactics and he felt it was not something he was going to be able to do in the short-term.

"He felt they could not understand what he was trying to do. Marcio is a proud man and and he is very anxious to get good results all the time.

"He gets very disappointed when there are bad results, and that is maybe why he asked to leave.

"He was in the Caymans for four years, so it was not as if he missed Brazil."

Dominic Keane revealed he had battled for the Brazillian to stay, but in the end understood his person reasons for leaving the club. A big row between Maximo and Allan Preston did nothing to help the Brazililan either, coming after a closed door friendly against Clyde which Livi lost 4-1.

The Brazillian was dignified in his departure, saying in a statement: "I know that it is often difficult to implement new ideas in football and I would like to thank Mr, Keane for the great support he has provided in both the good and bad moments we have experienced this term.

"I truly believe that Livingston Football Club has great potential and will, in the short term, affirm its place as one of the most influential and respected clubs in Scotland."

Keane was equally diplomatic: "I sympathize fully with the personal reasons which prompted Marcio's request to be allowed to leave, and I have assured Marcio that those reasons will remain a private matter between ourselves.

"It took great courage for him to come to Scotland and, as far as the history of Livingston FC is concerned, Marcio's efforts will be appreciated for years to come."

Davie Hay took control of the team for the next match, against Hibs and the players responded well for the new boss, Derek Lilley getting the game's two goals in the 38th and 83rd minutes. And while it wasn't the most skilful of performances, it did the job and fired the team up for a home game against Rangers, which ended up a 0-0 draw. Rangers were actually lucky to even get a point after Lee Makel had a penalty saved.

October was rounded out with a 1-0 cup win against Dundee United. And while fans of the tangerine team from Dundee only remember a gaffe by Willie Young leading to the goal – he gave Livi a free kick that looked as if it was meant for United, the Lions' took it quickly and scored – they were on poor form at the time and Livi were by far the better team, deserving to go through.

The start of November may be firework season, but it was a damp squib for the Lions' as Hearts took them to pieces, beating them 3-1 at Tynecastle. Livi didn't play too badly – they got the opening goal through Derek Lilley in the 52nd minute – but a failure to finish a high number of chances lead to the Lions' being beat in the last half hour of the game.

The winning ways returned for a game against Partick Thistle with two goals from a Derek Lilley penalty in the 26th minute and Lee Makel just before half time.

November was rounded out with 1-1 draws against Motherwell

and Dundee, but the club was looking ahead to December and a Scottish Cup game against Aberdeen.

It was an early Christmas present for the fans as Lee Makel broke a 2-2 deadlock in injury time – goals from Tosh for the Granite City team in the 34th and 59th minute, Lilley and Pasquinelli scoring for the Lions' in the 15th minute and just after half time – to take the club into the last four of the CIS Cup for the first time.

The club were brought back to Earth the following week with a 2-0 beating by Celtic, but on the bright side it was a better result than the last time they met. Dundee United then did the Lions' in by the same score, but Christmas cheer was found on December 20 as the Lions' took three points thank to three goals from Camacho, Pasquinelli and O'Brien.

The festive season is also said to be the time of goodwill to all men – it certainly was for Davie Hay who was told that for the remaining 18 months of his contract he would be the manager of the Lions' - and that's also perhaps the best way to consider the December 27 game against Aberdeen that ended in a 1-1 draw. Aberdeen fans probably weren't feeling that way though, Scott Booth having given them the lead in the first half only for Burton O'Brien to knock in an equaliser at the dying seconds of injury time.

Indeed, as one wag at the match put it: "If he had left that any later, it would have been next year."

New year, old scoreline as the Lions' drew 2-2 with Dunfermline. David McNamee started the scoring in the 15th minute, Barry Nicholson made it one each from the penalty spot after Oscar Rubio gave away another penalty. Livi took the game back in the 62nd minute thanks to Makel, but the lead was taken away with ten minutes to go as Stevie Crawford pulled it back to 2-2.

Given the decent performances over the season, it was taken as a given that third division Montrose would be no problem for the team in the third round of the Scottish Cup. Whoops. On the night, if it had not been for David Fernandez, the team could have faced cup humiliation.

Fernandez scored in the 17th minute with a great 30 yard shot, but Montrose made the rest of the game a struggle with defending that put clubs in higher leagues to shame.

Hibs must have fancied their chances against Livi after that performance, but the Lions' were able to face down their fellow

East Coast time to take in the three points.

This time it was Lee Makel in the 25th minute getting the goal and glory.

Another 1-0 game followed against Rangers, but sadly the goal was for them, scored by Christian Nerlinger. It could have been worse for Livi as they were lucky not to go 3-0 down after Jamie McAllister's arm blocked a shot in the box and Emmanuel Dorando brought down Nuno Capucho. In both cases ref Ian Brine ignored penalty cries - and booked Capucho for diving.

And while the fans may have thought getting beat by Rangers was bad, things were about to get a whole lot worse.

While the fans were looking forward to the next game, the CIS Cup semi-final against Dundee at Easter Road, the people who ran the club were looking at a more pressing problem - the bank. The Bank of Scotland were calling in the administrators on the club's debt, which Keane said was £3.5million and not the £10million that some had reported. There were rumours before the game and had been some speculation in papers, but here it was in black and white, confirmed.

But Livingston's situation was unique. They were not going into administration because of ridiculously high wages, which was the problem at most clubs. It was because the planned hotel and office complex at the stadium did not come to full and proper development. Not enough space was rented out and the debts associated with that part of the stadium rose - and rose to the point where the bank had to act.

Too rub salt into the wounds, the club earned a £500,000 windfall from beating Dundee that night to get to the CIS final.

The game itself lived up to the cliche of a game of two halves. The first half was Dundee constantly pushing forward, taking the three-man Livi defence to shreds, but unable to finalise that attacking.

Davie Hay made it four at the back at half time and that combined with whatever words he said to them, fired the team up a little and now it was Dundee's turn to feel under the cosh. But, like Dundee in the first half, they couldn't finish despite being roared on by 1800 fans.

As the ticked on the 90th minute, everyone though extra time was a given, but Brent Sancho and Lee Mair crunched sub Pasquinelli and ref Mike McCurry blew for a penalty. Derek Lilley - under God knows what sort of pressures - made no mistake with the shot from the spot and while there was celebrations, it was all tinged with sadness.

It was at high noon the day after the game that control officially went from Dominic Keane to the administrator, Fraser Gray of Kroll Buchler Phillips.

But Keane said he hoped he would be back one day - and would make sure no one could take the club off him again.

He said: "I am determined to get this club back at some point in the future.

"If I do, I will issue share to season ticket holders and make sure that the banks can never take it away from us again."

And while the administrators were given a bad rep, Mr Gray said he was there to try and save the club.

He said: "Our initial role is to evaluate the current financial position of the business. Our long-term role is to ensure the survival of the company if that is possible."

Stuart Lovell revealed that the players would be willing to play for nothing just so they could keep playing for the club and turn out in the final - something the Scottish Football League said it had no problems with.

A Scottish Football League spokesman said: "If they are still registered players, that is all that matters to us. What they are paid is a matter for them and the club, and if they came to a private agreement about turning out for nothing, it is a club agreement.

"If the players made no complaint about not being paid, it is a matter for them. The only criterion we have is that they are registered players. So it could very easily happen that they could play for nothing."

One thing that the fans were angry about was that, compared to other clubs, Livi's debt had been nothing.

Peter Dawson fumed at the time: "Celtic were £8million in debt before the Bank of Scotland went to them, Rangers owed over £40million at one point and the Bank of Scotland never bothered them, Dundee didn't get hit by administrators until their debt was £20million, so why did we get hit at £3.5million?"

Other fans decided to get proactive, setting up a trust called Livi for Life.

Committee member Gillian Wilson remembered: "Kay Robertson the Supporters Liaison manager was the instigator of the trust. Kay got information from Supporters Direct.

"Then a supporter Brian Whitehead asked Kay about trusts and

Kay passed on the information. Brian researched hoe to set up trusts and talked with James proctor from supporters direct.

"As part of the Supporters liaison meeting 'Fans forum' in Feb 2004, Brian presented the ethos of trusts and suggestions on how to go about setting up a trust. He posted information on the Livilions web site to gauge interest from supporters.

"However events over took the planning. At the fans forum meeting in Feb, we were forewarned that the club would go into administration the next day.

"Guest speakers at the meeting included James Proctor, a representative from Supporters Direct, which is a government backed body that assists fans in setting up their trusts, Kay Robertson, Supporters Liaison at LFC and Willie Dunne from West Lothian Council who discussed the implications of the lease for the club.

"In many ways this accelerated the development of the trust. A meeting was held where 400 fans turned up to hear about the trust movement.

"There was a working group of supporters who showed an interest and we started to work towards doing the back ground legal work to register as a trust.

"We rallied together and there was a flurry of activity like bucket collecting and T-shirt selling, doing what we could to raise funds."

LFL launched in September 2004, but in those dark February days, there were doubts if the club would see that far ahead.

However footballing life had to go on though and first up to face the skint Livi were the Edinburgh Spartans in the Scottish Cup. The Spartans had been applauded for reminding people of the romance of the cup - a role Livi had filled just a few years earlier - but it ended here with a Derek Lilley hat-trick in the 53rd, 61st and 70th minutes. David Fernadez got the other goal in the 59th minute.

Then it was time for a game againt Partick Thistle and the uncertaintly was starting to bite into the club.

The day before had seen the gutting of the team begin. for Juan Jose Camacho, Francisco Quino, Cherif Toure-Maman, Tom English, Guy Ipoua and Paul McLaughlin were all told that their contracts had been terminated immiediately, while Marvin Andrews, Emmanuel Dorado, Oscar Rubio, Fernando Pasquinelli, Stuart Lovell and Alan Main all had to take pay cuts of more than a third of their wages if they wanted to stay at the club.

And while the cuts did provoke outrage, anger and sadness. It was also noted that the six let go had less than 25 first team appearances and two of them had still to turn out for the top team.

Partick Thistle smelled blood and went for it. James Grady, Gerry Britton - twice, David McNamee and Andy Thomson had all scored before Livi pulled two back far too late in the game to make any impact.

Jags' fan Iain Hepburn remembers it well: Our brief flirtation with the SPL had some horror moments. But February 2004 has to go down as a weird one.

"Gerry and Derek hadn't long taken over from the nightmare that was Gerry Collins. Although it was too little too late, they pulled off some fantastic results, and that was one of the best. Did them 5-2 at Firhill in a midweek result. Five nil til the last few minutes, too.

"Was one of those games when everything just seems to come off ok - David McNamee even scored an own goal, which is always a great thing to watch.

"They weren't exactly bad that day, either. They've always given us a good game - had our measure when we were in the second division the first time, always been one of those sides we've struggled against, which made it even stranger when we smashed them."

The team bucked up for a Valentine's Day win against Motherwell. Three first half goals from McAllister, Lilley and Fernandez were enough with Derek Adams scoring in the 90th minute to pull one back for the Fir Parkers.

Then it was time for a trip to Dens Park and the result was almost a foregone conclusion, given that it was Livi's bogey ground, a win having never happened there for the Lions' since they were promoted to the SPL. This 1-0 game was no different. Steven Milne getting the only goal of the game for the Dundonians in the 58th minute.

The bad run continued just three days later with Hearts finally getting their first away SPL win over Livingston. It started well for the Lions' with Lee Makel scoring in the 2nd minute, but Mark de Vries made it 1-1 in the 25th minute and the Jambos took the lead in the 47th minute thanks to Andy Kirk. Livi equalised thanks to McMenamin just 9 minutes later but with six minutes on the clock Kevin McKenna made it three for the visitors.

This was one year Livi could have done without an extra day, especially as it was the 29th with a 5-1 humping by Celtic. Stephen Pearson opened the scoring for Celtic in the 12th minute, then Chris Sutton scored in the 36th minute. Derek Lilley pulled one back in the 41st minute to let Livi think they might have a chance in the second half, but goals from Thompson, Larsson in the 48th and 55th minutes and a penalty spot kick from Thompson in the 80th minute showed who was getting the result that day.

And while the league wasn't going brilliantly, the cup runs contined well. A game against Aberdeen ended in a replay – mostly thanks to Aberdeen captain Russell Anderson who scored an OG after getting onto the end of a David Fernandez cross and clearing it the wrong way.

At the other end – just six minutes later and just before the half hour mark – Scott Muirhead went for goal. Roddy McKenzie should have been able to get to it, but it took a cruel deflection off of Oscar Rubio to go in. The replay was set for 11 days later, but before that there was the cup final to attend to.

And while for most teams, a cup final is a cause for celebration, a time for the fans to rally round, it was a bit different for Livi.

Hibs had sold out of their allocation of more than 32,000 tickets for the game – and could have easily sold more.

Livingston had 9000 tickets and struggled to sell them – even after the players went to schools and tried to sell them, telling pupils that Livi might not be their first team, but people had second teams that they could also support.

But Hampden was packed on the day and the 9,000 that did make it for Livi were certainly in good voice.

The opening of the game was a nervy affair and it wasn't until after 10 minutes that both sides started to open up. Fernandez was lucky not to score early on, but after that it was Hibs who did all the attacking with Scott Brown and Derek Riordan having a go each.

Apart from Fernandez's decent chance early on, Livi's first real effort didn't come until the 36th minute via Derek Lilley. Fernadez then had another chance as half-time approached, but it ended up 0-0 at half time.

The Lions' upped a few gears in the second half. Derek Lilley knocked in the ball from eight yards out in the 50th minute to put the Lions' ahead. And then it was 2-0 just minutes later as McAllister knocked in a pass from outside the box. Hibs kept trying to get back into the game, but the Lions' had found their form and even five minutes injury time wasn't enough to get Hibs back in. The Lions' had won!

And the celebrations almost saw two of the team get arrested. Derek Lilley wanted to bring his family onto the pitch while Stuart Lovell saw a friend in the crowd he wanted to speak to, but the stewards hustled them away. As the players protested, one of Strathclyde Police's finest warned them that if they kept up their behaviour they could find themselves being lifted.

Fan Nick Wilson remembers it so well.

"The first half had been fairly lacklustre as far as Livi were concerned, Hibs had played the better football but with the scores level we were still in good spirits.

"I went to get the pies, my son Mark came with me but the youngest, Adam, stayed in his seat with our friends. The queue was quite long and the game restarted while we were still on the concourse.

"We were at the back of the queue so when the crowd got agitated about events on the field we would run back to the back of the stand to see what was happening.

"The first instance was a chance for Hibs, all I saw was the ball rolling out towards the corner flag. I would later learn from TV pictures how close Brown had come to putting Hibs in front. Next, it seemed like the Livi fans were getting expectant and we rushed back again to see Lee Makel play the ball out wide, the cross come back in and Derek Lilley's expert finish.

"Needless to say we went wild, leaping about the concourse like new born lambs! The other Livi fans in the queue clearly had no idea how to celebrate the fact their team was in the lead as the glumly stood watching us.

"By this time we had bought soft drinks from a mobile vendor and Mark started heading back to our seats. I went back to the queue. Another intake of breath by the Livi fans and I rushed back to see Fernandez release McAllister for the 2nd goal.

"Again I went wild, not caring that I was getting strange looks from the other folks in the queue.

"Next thing I knew Mark was beside me again, in the excitement he'd forgotten which stairway to go down! He'd seen the goal on the steps and come rushing back where once again we celebrated in style. I directed him to the right stairway and went back for the as yet unobtained pies. I finally got back to my seat with less than 30 mins to go. No one could believe I'd seen the goals that won the cup.

"That night we all went back to Almondvale, the boys both got to touch the cup as it was paraded round the ground. A great way to round off a day that we will never forget."

And the cup run ran on just days later with Aberdeen being beaten 1-0 in front of 4486 fans in the Scottish Cup replay thanks to a goal from Burton O'Brien.

Days later, it was the same teams in the league and Aberdeen were on the losing side again. McMenamin took the lead for the Lions' in 14 minutes. The Dons came back into it with six minutes left on the clock, but three minutes later any hopes of sharing points were dashed as Burton O'Brien grabbed a winner.

The winning run ended on with a 3-2 home defeat against Dundee United but March was ended with a 0-0 draw against Dunfermline.

April was not a kind month to the Lions'. It wasn't the worst, but it wasn't the best and there was a sense that the best of the season had passed with the CIS Cup win.

Hibs beat the Lions' 3-1 – Davie Hay dropping Fernandez for it on the basis that Celtic still paid a huge chunk of his wages, then there was a 1-1 draw against Kilmarnock before Celtic dumped them out the Scottish Cup via a 3-1 beating, which given some of the results this year against the 'tic was actually decent, and then there were draws against Rangers and Hearts. The month did end on a slightly better note – unless you were an Aberdeen fan, in which case Livi made it a rotten day again – with a 2-0 home win.

The last month of the season started terribly though with Kilmarnock beating the club 4-2, drawing against Partick and being beat by the club's hoodoo team Dundee 2-0. Things perked up on the last day of the season with a 4-2 beating of Hibs, but it left people in uncertain times, especially after the news that there may only be five full-time players at the club the following season. Marvin Andrews wasn't going to be one of them though as he had accepted a deal to go to Rangers on a two-year deal.

There was, for some, still a sense of positivity around the club as a consortium headed up by successful businessman Pearse Flynn was looking at taking the club out of administration. The process dragged on, but eventually Lionheart took control of the club – and there was certainly a lot of goodwill towards it. And that goodwill was quickly blown after Davie Hay was shown the door.

As fan Peter Johnson put it: "You just don't sack the guy who won you you're best trophy – and in those circumstances."

But another season dawned – one under the rule of Allan Preston. He wasn't the only new face, keeper Alan Main was out as well, thanks to back injury.

Preston brought in Kilmarnock's Colin Meldrum to replace him. Meldrum was just one of 16 players brought in to give the Livi squad a new look, but it didn't get off to the best of starts, beaing beat 3-1 by third division Berwick Rangers. To make matters worse, Berwick nabbed all three goals in the first half.

A friendly against Alloa was technically better - winning it for a start, but at 3-2 the defence still looked a bit ropey.

After that, Preston decided to try and bring in another signing - and it was one that looked very familiar. Derek Lilley.

Derek had left to join Boston United in Lincolnshire. But what had been dreams of a new start in a new country turned sour very quickly as his wife Shona hated life down south and failed to settle.

Preston was quick enough to spot the opportunity and brought him back after the SPL gave Livi permission to do so. Normally, the rules dictate that a player cannot resign for a club they left less than a year previously, but the much maligned institution called it right in showing some humanity to allow the family back to Scotland.

There were some more friendlies - including a draw against St Johnstone and a win over Brechin - and a trip to the Algarve before the season started properly on August 7 2004 and it whatever the team got up to abroad it must have done them some good as they thumped their Inverness rivals 3-0 at Almondvale to get the season off to a good start.

Livi played well, but the truth of the matter is that the trip down from the north must have done something to Caley, playing some of their worst football ever

But that's not to say the game was a classic. Far from it, though some of that is easily put down to the fact that Livi had no less than eight new players from the summer on the park at one point or another.

The game looked to be heading to a 0-0 half time when Stuart McCaffrey made a mistake allowing Livi's Burton O'Brien to pick up the ball from his awkward header and score from what was not only the first Livi shot on target of the game, but also the first goal of the SPL that year.

The second half picked up. Livi, encouraged by the goal, pushed more and more forward, taking chances. The second came in the 57th minute when David McNamee beat Stuart Golabek on the wing, put a neat ball in to the near post and Easton put the ball to the back of the net.

A nice run by Stuart Lovell - after a pass from super sub Jim Hamilton - caught Caley dreaming - or having a nightmare - and he slotted in the third in the 65th minute after rounding keeper Mark Brown to give Preston a great start to his Livi management career and to make the club top of the SPL. It might only have been the start of the season, but it was nice to see.

Defender Rubio took some knocks during the game and was a worry for the next match, an away game to Rangers. He made it back, but shouldn't have bothered as the team were wiped out by a hungry Rangers team.

Rangers' opener originated from a Shota Arveladze header from a wicked Vignal free-kick that was cleared off the line by Burton O'Brien.

But it wasn't all one-way traffic. Derek Lilley did test Stefan Klos with the game still in the balance at 1-0.

Stephen Hughes forced a Peter Lovenkrands shot over the line to make it 2-0 on 32 minutes.

He added his second 12 minutes from time, slotting home a ball from Shota Arveladze -who went on to complete the win three minutes from time.

Fan John Daley has the unfortunate ability to remember one thing from the game: "We had placed a lot of hope on Marc Libbra, but he seemed way too slow. This was a fast game, but not the fastest I'd seen and he looked as if he was out of his depth."

It was hoped the good run would continue with the game against Dundee United and it seemed promising at first.

They were given a boost early doors by an unfortunate collision between birthday boy and Dundee United debutant Paul Ritchie and Jim Hamilton before 10 minutes had even passed, leading to him being taken off for a dislocated collarbone and replaced by David McCracken.

The game carried on at fair pace with Livi providing much of the pressure during the game. Colin Easton in particular had a decent first half. Three times in the first 45 minutes he burst into the United box with superbly timed late runs.

He shot wide as he slid in on a Steven Boyack cross, then was let down by his control after a Burton O'Brien pass, while on the third occasion United keeper Tony Bullock produced a great save.

But there was a moment of drama at the other end of the pitch as well when Barry Robson had a shot just before half time that came back off the inside of a post.

Robson was right back into the thick of things at the start of the second half when he set up Mark Wilson, whose shot was only just off target.

United kept pressing and Wilson missed another chance, then, in 61 minutes, the visitors got their chance when Jason Scotland burst into the Livingston box, and Emmanuel Dorado hauled down the Trinidadian striker.

It was a blatant penalty, but one that wasn't necessarily going to get blown for as ref Willie Young had failed to wave cards for a number of harsh tackles throughout the game. In fact if he had gained better authoritative control of the game, Dorado might not have been so reckless wtith this challenge.

Regardless the penalty being scored by Billy Dodds put the Lions' one down and it fired them up for a while while United went defensive to hold on to their fragile lead.

Livi were given another fright though 10 minutes from the end when Andy McLaren had a good chance, but his header ended up at at the side netting.

Attack being the best form of defence got Livi going and Derek Lilley headed a deep Burton O'Brien cross for sub Colin McMenamin to knock the ball between the sticks.

And then it was time for the league cup and a new look against Stirling Albion for it. The Lions' turned into the all-blacks for the game because both regular Livi strips would have clashed with Albion's strips, so the training kit had to come out.

Dark was also the best way to sum up the team's performance and defence of their cup.

They may have had a few shots, but, just like earlier in the season, failed to net them. Burton O'Brien had the first go after just two minutes but Paul Hay cleared it off the line. Jim Hamilton - who was loved and hated by different sections of the Livi fans, judging by the crowd cheers and jeers - also had a few efforts but keeper Roddy Mackenzie managed to keep on top of it until the half hour mark when Craig Easton got the opener thanks to some nifty work by Burton O'Brien and Steven Boyack.

Only a fool would have written Stirling off though and throughout the second half they had a number of attacks, some of which actually beat the keeper but hit the posts or the underside of the bar.

However Livi didn't lie down and did try to get a second goal to try and control the game more. And they got one, but took their time about it - more than 45 minutes in fact.

Craig Easton also played a part in nabbing the second goal in injury time, finally letting Livi relax, after he passed to Jim Hamilton.

Allan Preston took the struggle as a good omen though, saying: "Last year we struggled early on in the competition and went on to win the cup."

Meanwhile Stirling boss summed up what he saw as the difference in the two teams - and the two leagues they were in when he said: "They had two good chances and scored with both. We had a few and didn't. I think that's where the difference between the SPL and the Second Division."

A game against Aberdeen should have been a chance for Livi to grab some more points as they hadn't been beaten by the north-east team in the last seven encounters, but thanks to a double by Steven Craig at Pittodrie, that wasn't the case.

And the Dons shirts weren't the only red on show that day as David McNamee was sent off just after the hour in what was to be the decisive moment for the match. Derek Lilley, Craig Easton and Gus Bahoken were also cautioned in the game.

Before it turned sour though, Livi had put on a fantastic defending performance with Roddy McKenzie playing a blinder, especially when he tipped a John Stewart header over the bar.

It looked as if Livi were on course for eight of out eight as the second half started and it was still nil-nil, but in the 62nd minute Steven Craig fired a shot at goal from just a few yards out.

It was a cert to be a goal, but McNamee's hand got in the road. To be more accurate, David didn't really have time to get his hand out the road of the rapid shot, but that wasn't how referee Mike McCurry saw it.

He banished the player from the pitch with a red card for deliberate handball and Craig made no mistake from the penalty spot, making sure that he got the goal bonus one way or another.

There was nothing controversial about the striker's second goal, in the 69th minute, pickeing up a pass from Kevin McNaughton and then cheekily chipping keeper McKenzie from outside the box.

Craig even had a chance to nab a hat-trick when he beat Emmanuel Dorado but put the shot wide of the post when he was one-on-one with the keeper.

Afterwards gaffer Preston felt that the red card moment was the decider in the game, though many felt Livi would have been lucky to get more than a point from the game even if they had stayed at 11 men.

He fumed: "The penalty was the turning point. How David is meant to get out of the way when the ball is being blasted at him from two yards away is beyond me.

"His reactions aren't that quick so there's no way he could have intentionally handled."

After that, there was a break for international football, giving everyone a chance to get their breath back after the frantic opening to the season.

Perhaps Livi were too relaxed because the first game after the rest saw them go down 2-0 to a determined Kilmarnock.

They weren't the only ones being relaxed. Crowds were staying under 4000 despite everything the club had done to try and bring in more people.

A draw against Dundee was the first time the two clubs would meet in a three day period. The second result – for the CIS Cup – went a lot better for them, a 2-1 win thanks to two goals from Jim Hamilton.

But the winning ways didn't last as Motherwell beat them 3-2 to finish off September.

October was not a great month, starting with a 0-0 draw against Hearts, but it did pick up with a 2-0 beating of Dunfermline. That was the only joy that month though as Celtic, Hibs and Caley Thistle all took three points off the club.

It got worse in November. As well as league defeats by Rangers, Dundee United, Aberdeen, they were dumped out of the cup – 5-0 – by Motherwell.

Clearly something had to be done and Pearse Flynn agreed. Preston and sidekick Alan Kernaghan were sacked.

A statement from the club read: "Lionheart Management confirms that Allan Preston is to leave the post of Manager of Livingston Football Club with immediate effect.

"The decision was taken by the Lionheart Board this week as part of a review of the club's football operation which included planning for its future development.

Alan Kernaghan is also to leave the post of Assistant Manager.

"Pearse Flynn, who leads Lionheart Management, commented: Allan Preston has done an excellent job in often very difficult circumstances.

"When Lionheart took over management of Livingston before the start of the new season the club had only four players under contract. Allan responded with a great deal of hard work and enthusiasm, and we were able to pull together a first-team squad very quickly at a time when the future of the club was less certain than it is today.

"Unfortunately we have come to the decision to find another manager after reviewing the football operations and also the club's recent performances.

We wish both Allan and Alan Kernaghan the best of luck for the future and thank them for their efforts to date.

"Reserve team coach, Alex Clelland, will take charge of the Livingston first team for this Saturday's match against Kilmarnock at Rugby Park."

The new manager effect must have worked as the Lions' won 3-1 thanks to goals from Hamilton and O'Brien.

And there were hopes it would work again the next game against Dundee because Rangers' legend Richard Gough was unveiled as the new boss.

It seemed to work again with a goal from McPake being enough to get the three points. But for the last two games of the year, Christmas magic didn't seem to be working as they were beaten 2-0 by Motherwell and drew 0-0 with Dunfermline.

The New Year started poorly with the Lions' going down 2-1 to Celtic at Parkhead. But confidence was boosted with a 2-1 win against Morton on January 11.

The league – and any hopes of a place in the top six – ran away from under them though as the club failed to take any points from games against Hibs, Caley Thistle, Hearts, Rangers, Dundee United, Aberdeen.

Hearts then put them out the Scottish Cup.

A brief return to form happened in March with a 3-1 win against Kilmarnock, a 1-0 win against Dundee and a draw against Motherwell.

The rest of the season was, quite frankly, a flurry of bad results, punctuated only by three draws – 1-1 each time against Motherwell, Dunfermline and Dundee on the last game of the season.

Fan David Black remembers: "Last game of the 04-05 season in which the Lions' only needed a draw to ensure SPL safety. An equaliser from Craig Easton kept Livi in the SPL but an injury time shot from Tam McManus which hit the post almost had us down."

For the fans this had been a struggle of a year. Not only had Davie Hay been kicked out, it had gone to the last day to see if the club would stay up Richard Gough had come in and while he kept the team up, he wasn't going to be about for next season, Paul Lambert was coming in to replace him and it was hoped he would get on better with Flynn than the ex-Rangers captain had rumoured to. At times it seemed as if more newspaper space was spent on discussing the alleged fallout between Gough and Flynn instead of the on-pitch performances. With hindsight that may have been a good thing.

But the end of the season wasn't the end of the drama.

Dundee asked the Scottish Premier League to investigate the circumstances in which Livingston signed and played Moroccan international Hassan Kachloul as an amateur.

Dundee chairman Bob Brannan wrote to SPL Secretary Iain Blair detailing Dundee's concerns about the signing and suggestions that Kachloul may have been paid by the Lions' despite his amateur status.

Livingston insisted the registration of Kachloul is in full accordance with the rules of the Scottish Football Association and SPL.

A Livi spokesman said at the time: 'We signed Kachloul as an amateur and we have the registration form.

"The only thing we would have paid him would have been expenses which he was due. We signed him on an amateur form and that was passed by both the SFA and the SPL."

In the end, the SFA and SPL both saw no need to relegate Livi instead of Dundee over the matter, but the club were fined £15,000.

Surely next season couldn't be as dramatic? Weren't the club due a break?

CHAPTER
12

THE LIONS' ROAR ON

And so it was, another season, where the club hoped to regain some of its early SPL glory days. And in a way, it would, showing an attacking style and courage reminiscent of the early days.

Like any manager. Paul Lambert wanted to get some new faces into the squad to give it a boost. Two of the players he brought in on three year contracts were ex-Hearts striker Ramon Pereira and Bosnian midfielder Dubi Tesevic, but he left it late as they were signed just a week or so before the season kicked off.

Having said that, they weren't last in, Aberdeen midfielder Derek Adams was pulled in just a few days before the end of July. What made signing Adams on a two-year deal even more sweet was the fact that Inverness Caley Thistle had also wanted him, but Livi won him.

The club was also able to bring back Hungarian Gabor Vincze. However he wouldn't turn up for the first game due to complications in trying to sign him and FIFA and the SFA helped get the player away from his Hungarian team, Gyori Eto.

One player who wouldn't be back though – at least not in a Livi strip – was David Fernandez, who had decided to go to Dundee United, despite Lambert's efforts to sign his ex-Celtic team mate.

Lambert couldn't have had a harder game for his SPL baptism of fire though with an away game at Ibrox to take on the league winners Rangers.

Rangers had been accused of stealing the league from Lambert's old team Celtic the previous season, only getting the trophy after Celtic conceded goals to Motherwell in the dying moments of the season.

While very few people expected Livi to actually pull in the three points, what was worrying for fans and Lambert was how easily the team capitulated. Rangers hammered Livi with attack after attack with Livi only getting the odd chance.

One of their better ones was Dubi Tesevic's long-range shot that forced Ronald Waterreus to make an effort to get to.

The first goal came in 23 minutes with Dado Prso slotting in a rebound from an Alex Rae volley.

The second goal took a while to come, but it was never in any doubt, and it was another follow-up with a cross from Peter Lovenkrands being deflected and Jose Pierre-Fanfan putting it away.

McKenzie did manage to deny Novo the third goal a few moments later. In fact McKenzie had not a bad game as he saved the club from a real roasting, denying Peter Lovenkrands and later on, Steven Thompson.

As if being two goals down wasn't bad enough, Livi went down to ten men when Richard Brittain was red carded for a late challenge on Ian Murray in the 74th minute.

Bizarrely that fired Livi up – or more likely the team felt they had nothing left to lose – and they briefly piled on the pressure and Waterreus did well to deny a shot by sub Scott McLaughlin round the post.

Injury time saw injury added to Livi's insult as Peter Lovenkrands finally grabbed the goal he had been chasing to make it 3-0.

Lambert tried to put a brave face on the result: "The players were terrific in terms of their work-rate. In the first half we were reasonably comfortable and we had a couple of chances, but at places like this you need a wee break."

Eto didn't actually play in the Falkirk game – and cynics would argue that neither did any of the eleven people representing Livingston on the pitch.

Russell Latapy was the player of the day, taking the game to Livi more or less from the kick-off. He set up other people's shots on goal, had a few himself and was a general pest all over the pitch. The only surprise was that it took 28 minutes for the goal to come as he got on the end of a pass from Danny McBreen and then thumped it past Roddy McKenzie.

Falkirk's confidence soared after the goal and as they pushed on the pressure, Livi found themselves getting frustrated and Ramon Pereira was booked for a harsh tackle on Lima.

The attacks continued more or less one-way – all Falkirk – and half time couldn't come quick enough, giving Roddy McKenzie a deserved breather. Like the Ibrox game, at times he was all that was standing between Livi and a hiding.

Lambert made some changes with Pereira and Scott McLaughlin being swapped for Robert Snodgrass and Dubravko Tesevic.

This gave the Lions' a bit of a boost and they were unlucky not to get an equaliser just after 50 minutes when McPake had a few good shots, wasting a one-on-one against keeper Matt Glennon. McPake kept up the pressure and he was joined by Emmanuel Dorado, both of them giving the fans a number of edge-of-the seat moments. Sadly none let them jump off their chairs to celebrate.

And then they were given a reason to slump in their chairs in despair as the ball came off Dave Mackay during a Falkirk attack in the 72nd minute. Duffie claimed it, and many are still split over who actually put it in. Mackay would probably prefer to think that he didn't sink the game for the Lions'.

As well as the defeat, Harald Pinxten pulled a groin injury.

The defeat was so bad that Paul Lambert hinted that he might even give up retirement to help motivate the Lions'.

He added: "If you don't show enthusiasm and the will to win, then you won't get anything from this game.

"We weren't even there during the first half and it was that spell that cost us the points. I am disappointed that we didn't raise our game."

The only consolation Lions' fans had from the next game – an away game against Hibs – was that they didn't have too far to travel home after being despondent at the result. Livi failed to score while Hibs bagged three at the other end, largely thanks to Scott Brown ripping the Lions' apart.

And then there was the return of the Bhoy. Forced by the bad results to come out of retirement, Paul Lambert found himself amongst the starting 11 for the game against Dunfermline.

While the Man of the Match award he received no doubt touched him, he was probably even happier with the point that the team nabbed from the game.

But it wasn't looking so rosy at the start of the match as Dunfermline went one up thanks to a goal from ex-Livi player Lee Makel.

The Lions', throughout the game, seemed to be more intent on not losing than winning – and apart from the goal did admirably in holding the Pars at bay – but the second half saw them try and attack a little more. Lambert came off just before an hour was on the clock, letting Pereira come on. And it was an inspired move as that was who bagged the goal in the 64th minute, getting on the end of a Jason Dair cross.

Then on top of Lambert, the club signed Dalglish. Not Kenny, but his son Paul, who had played at a number of clubs including Newcastle and Celtic.

And it was a fortuitous signing as he saved the club from cup disaster just days later.

Playing against Raith Rovers has always been a nervy affair for the Lions' and this game was no different – especially after five minutes when Paul Lambert hobbled off with what seemed to be a thigh injury.

Still, there was a belief about the team and they weren't afraid to actually have a go against the Rovers with captain Dave Mackay and Scott Boyd both having excellent chances, only to be thwarted by keeper Alistair Brown.

As half-time approached, many fans felt that they had been unlucky not to be one up. The Raith players must have felt the same because in the 44th minute they slotted one away with Paul McManus getting the glory.

It was nearly two within minutes of the second half, as Dave Mackay nearly scored an own goal, but from that fright the team found their purpose and started attacking again like they had in the second half.

This time there was one difference – they were actually able to score and the equaliser turned up in the 54th minute from a corner and Jason Dair taking control of the ball to put it beyond Brown.

Just as the clock was about to hit 70 minutes, Dalglish nabbed his opener for the club with a cheeky nutmeg on the keeper and set up a cup tie game against on-form SPL team Hearts.

The win may have given the team – and the club coffers – a boost, but the euphoria didn't last too long with Kilmarnock bringing the team back to earth with a three-goal pounding at the end of August.

Colin Nish was the man singularly responsible for the damage against a weakened Livi side, which was missing David McNamee, Harald Pinxten, Greg Strong and Paul Lambert. Derek Adams was added to the injury list in the 34th minute, but before that Nish had put Killie one up with a top corner shot that McKenzie had no chance of saving.

As if losing Adams wasn't bad enough, Nish scored his second just after the player went off, nodding home a cross from Gary Locke.

And just to show Livingston how exposed they were from that sort of attack, Locke and Nish did it again in the 44th minute.

The second half could have seen Killie score more, but the team knew they had done all they needed to secure the points. Livi did have some attacking moments, but they were scarce and more importantly, not of the quality required for results in the SPL.

The last day of August saw transfer flurry-a-go-go at Almondvale with Lambert bringing in Coventry's Irish international striker Graham Barrett on a one year loan deal while also letting go – on free transfers or loan deals – Graham Dorrans and Scott McLaughlin.

Five games into the new season and it wasn't looking good for the new town team, having played five, lost four, drew one and they had just one point, putting them smack bottom of the league.

No one expected the next game to see Livi acquire more points as it was against league leaders Hearts, who were enjoying something of a renaissance.

It was all Hearts from the kick-off and they enjoyed all the early pressure, so it was no great surprise – but no joy for the Livi faithful either - when they opened the scoring after 11 minutes.

Rudi Skacel's close-range header, his sixth goal in six games, got the ball rolling.

The Czech midfielder headed into the unguarded net after Hartley had directed Roman Bednar's cross back across goal.

Edgaras Jankauskas almost doubled the lead midway through the half when he met Steven Pressley's cross beyond the back post, but his shot from a tight angle was well kept out by Roddy McKenzie.

But Hearts did go two goals up after 26 minutes. McAllister curled in a free kick from the right and Andy Webster took advantage of some really poor marking by Dave Mackay to head past McKenzie.

The first threat to the Hearts goal almost brought about a goal, but Craig Gordon did brilliantly to push Mackay's shot on the turn round to the post.

Thirty four minutes gone and Paul Hartley managed to tap in a third from six yards out thanks to a Bednar square ball pass.

But it wasn't all one-way traffic. Barrett had a chance to make it 3-1 with a fantastic free kick in the 44th minute that was just saved by Hearts' keeper Craig Gordon.

Paul Dalglish managed to reduce the difference between the teams just before half time though, forcing the ball into the net from close range after he got onto the rebound from a Barrett free kick.

Hearts had started the second half poorly, and Livi might have pulled another goal back just after the break when Barrett headed just over the bar, and then Dalglish poked a great chance wide with just Gordon to beat.

Hearts came back into it though in the 63rd minute after Barrett was said to have pulled the shirt of McAllister in the box and Hartley sent McKenzie the wrong way from the penalty spot.

Bednar could have got on the scoresheet with 15 minutes to go but his header from Robbie Neilson's cross was wide.

Gordon produced his third excellent save of the game when he pushed a Derek Adams volley over the bar despite being on the ground as the result of a prior challenge.

Then it was a real sickener. As if being bottom of the league wasn't bad enough, the salt was then rubbed into the wound during a game against Dundee United.

The fact that United won 2-0 was bad enough, but what made it sickening was the fact that their best player on the day was David Fernandez. Indeed it's easy to say that he was the difference in the two sides and Livi fans could only look on and wish that he was still one of them.

It would be unfair though to say that this was a one-way game. Livi did have a fair chunk of possession; it's just that they did very little with it while Dundee United made every pass look like a threat.

The first opportunity of the game came in the eighth minute when Fernandez was first to an in-swinging Robson corner only to see his near-post flick clear the bar.

In the 15th minute, after solid work by Mark Wilson had carved out a chance for Canero, McKenzie made a good save.

Fernandez lifted the game when he tried his luck with a 25-yard drive which was well saved by McKenzie.

United piled on the pressure and then McKenzie made a great save from Mark Wilson's left-footed curling shot from outside the penalty area.

In the 32nd minute McKenzie made another terrific finger tip save from Fernandez's 25-yard free-kick but from the following corner the Spaniard headed the home side into the lead.

Robson's in-swinger from the right was again met by Fernandez whose header from eight yards flew past the despairing Derek Adams on the line who could only help the ball into the net.

Livingston finally found the target when United keeper Derek Stillie had to punch clear Graham Barrett's 30-yard free-kick.

In the best move of the match, Fernandez cleverly set up Mark Kerr but the United midfielder sent his angled shot from close range into the side netting.

In the 64th minute Fernandez's pass sent Robson through on goal but the winger missed the target from 12 yards.

Robson later skinned Richard Brittain inside the penalty area and sent his shot from 10 yards crashing off the near post before the ball flew to safety.

In the 76th minute the home side eventually sealed their victory with Canero getting the goal this time.

However Fernandez was, yet again, involved when his overhead kick was blocked but the ball broke to the former Kilmarnock player 12 yards from goal and he wasted no time in driving his right-footed shot past the helpless McKenzie.

Next up was the cup game against Hearts and no one expected anything given the earlier result from the two teams meeting and everyone expected Hearts would be going into the quarter finals to face Inverness Caley Thistle. In fact many thought Livi had as much chance of being in the quarter finals of the CIS-sponsored cup as the Champions League final.

Oh ye of little faith.

There may have been a number of factors in Livi's favour – terrible weather conditions, it was a home leg, Hearts' gaffer George Burley rested club top scorer Rudi Skacel while first team Stalwarts, Takis Fyssas, Julien Brellier and Roman Bednar were all out – but at the end of the day it boiled down to two teams of 11 men facing off, and the better team won.

Hearts started the game as the more attacking team from early in the game though.

Just seven minutes in, Jamie McAllister tried his luck with a shot from outside the box but ex-Jambo keeper Roddy McKenzie saved his effort without any great difficulty.

Hearts kept the pressure on with an attack in the 18th minute that saw Robbie Neilson put the ball into the box, only for Livi's Manu Dorado to put it out of play.

Then Livi decided to have a go and it was another ex-Hearts player who was instrumental in the attack. Ramon Pereira set up an unmarked Paul Dalglish, but his dad's skills weren't with him at that moment and he put the ball wide on the right hand side.

But it was Hearts who had the majority of attacks in the first half with Simmons and Hartley having a go and Mole may have as well, in the 40th minute if he hadn't been brought down by Allan Walker first, earning Livi their first booking of the night.

Livi seemed more fired up in the second half and in the 54th minute, the home fans were given something to celebrate when the Lions' scored. As if that wasn't bad enough for the travelling Jambo support, it was their ex-player Pereira who scored, getting on the end of a cross by Adams.

Minutes later it was nearly two as Simmons sliced the ball past his own goal while trying to clear a Brittain corner.

Clearly changes had to be made and Skacel came on for Camazzola while Calum Elliot replaced Mole. Skacel made Hearts look sharper and he came close with a late shot parried by Roddy McKenzie and Stephen Simmons having a chance with the rebound, but whacking it off Greg Strong.

But the comeback effort was not sharp enough and even though it was blustery winds, it wasn't enough to silence the blustery howls of the Hearts' fans facing their first defeat of the season and being kicked out the cup to boot. Some tried to put a brave face on it by saying that it was good as it allowed them to concentrate on the league, but the majority were sickened.

Not so the home support. And no one was more delighted than Paul Lambert who said: "I thought we were terrific straight from the kick-off and we gave everything we had and it was also a good goal we scored.

"Our general play was excellent. Although Hearts made changes they still had internationals on the pitch. I hope this is the kick-start to our season."

And the win did seem to bring back the Livi of old as the Lions' squared off against Aberdeen and managed to come back with a point. Not as glorious as nabbing three points perhaps but better than losing three.

Jimmy Calderwood's Aberdeen side failed to find any early rhythm but created a chance after just 12 minutes when Kevin McNaughton found space to deliver a delightful cross to the back post.

Jamie Smith beat Jason Dair in the air, but could only direct his header straight at Roddy McKenzie in the Livingston goal.

With the Dons struggling to pass the ball effectively Livingston nearly snatched an unlikely lead, much to the shock of the home crowd.

Paul Dalglish shrugged off the physical attention of Chris Clark and Esson did well to block his shot from the edge of the box, before Zander Diamond cleared the follow-up off the line.

The Dons continued to struggle and there was another scare for the home fans when McNaughton headed just over his own crossbar from a corner.

At the other end McNaughton was narrowly wide of the mark with a shot after a neat Crawford lay-off.

As the first half came to a close, Livi's Derek Adams saw his chip from 18 yards well gathered by Esson, before McKenzie beat away a stinging Scott Severin free-kick from 25 yards out.

Aberdeen continued to huff and puff after the break and Livingston were able to repel their advances without too much trouble.

However, Livi were fortunate when Crawford latched on to a Smith pass, cut inside Greg Strong and hit a shot with the outside of his right foot against McKenzie's post.

The Lions' luck would hold a minute later when Aberdeen were presented with an even better chance to open the scoring when Walker conceded a penalty after handling the ball in the box, but Lovell blazed the spot-kick too high.

Crawford later tested McKenzie with a low effort from the edge of the box, as the away side restricted Aberdeen to efforts from a distance.

But delightful link-up play between Walker and substitute James McPake almost led to a Livi winner against the run of play.

McPake fired a shot across goal from 16 yards out, but Esson plunged low to his right to steer the effort wide of goal.

Afterwards, Lambert said he felt justice had been done with Lovell skying the penalty.

He said: "I cannot believe someone can cross the ball from 50 yards and a defender is expected to clear it by jumping with their hands by their side.

"I believe we got the break we deserved when it was missed."

Then October kicked off with a game against Celtic - but it's not one anyone at Livi will want to remember.

Just like Lambert, new Celts boss Gordon Strachan had plenty to prove. And prove it he did with this 5-0 gubbing of the Lions'. In fact, the only good thing that happened for Livi was the weather – though there were enough clouds over the fans after this result to fight against that.

It was the same time for the Lions', who had done so decently against Aberdeen, and they were more than decent here – they were just incredibly outplayed.

It was nearly 6-0 if not for the efforts of Roddy McKenzie, who did well to put a shot from Shunsuke Nakamura past in the sixth minute.

For the first half hour or so, the Lions' defended well, frustrating Celtic almost every minute – though this was at a cost of their own attacking chances, but the goal deluge started just 10 minutes before half time with McManus getting onto the end of a header. Maloney made it two on the edge of half time with a shot from around 15 yards out.

It didn't take 35 minutes in the second half for the goals to come. The first was headed in by Magic Zurawski in the 51st minute, Chris Sutton nabbed another ten minutes later and Craig Beattie got the last of the day 10 minutes after that.

And while there was little to take from the second half, it did have to be said that Lambert's Lions' had played well in patches.

The decent playing carried on into the next game – against Motherwell. But sadly so did the results going the wrong way. At least this time, it was only a 1-0 defeat, courtesy of Richie Foran getting onto the end of a Phil O'Donnell cross in the 22nd minute.

But the next game – against Caley Thistle – would see the club hit a three game decent patch. Decent, that is, compared to what had gone before.

And while there were no wins, there were no losses either as the Lions' took a point from each match.

But they did so in a fairly dramatic fashion. First up against Caley, they scored in the 13th minute after Harold Pinxten put it away.

Caley drew level in the 71st minute thanks to a Roddy McKenzie gaffe at a free kick and then the Lions' were made to sweat as Graham Barrett was stretchered off after a nasty-looking fall. The problem stemmed from the fact that Livi had already played their three substitutes, so under the rules no one else could come on and the team had to get by with 10 men.

They managed to hang on though and Lambert couldn't praise the lads enough: "All credit to the players for hanging on. We're looking forward to taking on Rangers.

"As for the free-kick, Roddy knows he should have saved it."

And there was signs of the old Livi at the next game –a smashing 2-2 draw against Rangers, but just before the hour mark, it looked as if the game was going to be a humping for the home team as Barry Ferguson had scored in the 15th minute and Chris Burke had knocked in a second just before 55 minutes on the clock.

As fan John Belton put it: "It was shaping up to be a bad one. You had the feeling that Rangers were just getting ready to crack in a third and fourth to make it a lousy day for us."

Two minutes after Burke's goal that all changed. A gaffe by Ricksen let Robert Snodgrass line up a shot that beat Waterreus and flew inside the far post.

Sensing an opportunity, Paul Lambert put on another striker, James McPake, but it was Snodgrass again who scored eight minutes later with a header.

Afterwards Lambert said: "Robert dug us out of a hole there."

But a bit of the old Jim Leishman confidence also shone through when he added: "I have mixed emotions because I think we could have won the game. To come back from 2-0 down was unbelievable, it really was. It was terrific for us. I don't think there are too many times when you will see a team come back from 2-0 down against Rangers."

It was Snodgrass again in the next game who saved the day. Technically the score here was 2-0 Livi and not the 1-1 against Falkirk that history records, but that's because Harold Pinxten scored the opener in the 20th minute – just at the wrong end of the ground.

Falkirk owned the first half and the pressure was showing early on. If Roddy McKenzie had been more composed at the 20th minute, he could have got a hold of Craig McPherson's corner. Instead, he missed it and it bounced off Pinxten's head to go in.

The scoreline stayed that way until the second half, but Snodgrass began testing Matt Glennon at the other end. There was some more dominance in the game by the Lions', but the vast run of play was still Falkirk. As the game wound down, Snodgrass refused to give up and grabbed an equaliser in the 88th minute.

A late point was better than none and there was more cheerful news for the fans after the game as it was revealed that Allan

Walker signed a new contract keeping him at the club, in theory, until the end of the 2007-2008 season.

Not that he was much use in the next game against Hibs, unless you count being booked as useful. To be fair, he wasn't the only one. Paul Dalglish and Paul Tierney also going into the ref's book.

Livi opened the scoring just before half time. Snodgrass had threatened the goal a number of times but it was Greg Strong who got the glory with a 12 yard shot in the 42nd minute.

It looked as if the Lions' were on course for their first league three points until the 83rd minute when the clumsy-playing Hibs pulled their act together – and had a bit of luck – with Shiels scoring from a deflection and Garry O'Connor getting the winner three minutes later after his shot deflected off Allan Walker to beat McKenzie.

Afterwards Paul Lambert said: "That was a sore one, there is no doubt about that. But that's football, it can be a cruel game at times.

"I don't think we deserved that. Hibs are a good side but we gave them a game. Two deflections went against us but that can happen."

There was no time for self-pity though as next up was a cup game against Caley. Up for grabs was a place in the CIS Insurance Cup semi finals, something both teams could do with the cash from.

It started badly with Craig Dargo getting the opener for Caley in the 55th second, beating Ludovic Roy, who was between the posts covering for an injured Roddy McKenzie.

There was about 55 seconds left in the half when Livi brought themselves back into the game, after a fiercely competitive first half that Caley had the best of, with Dave Mackay thumping one in from the edge of the box to beat Mark Brown.

The second half saw Livi gain confidence and both sides had chances to take the lead - James McPake from eight yards out for the Lions', but after 90 minutes it was all square.

Extra time went on – and on – and just when it looked as if the extra 30 minutes wouldn't be enough, Paul Dalglish received a pass from Ramon Pereira to go round Brown and score.

Caley insisted the 117th minute goal was offside but referee Mike McCurry was having none of it.

Caley Thistle's Ian Black nearly made it all level when he struck the post in the dying seconds, but the valiant effort wasn't enough and it was the Lions' who went through to the semi final.

As the middle of November approached, the club were in a strange position. They had beaten the team everyone was talking about – Hearts – and were through to a semi final, but at the same time, the league position was precarious to say the least, bottom of the league with just five points and no wins. Granted all that was keeping them on the bottom spot was a goal difference of minus 23, compared to equally-pointed Dunfermline's minus 20. After that, though, there was a leap of eight points to try and catch up with Falkirk or Dundee United.

Signs were promising though.The football at times was great to watch, Lambert was a good manager, the team certainly had a cavalier style to their play and they were bonding better with each outing. One thing was for sure: it would go down to the wire in May no doubt.

After all, when have Livi ever done anything the easy way?

WHERE DOES THE MIGHTY LION GO FROM HERE?

Livingston have survived by the whiskers more often than not and the sceptical amongst the fans might think that the nine lives are up this season. However only a fool would rule Livingston out of anything at this stage. The team are experts at going to the wire before pulling off another season in the SPL.

Given that over the years the club seems to have gone through more incarnations than Doctor Who, a period of stability is required for the club. What it also needs is more fans.

There's no denying that the people who do go to the games are very committed and many people in the area are happy to have Livi as their second team normally after the Old Firm or one of the Edinburgh sides but they rarely go to see them or spend any money on the club.

Over years this may change but it will take long lifetimes. After all most children who go into football will go with their father and end up supporting their father's team, so if the dad isn't taking the kids to Almondvale, then that's another future fan lost.

It may be that Livi have to get radical with their ticket policies to entice more people in with buy one get one free offers or bring along a pal schemes where a friend who has never been to a Livi game gets to come along free.

This sort of offer especially when the team are on the telly might help, but it will take years.

Success would also help. Many fair-weather fans will jump ship to see a winning team that pulls off good results on a regular basis. Livi had one great season but as it didn't keep going, some of the fans drifted away.

It may be horror of horrors that the best thing for the club would be to actually go down. This worked wonders for Hibs as they went down, got some good results, won the league, giving everyone a boost and came back up. A drop may also allow Paul Lambert to get some more managerial nous under his belt, not that he's done too badly with what he has to work with. The club has played some decent and attractive football.

Whatever the future holds, one thing is for certain, it won't be dull!

Thank you, for buying a Lipstick Publishing title.
Why not check out our website for other great books?
www.lipstickpublishing.com

If you would like to be added to our mailing list for new books we
are publishing just drop us an e-mail at:
admin@lipstickpublishing.com

Customers who bought this book also bought:

Raising The Kursk ISBN: 1904762050
Winning Mentality ISBN: 1904762115
Nocturne in Bleu   ISBN: 1904762239

All our titles are available from all good book shops and online
ordering at: www.amazon.co.uk
Or www.lipstickpublishing.com

Our next title for publication is 'On The Puffin's Wings'
The adventures with the birds of Scotland and Ireland.
ISBN: 1904762263